Ways of
MAKING
LITERATURE
MATTER

A BRIEF GUIDE

Ways of
MAKING
LITERATURE
MATTER

A Brief Guide

John Schilb

Indiana University

John Clifford

University of North Carolina at Wilmington

BEDFORD / ST. MARTIN'S   Boston   ◆   New York

FOR BEDFORD/ST. MARTIN'S

Executive Editor: Stephen A. Scipione
Production Editor: Lori Chong Roncka
Production Supervisor: Catherine Hetmansky
Director of Marketing: Karen Melton
Editorial Assistant: Tracey Lynne Finch
Production Assistant: Thomas P. Crehan
Copyeditor: Lisa A. Wehrle
Text Design: Geri Davis, The Davis Group, Inc.
Cover Design: Trudi Gershenov Design
Cover Art: Bill Jacklin, *The Park*, 1996 (tapestry detail)
Composition: Stratford Publishing Services
Printing and Binding: Quebecor Printing Kingsport

President: Charles H. Christensen
Editorial Director: Joan E. Feinberg
Editor in Chief: Karen S. Henry
Director of Editing, Design, and Production: Marcia Cohen
Managing Editor: Elizabeth M. Schaaf

Library of Congress Control Number: 00–103105

Manufactured in the United States of America.

5 4 3 2 1 0
f   e   d   c   b   a

For information, write: Bedford/St. Martin's, 75 Arlington Street, Boston, MA 02116 (617-399-4000)

ISBN: 0–312–25913–1

Preface for Instructors

This book shows students how to think and write critically about any literary work. Therefore, it will be especially useful for courses that teach literature and composition together. All seven chapters come from our larger volume *Making Literature Matter: An Anthology for Readers and Writers*. Some instructors of literature and composition, while valuing that book's lessons in criticism, have asked us to package them in a brief guide. So for these teachers, and for others like them, here is *Ways of Making Literature Matter*. Each chapter presents what we think are new and productive ways of reading, analyzing, and writing about literature. Also included are twenty stories, poems, plays, and essays, drawn from the 153 selections in our larger book.

What This Book Emphasizes

In our decades as English faculty, we have enjoyed reading literature, teaching about it, and writing about it. We have also dedicated ourselves to writing instruction, both in our classroom practice and our research. We know that literary studies and composition studies can be difficult to synthesize, especially given their different institutional circumstances. But each has much to teach the other, and our aim in these pages has been to connect them in ways that will lead students to better reading, writing, and critical thinking. You will notice that throughout this book we emphasize the following:

The importance of writing. Our cornerstone belief is that students make literature matter to themselves, and to others, when they write about it. Accordingly, *Ways of Making Literature Matter* prompts them to write almost immediately and keeps them writing as they work through the activities and assignments in the text. We depict writing as a perpetually useful and rewarding means of exploring various dimensions of a literary work.

Each chapter takes students step-by-step through the process of writing about literature. In part, our discussions draw on classical rhetoric; for instance, we build on Aristotle's definition of rhetoric as "the discovery of the available means of persuasion." We also incorporate insights from contemporary rhetoricians like Stephen Toulmin, who has influenced our treatment of claims and warrants.

The value of argument.   As these rhetorical influences suggest, our text is distinguished by its emphasis on how to write *arguments* about literature. Of course we don't encourage students to prepare diatribes; instead we ask them to see argument as civil inquiry, a process requiring writers to clarify, support, and often revise their ideas. This concept of argument is, we believe, vital to classes in literature and composition. Quite simply, students need to see argument as careful, well-grounded thought.

To help them see this, our first two chapters refer continually to several poems about work, as a way of showing students how to write arguments about particular texts. Chapters 3 through 6 move through all four genres in this book: stories, poems, plays, and essays, using the works to explain the process of arguing about that genre. Throughout these chapters, brief writing tasks and exercises (about fifty of them) help students to formulate issues and claims. We also include five sample arguments by students, showing how these writers developed informal jottings into full-fledged drafts. Our goal throughout is to help students build their personal responses to literature into compelling arguments about it.

Critical issues in literary studies.   Another distinctive feature is our emphasis on specific issues currently pursued in literary studies. Typically, literature textbooks refer to the discipline's present state by identifying schools of critical thought, such as feminist criticism, New Historicism, psychoanalytic criticism, or cultural criticism. But the average critic is more eclectic than these categories suggest, and the time spent explaining these categories is better spent cultivating students' own reading and writing. Therefore, instead of taking a "schools" approach, Chapter 1 introduces students to the kinds of questions that literature specialists now address: questions of fact, definition, genre, pattern, symbolism, evaluation, history, cause and effect, and policy.

Similarly, we point out particular subjects that currently engage the discipline—what classical rhetoricians would call its special topics. These include gender, race, memory, subversion, and the body as well as relations between "high" culture and mass culture. Again, we do more than just list these issues and topics. Rather, we demonstrate their usefulness by applying them to particular literary works and provide opportunities for students actually to implement the principles and strategies we discuss.

The process and tools of research.   The final writing project in a literature-based composition course or an introductory literature course is often a research paper, and the final chapter of this book explores how to develop a well-researched argument about literature. Chapter 7 follows the research process of a student, offering detailed advice on finding a topic, locating and working with library and electronic sources, and drafting and documenting. It concludes with the student's research paper, annotated to call out important features of her argument.

Electronic Resources

Classes using our book may want to visit our publisher's Web site, *www.bedfordstmartins.com*, where a companion Web site to *Making Literature Matter* can be found by clicking the Literature link. The companion site includes resources that may be helpful to students (for example, information about the authors in *Ways of Making Literature Matter*) and to instructors (especially an annotated bibliography of resources useful in teaching literature-and-composition courses).

Acknowledgments

At Bedford / St. Martin's, we thank the same fine group of people who worked with us for the years it took to prepare *Making Literature Matter*, especially publisher Chuck Christensen, editorial director Joan Feinberg, executive editor Steve Scipione, production editor Lori Roncka, and director of marketing Karen Melton. Those whose behind-the-scenes work was indispensable include Maura Shea, Nicole Simonsen, Tracey Finch, Elizabeth Schaaf, John Amburg, Lisa Wehrle, and Sandy Schechter.

John Schilb thanks his former colleagues at the University of Maryland. He is especially indebted to Jeanne Fahnstock, whose knowledge of rhetoric and argumentation continues to awe and inspire him. John appreciates, too, the support of his new colleagues at Indiana University, especially Christine Farris. John Clifford thanks his colleagues at the University of North Carolina at Wilmington, especially Joyce Hollingsworth. Our thanks go also to Janet E. Gardner of the University of Massachusetts at Dartmouth for her excellent work on the research chapter.

We once again take the opportunity to thank those who reviewed our manuscript of *Making Literature Matter*, especially those who had valuable things to say about the text chapters: Jonathan Alexander, University of Southern Colorado; Virginia Anderson, University of Texas at Austin; Carolyn Baker and Rance G. Baker of San Antonio College; Barbara Barnard, Hunter College; Linda Bensel-Meyers, University of Tennessee, Knoxville; Kevin J. H. Dettmar, Southern Illinois University at Carbondale; Thomas Dukes, University of Akron; Irene R. Fairley, Northeastern University; Iris Rose Hart, Santa Fe Community College; Carol Peterson Haviland, California State University, San Bernardino; John Heyda, Miami University–Middletown; Margaret Lindgren, University of Cincinnati; Phillip Mayfield, Fullerton College; Julie Segedy, Chabot College; Sharon Winn, Northeastern State University; Bertha Wise, Oklahoma City Community College.

As with *Making Literature Matter*, we dedicate this book to our wives, Wendy Elliot and Janet Ellerby, whose presence in our lives still matters most.

J.S.
J.C.

Contents

2. Writing   41

3. Writing about Stories   71

7. **Writing a Research Paper**   176

Ways of
MAKING
LITERATURE
MATTER

A Brief Guide

INTRODUCTION

What Is Literature? How and Why Does It Matter?

> Art lives upon discussion, upon experiment, upon curiosity, upon variety of attempt, upon the exchange of views and the comparison of standpoints. . . .
> — Henry James, "The Art of Fiction"

The title of this book, *Ways of Making Literature Matter*, may seem curious to you. Presumably your school assumes that literature already matters, for otherwise it would hardly offer courses in the subject. Quite possibly you are taking this course because you think literature is important or hope it will become so for you. But with our title, we want to emphasize that literature does not exist in a social vacuum. Rather, literature is part of human relationships; people *make* literature matter to other people. We will be especially concerned with how you can make literature matter to others as well as to yourself. Above all, we will point out ways you can argue about literature, both in class discussions and in your own writing.

First, though, we need to address three questions:

- How have people defined literature?
- What about literature has mattered to people?
- What can you do to make literature matter?

How Have People Defined *Literature?*

Asked to define *literature*, probably most people would say that the term encompasses fiction (novels and short stories), poetry, and drama. Although this definition is common, it is somewhat misleading. It fails to acknowledge that fiction, poetry, and drama are rooted in everyday life. Often these genres make use of ordinary forms of talk. For example, much of Philip Levine's poem "What Work Is" (p. 41) reads like the talk you might overhear spoken by someone waiting at the gate of an automobile plant, hoping to be called for work. But it is no less "poetic" for its plain language and its often-conversational tone.

The genres regarded as "literary" are tied in other ways to daily behavior. Most likely you are often poetic, in the sense that you use metaphors in your

1

conversations and you quote or sing lyrics of songs. Probably you are often theatrical, too, carrying out various kinds of scripts and performing any number of roles. Furthermore, you probably engage in storytelling even when you are not actually writing works of fiction. Imagine this familiar situation: You are late for a meeting with friends because you got stuck in traffic, and now you must explain to them your delay. Your explanation may very well become a tale of suspense, with you the hero racing against time to escape the bumper-to-bumper horde. As the writer Joan Didion has observed, "We tell ourselves stories in order to live." Almost all of us spin narratives day after day, because doing so helps us meaningfully frame our lives.

Many people would admit that literature is grounded in real life and yet still insist on applying the term only to written texts of fiction, poetry, and drama. But this attitude is distinctly modern, for the term *literature* has not always been applied so restrictively. *Literature* was at first a characteristic of *readers*. From the term's emergence in the fourteenth century to the middle of the eighteenth, *literature* was more or less a synonym for *literacy*. People of literature were assumed to be well read.

In the late eighteenth century, however, the term's meaning changed. Increasingly it referred to books and other printed texts rather than to people who read them. At the beginning of this shift, the scope of literature was broad, encompassing practically all public writing. But as the nineteenth century proceeded, the term's range shrank. More and more people considered literature to be imaginative or creative writing, and they distinguished it from nonfiction. This trend did take years to build; in the early 1900s, literature anthologies still featured essays as well as excerpts from histories and biographies. By the mid-1900s, though, the narrower definition of literature prevailed.

As we have noted, many people still associate literature with just fiction, poetry, and drama. Nevertheless, this limited definition has become newly vulnerable. From the early 1970s on, a significant number of literature faculty have called for widening it. In 1979, for instance, a National Endowment for the Humanities–Modern Language Association summer institute entitled "Women's Nontraditional Literature" applied the term *literature* to genres that had not been thought of as such. Participants studied essays, letters, diaries, autobiographies, and oral testimonies. To each of these genres, women have contributed much; in fact, the institute's participants concluded that a literature curriculum slights many works by women if it focuses on fiction, poetry, and drama alone.

Of course, even within these three categories, the term *literature* has been selectively applied. Take the case of novelist and short-story writer Stephen King, whose books have sold millions of copies. Despite his commercial success, a lot of readers—including some of his fans—refuse to call King's writing literature. They assume that to call something literature is to say it has artistic merit, and for them King's tales of horror fall short.

Yet people who use the term *literature* as a compliment may still disagree about whether a certain text deserves it. Plenty of readers praise King's writing as literature, while others deem it schlock. In short, artistic standards differ. To be sure, some works have been constantly admired through the years; regarded as classics, they are frequently taught in literature classes. *Hamlet, Othello, The Tempest*, and other plays by William Shakespeare are perhaps the most obvious examples. But in the last twenty years, much controversy has arisen over the literary canon, those works taught again and again. Are there good reasons why the canon has consisted mostly of texts by white men? Or have the principles of selection been skewed by sexism and racism? Should the canon be changed to accommodate a greater range of authors? Or should literary studies resist having any canon at all? These questions have provoked various answers, the result being continued debate. Nowadays even Shakespeare's works are not universally beloved. For example, Aimé Césaire, a contemporary writer from Martinique who associates Shakespeare with the dominant colonialism of the Elizabethan age, rewrote *The Tempest* to reflect his political discontent. Shakespeare still has legions of defenders, as do many writers long acclaimed as great, but disputes about what constitutes greatness are likely to persist.

Also in question are attempts to separate literature from nonfiction. Our notion of the literariness of everyday life acknowledges that much "nonfiction" shows imagination and relies on devices found in novels, short stories, poems, and plays. The last few years have seen the emergence of the term *creative nonfiction* as a synonym for essays, autobiographies, and histories that use evocative language and strong narratives. Conversely, works of fiction, poetry, and drama may center on real-life events. One example is Nobel laureate Seamus Heaney's poem "Punishment." It juxtaposes two actual incidents: the discovery of an ancient woman's body and the violence suffered by women of Northern Ireland for consorting with British soldiers.

Works like Heaney's confirm that poetry can embrace actual history. Some people, however, argue that poems about real events are still "literary" because they inspire contemplation rather than action. This view of literature has traditionally been summed up as "art for art's sake." Yet this notion brushes aside all the poems, novels, short stories, and plays that do encourage audiences to undertake certain acts. Spokane Indian writer Sherman Alexie's "Capital Punishment," for example, is typical of poems that are designed to spark resistance to the death penalty.

In this book, we resist endorsing a single definition of *literature*. Rather, we encourage you to review and perhaps rethink what the term means to you. At the same time, we do want to expand the realm of literature, so we include several essays in addition to short stories, poems, and plays. We also invite you to make connections among these different kinds of texts: You need not treat them as altogether separate species.

What about Literature Has Mattered to People?

People have studied literature for all sorts of reasons. You may be surprised to learn that in the late 1800s, English departments in American universities taught Shakespeare's plays mostly by having students trace the origins of particular words he used. Shakespeare's plots, characters, and themes received little attention. Today, by contrast, most classes in Shakespeare consider these things important; they are not content to use his plays as a springboard for dictionary research. In fact, literary history can be seen as a history of changing responses to literature. Nevertheless, if you were to ask people today why they read literature, probably you would get several common answers. The following are some we have heard. As we list them, compare them with what you might say.

One common reason for reading literature has to do with proving sophistication. Ever since the eighteenth century, people have sought to join the cultural elite by proving their familiarity with literature. Read Shakespeare's plays, their thinking goes, and you can then impress high society with quotations from him. The desire to raise one's status is understandable. Still, this motive is rarely enough to sustain a person's interest in literature. Frankly, we hope you will find other reasons for reading it. At the same time, we encourage you to analyze how knowledge of literature has served as *cultural capital:* that is, as a sign of a person's worth. In coining the term *cultural capital*, sociologist Pierre Bourdieu suggested there is something wrong when a society makes literature a means of achieving status. Do you agree?

Another common reason for reading literature has to do with institutional requirements. Millions of students read literature simply because they have to take courses in it. Probably Roland Barthes, the French critic, had this situation in mind when he wryly defined *literature* as "what gets taught in schools." Barthes was being provocatively reductive; if pressed, perhaps he would have conceded that people read literature outside school, too. Across the United States, college graduates and others meet regularly in book discussion groups, studying literature together. Even if you are taking this course only because you must, the obligation may turn out enjoyable. When required to read literature, students have found value in it. While inevitably they end up preferring some works to others, they learn that literature provides them with more pleasures and insights than they had expected. Stay open to the possibility that you will find the same rewards.

Still another popular reason for reading literature is the enjoyment it provides. Quite simply, lots of people find the experience entertaining. Specifically, they may revel in literature's ability to render human existence concretely. They may delight in its often eloquent and evocative language. They may like finding all the various patterns in a literary text. They may prize the moments when literature makes them think, laugh, or cry.

People have also turned to literature because, as scholar and critic Kenneth Burke has noted, it serves as "equipment for living." Perhaps you have found that a certain story, poem, play, or essay helped you understand your life and conduct it better. Of course, even readers who look to literature for guidance may have different tastes. While some readers prefer literature that reflects their own lives, others like it most when it explores situations that they have not experienced or have not pondered much. "When it's the real thing," critic Frank Lentricchia notes, "literature enlarges us, strips the film of familiarity from the world; creates bonds of sympathy with all kinds, even with evil characters, who we learn are all in the family."

Some people *dislike* literature because they find it too indirect. They resent that it often forces them to figure out symbols and implications, when they would rather have the truth presented straight. But in life, truth can be complicated and elusive. In many ways, literature is most realistic when it suggests the same. Besides, many readers appreciate literature most when it resists simple decoding, forcing them to adopt new assumptions and learn new methods of analysis. Indeed, throughout this book we will suggest that the most interesting and profitable conversations about literature are those in which the issues are not easily resolved. One of the best things your course will provide you is the chance to exchange insights with other students about texts whose issues prove challenging.

We hope that any literature you read in this book strikes you as "equipment for living." If a particular selection leaves you cold, use the occasion to identify and review the standards you are judging it by. Even if you like a piece, think about the values you are applying. Probably your values will grow clearer to you in class debates, especially if you have to support your own view of a work.

What Can You Do to Make Literature Matter to Others?

Look again at our opening quotation, which comes from an 1895 essay called "The Art of Fiction" by the American novelist, short-story writer, and critic Henry James. When James declared that "art lives upon discussion, upon experiment, upon curiosity, upon variety of attempt, upon the exchange of views and the comparison of standpoints," certainly he was suggesting that the creators of literature play a big role in making it matter. But James was suggesting, too, that plenty of other people contribute to literature's impact. Today, these people include publishers, printers, agents, advertisers, librarians, professional reviewers, bookstore staff, and even show business figures such as Oprah Winfrey, who got millions of viewers to participate in her "book club." Teachers of literature also make it matter — or at least they try to! Perhaps your parents or other family members have contributed to your appreciation of certain literary texts; many adults introduce their children and grandchildren to books they loved when young. Moreover, friends often recommend works of literature to one another.

We concede that some people think of literature negatively, believing that it matters in a way they don't like. The ancient Greek philosopher Plato wanted to ban poets from his ideal republic because he thought they merely imitated truth. Today, reviewers sometimes want to stop a book from being widely read, believing it will do more harm than good. One recent example is Kathryn Harrison's *The Kiss*, a memoir about the author's incestuous relationship with her father. Many reviewers hated the book, regarding it as a superficial and tasteless treatment of its subject. At the same time, some of these reviewers feared that *The Kiss* would attract a large audience, so they made their criticisms of it sound like public health warnings.

Throughout history, various forces have worked actively to censor or abolish a great deal of literature. In communities across the contemporary United States, pressure groups have succeeded in getting particular novels removed from library shelves. These novels include such classics as *The Catcher in the Rye* and *Adventures of Huckleberry Finn*. History has also seen many writers of literature killed, jailed, or harassed for their work. In recent years, the most conspicuous example of such persecution has been the Ayatollah Khomeini's indictment of author Salman Rushdie. The ayatollah was so enraged by the portrayal of Islam in Rushdie's novel *The Satanic Verses* that he commanded his followers to hunt Rushdie down and slay him. Even after the ayatollah died, Rushdie was still in danger, for the *fatwa* against him remained in effect. Not until eight years after the original edict did the Iranian government back away from it, thereby granting Rushdie at least a measure of safety. But the Rushdie affair stands as a reminder that some writers of literature risk their lives. Ironically, the ayatollah's execution order was a sort of homage to literature, a fearsome way of crediting it with the power to shape minds.

Our book aims to help you join the conversations that Henry James saw as nourishing literature. More specifically, our book focuses on helping you argue about literature, whether your audience is your classmates, your teacher, or other people. While arguments involve real or potential disagreement, they need not be waged like wars. When we use the term *argument* in this book, we have in mind civilized efforts through which people try to make their views persuasive. When you argue about literature, you are carefully reasoning with others, helping them see how a certain text should matter to them.

In particular, we will say much about you as a writer. The main goal of your course is to help you compose more effective texts of your own. By writing arguments about literature, you make it matter to others. Moreover, you learn about yourself as you analyze a literary text and negotiate other readers' views of it. We will emphasize that, at its best, arguing is indeed a process of inquiry for all involved. This process entails a great deal of re-vision: Both you and your audience may wind up changing your minds.

The Rest of This Book

Chapters 1 and 2 introduce you to activities that are at the heart of making literature matter: reading, thinking, and writing. Chapters 3 through 6 focus on writing about the four literary genres we include in this book. Each of these four chapters identifies traditional features of each genre — fiction, poetry, drama, and essays — and lays out strategies for developing, drafting, and revising the sorts of papers you will write in this course. As examples, we include writing by other students of literature.

Finally, Chapter 7 explains how to write a literary research paper: how to discover and focus on a topic; how to find and use sources; and how to draft, revise, and document the paper. Throughout this chapter, we follow the active research process of one student as she proceeds from her preliminary response to a short story through her investigation of some of the key issues it raises. The results of her work are presented at the end of the chapter in a completed research paper, documented in the style recommended by the Modern Language Association (MLA).

WRITING ASSIGNMENTS

1. Write a brief essay in which you explain what you value in literature by focusing on a literary work you have liked and why you liked it. Don't worry about whether you are defining *literature* correctly. The aim of this exercise is for you to begin reviewing the values you hold as you read a work that you regard as literary.

2. Sometimes a literary work matters to you in one way, and then, when you read it again, it matters to you in another way. Write a brief essay in which you discuss a work that did, in fact, matter to you differently when you reread it. In what way did it matter to you the first time? What significance did it have for you later? What about your life had changed in the meantime? If you cannot think of a literary work, choose a film you have seen.

3. Write a brief essay in which you identify the values that a previous literature teacher of yours seemed to hold. Be sure to identify, too, ways in which the teacher expressed these values. You may want to bring up one or more specific events that took place in the teacher's classroom.

4. Many bookstores sell computer instruction manuals. Examine one of these. Do you consider the manual literature? Write a brief essay answering this question. Be sure to explain how you are defining *literature* and refer to the manual's specific features.

5. Visit your school's bookstore or another bookstore. Spend at least a half hour looking at books in various sections, noting how the publishers of these works try to make them matter. Look at such things as the books' physical formats, the language on their covers, and any introductory material they include. Then, write a brief essay in which you identify and evaluate the strategies for "mattering" used by at least three books you came across.

6. Visit a Web site that includes readers' comments about particular works of fiction. A good example is www.amazon.com, a commercial online "bookstore." Choose a novel or short story collection on the site that readers have commented about a lot. Then, write a brief essay in which you identify the values that seem reflected in the comments. In what respects, apparently, does literature matter to these readers? What do they evidently hope to find in it?

7. Write a brief essay in which you recall an occasion when someone made something matter to you. Presumably this exercise will get you thinking about what it means to "make something matter." At some point in your essay, try to define this phrase, using your specific experience as an example.

8. Write a brief essay in which you summarize your history as a writer. What are the main kinds of writing you have done? What successes and problems have you experienced as a writer? How might this course help your writing most?

1

Reading and Thinking

Reading Comparatively:
Three Poems about Work

Let's assume that you are analyzing a poem. How might you develop ideas about it? One good way is to see how the poem resembles, and differs from, others on the same topic. To get a better sense of this method, read the following three poems, each of which concerns work.

JOHN MILTON
When I consider how my light is spent

When I consider how my light is spent,
    Ere half my days in this dark world and wide,
    And that one talent which is death to hide
Lodged with me useless, though my soul more bent
To serve therewith my Maker, and present   5
    My true account, lest He returning chide;
    "Doth God exact day-labor, light denied?"
I fondly ask. But Patience, to prevent
That murmur, soon replies, "God doth not need
    Either man's work or His own gifts. Who best   10
    Bear His mild yoke, they serve Him best. His state
Is kingly: thousands at His bidding speed,
    And post o'er land and ocean without rest;
    They also serve who only stand and wait."   [c. 1652]

FRANCES E. W. HARPER
Free Labor

I wear an easy garment,
    O'er it no toiling slave
Wept tears of hopeless anguish,
    In his passage to the grave.

And from its ample folds   5
    Shall rise no cry to God,
Upon its warp and woof shall be
    No stain of tears and blood.

Oh, lightly shall it press my form,
    Unladen with a sigh,   10
I shall not 'mid its rustling hear,
    Some sad despairing cry.

This fabric is too light to bear
    The weight of bondsmen's tears,
I shall not in its texture trace   15
    The agony of years.

Too light to bear a smother'd sigh,
    From some lorn woman's heart,
Whose only wreath of household love
    Is rudely torn apart.   20

Then lightly shall it press my form,
    Unburden'd by a sigh;
And from its seams and folds shall rise,
    No voice to pierce the sky,

And witness at the throne of God,   25
    In language deep and strong
That I have nerv'd Oppression's hand,
    For deeds of guilt and wrong.   [1874]

MARGE PIERCY
To be of use

The people I love the best
jump into work head first
without dallying in the shallows
and swim off with sure strokes almost out of sight.
They seem to become natives of that element,   5

the black sleek heads of seals
bouncing like half-submerged balls.

I love people who harness themselves, an ox to a heavy cart,
who pull like water buffalo, with massive patience,
who strain in the mud and the muck to move things forward, 10
who do what has to be done, again and again.

I want to be with people who submerge
in the task, who go into the fields to harvest
and work in a row and pass the bags along,
who are not parlor generals and field deserters 15
but move in a common rhythm
when the food must come in or the fire be put out.

The work of the world is common as mud.
Botched, it smears the hands, crumbles to dust.
But the thing worth doing well done 20
has a shape that satisfies, clean and evident.
Greek amphoras for wine or oil,
Hopi vases that held corn, are put in museums
but you know they were made to be used.
The pitcher cries for water to carry 25
and a person for work that is real. [1974]

These poems differ in their styles and cultural references, in part because they come from different historical periods. Whereas John Milton wrote his poem around 1652 and published it in 1673, the other two poems were published much later: Frances Harper's in 1874, Marge Piercy's in 1974. But if you look at the poems together, you can better see the specific approach each takes to the subject of work.

A WRITING EXERCISE

Once you have read the three poems as a group, write brief responses to each. You might jot down things you especially notice about them, feelings they evoke in you, and questions you have about them. You might also note work experiences of your own that they lead you to recall. With each poem, write for ten minutes without stopping — off the top of your head, so to speak. Don't feel that you have to pour forth terrific insights right away. This exercise, often called **freewriting**, simply helps you begin responding to a text.

If the poems puzzle you at first, take heart. Few people make brilliant observations about a work of literature when they first read it. Examining literature is best seen as a process, during which you gradually construct, test, revise, and refine your sense of a text. Practically everyone would need to reflect on these three poems a while before developing substantial ideas about them. We think literature is most worth reading when it challenges your current understanding of the world, pressing you to expand your knowledge and review your beliefs.

You need not read in isolation, relying solely on yourself to figure out a text. If you have trouble understanding a literary work, try consulting other readers. In the course you are taking, you will have plenty of chances to exchange insights with your classmates and teacher. All these people are resources for your thinking. Encourage them to see you as a resource, too.

Still another good way to ponder a literary work is to write about it. Again, do not feel obliged to churn out a polished, profound analysis of the text right away. If reading literature is best seen as a process, so too is writing about it. To begin your study of a work, you might freewrite in a notebook or journal. Then, you might try extended drafts, in which you experiment with sustained analysis. Only later might you attempt a whole formal paper on the text, aiming to show others that you have arrived at a solid, credible view of it. In each of these activities, your thinking might be helped by class discussions. Perhaps classmates will even be able to give you direct feedback on your writing, including the freewriting you have just done on the three poems about work.

As you read through these chapters, we hope that you find them to be emotionally engaging as well as thought-provoking. Moreover, we hope our advice helps you to become a more learned and thoughtful reader of other literature you may read in the course where you use this book, or elsewhere. But we have yet another goal. With the texts we present, the background information we provide, the questions we raise, and the assignments we suggest, we seek to help you become a more thoughtful and effective writer. That is why we began by asking you to freewrite about the three poems.

Probably you have already taken courses that required you to write a great deal. On your own, perhaps you have enjoyed writing poems, short stories, plays, essays, or other kinds of texts. Actually, almost everyone does some kind of writing outside of school, whether it's merely a letter or a full-fledged essay. Nevertheless, you may hesitate to call yourself a writer out of a belief that your writing is often flawed. Yet everyone brings strengths to the act of writing, and we hope this course helps you recognize yours. While obviously the course is a chance for you to improve as a writer, believing that you deserve to be called a writer is an important step in your growth.

A WRITING EXERCISE

Introduce yourself to the rest of the class through a letter that describes your career as a writer. You might recall particular works you have written and memorable writing teachers you have had. Also, you might identify whatever kinds of writing you like to do, your current strengths as a writer, and aspects of your writing that you hope to strengthen in this course.

LITERATURE AS SOCIAL ACTION

We began this chapter with poems by Milton, Harper, and Piercy because each of these poets views writing as we would like you to view it: as a form of social action. Perhaps you see writing as a form of communication, a way to express your ideas. This is a logical and important concept of writing to hold. But these three poets also see writing as a way to have impact on other people. They write not just to express themselves but also to shape the world around them. As writers, they contributed especially to the political debates of their day.

John Milton (1608–1674) played a leading role in England's Puritan revolution, which sought to make dominant its own version of Christianity. Ultimately, the Puritans executed King Charles I and installed their leader Oliver Cromwell as head of state. Milton supported the Puritan movement through his poetry and prose. He wrote "When I consider how my light is spent" while working as an official in Cromwell's government. Obviously autobiographical, the poem refers to Milton's growing blindness, which threatened to prevent him from serving both his political leader and his religious one, God. Milton was further discouraged a few years later when the monarchy was restored with the crowning of Charles II. Even then, however, Milton remained active as a social critic. In 1667, with the publication of his epic poem *Paradise Lost*, he aimed "to justify the ways of God to man."

Like Milton, African American writer Frances Ella Watkins Harper (1825–1911) saw social injustice as a sin to be eradicated. Through her poems, essays, fiction, and speeches, she specifically challenged the oppression of African Americans and women. Born free, Harper spent the pre–Civil War period campaigning against slavery. After emancipation, she worked on behalf of the former slaves, striving to help them prosper and to secure their legal rights. During this post–Civil War period, she wrote "Free Labor." At the same time, Harper participated in the campaign to obtain voting rights for women, although she had to fight racial prejudice even within the suffrage movement.

Marge Piercy (b. 1936) is a veteran of the contemporary civil rights and women's movements. During the 1960s and 1970s, she also protested America's involvement in Vietnam. Subsequently she has used her writing to promote various social causes, especially feminism. Piercy is the author of several novels, including the 1976 science-fiction classic *Woman on the Edge of Time*. But she has published several books of poetry as well. The title "To be of use" suggests how Piercy conceives a poet's responsibilities. In her introduction to *Circles on the Water*, a 1982 collection of her poems, Piercy hopes that her readers "will find poems that speak to and for them, will take those poems into their lives and say them to each other and put them up on the bathroom wall and remember bits and pieces of them in stressful or quiet moments" (xii).

In presenting these three poems by Milton, Harper, and Piercy, we are not asking you to adopt the writers' political beliefs. Were these writers to meet, probably they would disagree among themselves about various issues. Nor is all their writing explicitly political: Each has written poems focused more on private life than on public affairs. And yet, each of these writers has often explored how the private and public realms are related. For instance, even as Milton wrote about the loss of his sight, he raised the question of how to define public service and prodded his readers to share his abiding faith in God. Furthermore, each of these poets wrote to affect readers' hearts and minds. Each of them is a good model for thinking about the social context and possible effects of your writing as you produce your own texts.

Thinking Critically: The Value of Argument

We believe that there are three good reasons for you to learn to argue about literature. First, the term **argument** refers to a kind of talk as well as a kind of writing; thus, focusing on this term can help you relate your own written work to discussions in class. Second, you will read a work of literature with greater direction and purpose if you are working toward the goal of constructing arguments about it. Finally, when you argue, you learn a lot, because you have to ponder things you may have taken for granted as well as things unfamiliar to you.

Specifically, *arguing* is a process in which you identify a subject of current or possible debate; you take a position on that subject; you analyze why you view the subject the way you do; and you try to persuade others that your view is worth sharing or is at least reasonable. Often the process of arguing is not straightforward. Just when you think you have decided how you feel about a subject, class discussion may lead you to change your position or shift to a completely different topic. Whatever the case, to argue well means to engage in self-examination. Also, it means attending to the world around you: especially to the ways that other people think differently from you.

For many, *argument* is a negative term. Perhaps it makes you think of unpleasant shouting matches you have been in or witnessed — times when people have bitterly disagreed with one another and refused to compromise. Almost everyone has experienced arguments of this sort. Moreover, they are a kind of argument that the media promote. On talk radio, hosts as well as callers are often brutally argumentative, mixing strong opinion with outright insult. Similarly, television's political talk shows regularly become sheer quarrels; on *Crossfire, The McLaughlin Group,* and *The Capital Gang,* panelists fall again and again into nasty, noisy debate. Spats are even more spectacular on daytime talk shows like Jerry Springer's, which invite friends and family members to clash in public on such high-voltage topics as "You Stole Him from Me and I Want Him Back!" On occasion, these shows actually get violent, the participants turning from words to fists. No wonder many people see argument as fierce competition, even as a form of war.

A WRITING EXERCISE

Although this book emphasizes written argument, a good way of starting to think about argument is to consider its oral forms. Recall a specific oral argument you recently observed or one in which you recently participated. Do not worry about whether your understanding of the term *argument* is correct; the aim of this exercise is for you to review what you associate with the term.

Write an informal account of the argument you recall. Who engaged in this argument? What did they argue about? What views did they express? What tones did they use? How willing were they to compromise? What were the stages of this argument? What was the outcome? Besides addressing these questions, evaluate the participants' thinking and behavior. To what extent was each person's position reasonable? In what ways, if any, might they have talked more productively?

ARGUMENT AS INQUIRY

Although many people view argument as war and have plenty of reasons to do so, we encourage you to argue in a more positive sense. In any meaning of the term, to *argue* is to disagree with others or to set forth a view that you suspect not everyone holds. But argument need not be a competition in which you aim to prove that only you are right. For one thing, at times you might collaborate with someone else in arguing a position. Also, in an argument you can concede that several views on the subject are possible, even as you develop your own position. Actually, you are more apt to persuade your audience if you treat fairly opinions other than yours. Furthermore, successful arguers establish common ground with their audience; they identify and honor at least some of the beliefs that their readers or listeners hold.

Keep in mind, too, that participants in an argument ought to learn from one another. If you take seriously other people's responses to your position, you will find yourself reexamining why and how you express that view. As we have already noted, you may even change your mind. Above all, we hope you will see argument as *inquiry*, a process in which you think hard about your beliefs rather than just declare them.

THE ELEMENTS OF ARGUMENT

When you argue, you attempt to *persuade* an *audience* to accept your *claims* regarding an *issue* by presenting *evidence* and relying on *warrants*. The italicized words are key to this book; we will bring them up often. Here we will explain what we mean by each, beginning with *issue* and then moving to *claims, persuasion, audience, evidence,* and *warrants*. As we discuss these terms, we will refer mostly to the process of arguing about literature. In particular, we will mention arguments that might be made about the three poems by Milton, Harper, and Piercy. Also, we will stress the usefulness of comparing these poems. Therefore, before going further, you may want to read them again.

Issues

An **issue** is something about which people have disagreed or might disagree. Even as you read a text, you can try to guess what features of it will lead to disagreements in class. You may sense that your own reaction to certain aspects of the text is heavily influenced by your background and values, which other students may not share. Some parts of the text may leave you with conflicting ideas or mixed feelings, as if half of you disagrees with the other half. At moments like these, you come to realize what are issues for you, and next you can urge the rest of your class to see them as issues, too.

An issue is best defined as a question with no obvious, immediate answer. Thus, you can start identifying issues by noting questions that occur to you as you read. Perhaps this question-posing approach to texts is new for you. Often readers demand that a text be clear, and they get annoyed if it leaves them puzzled. Of course, certain writing ought to be immediately clear in meaning; think of operating instructions on a plane's emergency doors. But the value of a literary work often lies in the work's complexities, which can lead readers to reexamine their own ways of perceiving the world. Also, your discussions and papers about literature are likely to be most useful when they go beyond the obvious to deal with more challenging matters. When your class begins talking about a work, you may feel obliged to stay quiet if you have no firm statements to make. But you can contribute a lot by bringing up questions that occurred to you as you read. Especially worth raising are questions that continue to haunt you.

In the case of "When I consider how my light is spent," one possible issue concerns its ending. Milton's speaker wonders how he can serve God now that he is blind. Specifically, the speaker asks, "Doth God exact day-labor, light denied?" But it is Patience, not God, who responds to the speaker's question, proclaiming in the last line that "they also serve who only stand and wait." Why does Milton have Patience, rather than God, reply to the speaker? This issue deserves to be raised because Milton does not thoroughly explain what he means by *patience*, a word that can be defined in various ways. When Piercy's speaker in "To be of use" celebrates those people "who pull like water buffalo, with massive patience," she may or may not be endorsing the kind of patience to which Milton refers.

A possible issue with Harper's "Free Labor" concerns the last two lines of the third stanza. There, the speaker denies hearing "some sad despairing cry." If you wish, you can accept her denial at face value, taking her to mean that slave labor has really ended and that an era of truly free labor has arrived. But this interpretation is not the only conceivable one. You may see the speaker's use of the words "sad despairing cry" as indicating that she still hears such a sound. Maybe she cannot forget slavery after all; maybe she believes African Americans remain slaves in some sense. Whatever you conclude, you can raise this issue: How should the lines be interpreted?

Similarly, Piercy's first stanza presents an apparent paradox. Like the whole poem, the stanza emphasizes work. Yet it ends with an image of play: "the black sleek heads of seals / bouncing like half-submerged balls." Therefore, a possible issue is, What should Piercy's readers conclude when the stanza brings work and play together?

You may feel that at present, you are far from able to answer questions like these. But again, you achieve much when you simply formulate questions and bring them up in class. Then, as other students help you ponder them, you will grow more able to explore issues through writing as well as through conversation.

You are more likely to come up with questions about a text if you do not assume that the text had to be written exactly the way it was. For every move the writer made, alternatives existed. Milton might have had God speak directly rather than having Patience speak. Harper might have let her speaker admit to hearing the cry. Piercy might have stuck entirely with images of work. When you bear in mind writers' options, you grow more inclined to explore why they made the choices they did and what the effects of those choices may be.

You will recognize writers' options more easily if you compare their texts with others. As we have said, we invite comparison throughout this book. Milton's reference to Patience is more apt to strike you as a calculated decision if you note Piercy's use of the word. Recall that she doesn't capitalize *patience* or treat it as a being who can speak. Also, whereas Milton associates the word with waiting, Piercy seems to associate it with hard labor, which is not necessarily the same thing. In light of Piercy's poem, then, Milton's reference to Patience comes across as thoroughly questionable. That is, it emerges as a strategy whose aims and effects are worth pondering.

Next we identify ten kinds of issues that come up in literature courses. Our list will help you detect the issues that arise in your class and discover ones to bring up in discussions or in your writing. The list does not include every kind of issue; you may think of others. Moreover, you may find that an issue can fit into more than one of the categories we name. But when you do have an issue that seems hard to classify, try nevertheless to assign it to a single category, if only for the time being. You will then have some initial guidance for your reading, class discussions, and writing. If you later feel that the issue belongs to another category, you can shift your focus.

1. Issues of fact.   Rarely does a work of literature provide complete information about its characters and events. Rather, literature is usually marked by what literary theorist Wolfgang Iser calls "gaps," moments when certain facts are omitted or obscured. At such times, readers may give various answers to the question, What is happening in this text? Recall, for instance, Milton's first line: "When I consider how my light is spent." The word *when* is ambiguous, leaving unclear how often the speaker has brooded about his apparent uselessness. Is it just on this occasion that he worries about the effects of his blindness? Or does he repeatedly sink into despair and need Patience's response every time? Of course, readers tackle questions of fact only if they suspect that the answers will affect their overall view of the text. Imagine one reader who believes that Milton's *when* refers only to the present occasion, and a second reader who believes that the word refers to repeated brooding. How might they see the whole poem differently because of their different assumptions?

2. Issues of theme.   You may be familiar with the term **theme** from other literature courses. By *theme* critics usually mean the main claim that an author seems to be making with his or her text. Sometimes a theme is defined in terms of a single word—for example, *work* or *love*. But such words are really mere topics. Identifying the topics addressed by a text can be a useful way of starting to analyze that text, and later in Part One we will list several topics that currently preoccupy literary studies. A text's theme, however, is best seen as an assertion that you need at least one whole sentence to express.

With many texts, an issue of theme arises because readers can easily disagree over what the text's main idea is. In literature classes, such disagreements often occur, in part because literary works tend to express their themes indirectly. Readers of Harper's poem may give several different answers to the question, What is Harper ultimately saying about "free labor"? Some readers may accept the speaker's statements at face value, assuming that the speaker truly believes slavery is over and that an era of free labor has begun. Furthermore, these readers may figure that Harper, the author, holds the same belief. But other readers may feel the speaker is being ironic, since she continually refers to the horrors of slavery even as she vows to wear her garment "lightly." These readers may feel that the author, too, remains highly conscious of African Americans' servitude. Perhaps Harper assumes that African Americans' work should *never* be taken lightly, because it is connected with their history of pain. Maybe she is even criticizing the term *free labor*, fearing that it will obscure the past and the present suffering of her race. Or perhaps Harper does like the term but wants to point out that black freedom is a recent, fragile achievement, with slavery always threatening to return.

If you try to express a text's theme, avoid making it a statement so general that it could apply to an enormous number of works. Arguing that Milton's theme is "Have faith in God" hardly gets at the details of his poem. On the other hand, do not let the text's details restrict you so much that you wind up making the theme seem relevant only to a tiny group. If you argue that Milton's theme is "Blind poets shouldn't let their condition make them doubt God," then the many people who are *not* blind poets will wonder why they should care. In short, try to express themes as midlevel generalizations. With Milton's poem, one possibility is "Some people's conditions may prevent them from serving God in obvious ways, and they may therefore question His plan for them, but in the long run they may be able to maintain their faith and believe they are fulfilling His will." A statement like this seems both attentive to Milton's specific text and applicable to a fairly large portion of humanity. Of course, you are free to challenge this version of Milton's theme by proposing an alternative. Moreover, even if you do accept this statement as his theme, you are then free to decide whether it is a good principle to live by. Identifying a theme is one thing; evaluating it is another.

Sometimes an author will appear to state the theme explicitly in his or her text. Such moments are worth studying as you try to determine what the theme is. For instance, you may believe that Milton's theme is the concluding line of his poem: "They also serve who only stand and wait." Yet remember that a theme ties together various parts of a text. Focusing on a single passage, even if it seems "thematic," may lead you to ignore other passages that a statement of theme should encompass. With Milton's poem, someone may argue that the last line does *not* seem to state the theme. After all, much comes before that line: in particular, the speaker's extensive expression of doubt.

Often you will sense a work's theme but still have to decide whether to state it as an **observation** or as a **recommendation**. You would be doing the first if, for example, you said Piercy's theme is that "People need to feel that the work they do is real." You would be doing the second if you said Piercy's theme is that "People should look for work that they find real." Indeed, when they depict a theme as a recommendation, people often use a word like *should*. Neither way of expressing a theme is necessarily better than the other. But keep in mind that each way conjures up a particular image of the author. Reporting Piercy's theme as an observation suggests that she is writing as a psychologist, a philosopher, or some other analyst of human nature. Reporting her theme as a recommendation suggests that she is writing as a teacher, preacher, manager, or coach: someone who is telling her readers what to do. Your decision about how to phrase a theme will depend in part on which of these two images of the author you think appropriate.

You risk obscuring the intellectual, emotional, and stylistic richness of a text if you insist on reducing it to a single "message." Try stating the text's theme as a problem for which there is no easy solution. This way you will be suggesting that the text is, in fact, complex. For instance, you might state the theme of Harper's poem as follows: "It is important to value African Americans' new ability to engage in free labor, but such appreciation threatens to obscure their painful history of slave labor, a history that may come back to life if the gains of Reconstruction are reversed."

Also weigh the possibility that a text is conveying more than one theme. If you plan to associate the text with any theme at all, you might refer to *a* theme of the text rather than *the* theme of the text. To be sure, your use of the term *theme* would still have implications. Above all, you would still be suggesting that you have identified one of the text's major points. Subsequently, you might have to defend this claim, showing how the point you have identified is indeed central to the text.

Issues of theme have loomed large in literary studies. We hope that you will find them useful to pursue. But because references to theme are so common in literary studies, students sometimes forget that there are other kinds of issues. As you move through this list, you may find some that interest you more.

3. *Issues of definition.*   In arguments about literature, issues of **definition** arise most often when readers try to decide what the author means by a particular word. Look back at the last line of Milton's poem: "They also serve who only stand and wait." What, conceivably, does Milton mean by *wait*? Readers may express different notions of how Milton defines this activity. Perhaps he sees waiting as altogether passive; then again, perhaps he believes it can involve several actions, including the writing of poems. To address this issue of definition, readers would also have to consider what the poem's speaker is waiting *for*. Evidently, the speaker hopes for something from God, but what exactly might that something be?

An issue of definition may come up even when the author straightforwardly explains terms. For one thing, readers may argue about whether the author's definitions make sense. Think again of Piercy's poem, which suggests that work is "real" when people "submerge" themselves in it. Perhaps a number of readers would disagree with her, choosing to define "real" work differently. Moreover, even readers who like Piercy's definition may disagree with one another as they seek to apply it. They may have different opinions about what jobs are "real" in her sense.

Like all kinds of issues, those involving definition can emerge more clearly when you compare texts. Recall Milton's and Piercy's references to "patience." Looking at their different uses of the word will probably lead you to reflect at length on how each of them defines it.

4. Issues of symbolism.   In literary studies, an issue of **symbolism** is often a question about the meaning and purpose of a particular image. A good example is Harper's use of the word *garment*. Readers may have different ideas about why she uses this image, her specific adjectives for it, the effects of her building the whole poem around it, and the exact kind of clothing this "garment" may be. An issue of symbolism is also involved if you find yourself wondering whether some element of a text is symbolic in the first place. Milton uses the word *light* as he describes his loss of vision. What various things can *light* symbolize?

5. Issues of pattern.   With issues of **pattern**, you observe how a text is organized. More precisely, you try to determine how certain parts of the text are related to other parts of it. But in thinking about how elements of the text may be grouped together, keep in mind the meaning and purpose of any pattern you find, especially since readers may disagree about that pattern's significance.

Many poems exhibit patterns in their rhymes and stanza lengths. You may have noticed that Milton's poem rhymes, although you may not know the technical term for the structure he is using. His poem is an **Italian sonnet**, in his time a popular form of verse. Following the conventions of this form, Milton has written fourteen lines: eight lines with one pattern of rhyming followed by six lines that rhyme in a different way. (Try to identify each rhyme scheme.) Even if you already possess this information about Milton's poem, there is still the issue of how the poem's form relates to its content. Do the first eight lines differ from the last six in subject matter? If so, do these sections' different rhyme schemes affect your response to their subjects?

Another common pattern in literature is **repetition**. Perhaps you have noted already that Milton uses the word *serve* three times. Moreover, Harper uses *sigh* three times, *lightly* twice, and the phrase *too light* twice. Yet even when repetition is easy to detect, readers may have different ideas about its function. Again, the issue then becomes not so much whether the author is repeating words, but how this repetition contributes to the work as a whole. What might Milton and Harper be trying to achieve when they use certain words more than once?

Often a text's patterns are more elusive. In the words of literary theorist Kenneth Burke, readers must spend time figuring out "what goes with what," besides having to determine the significance of the patterns they find. With Milton's poem, you may not have realized immediately that the words *spent* and *account* can be linked. Both of these words come from the world of finance. Even if you do make this connection, you still face the task of deciding why economic terms appear in a poem about religious matters.

A text's apparent oppositions are also patterns to be debated. For instance, when Milton contrasts "my light" with "this dark world," readers may have different notions of what he associates with each phrase. And while some readers may readily point out Harper's contrast between free labor and slave labor, others may say she is implying that the two really should not be distinguished.

6. *Issues of evaluation.*   Consciously or unconsciously, **evaluation** always plays a central role in reading. When you read a work of literature, you evaluate its ideas and the actions of its characters. You judge, too, the views you assume the author is promoting. Moreover, you gauge the artistic quality of the text.

Specifically, you engage in three kinds of evaluation as you read. One kind is philosophical: You decide whether a particular idea or action is wise. Another kind is ethical: You decide whether an idea or action is morally good. The third kind is aesthetic: You decide whether parts of the text, or the work as a whole, succeed as art. Of course, another reader may disagree with your criteria for wisdom, morality, and art; people's standards often differ. It is not surprising, then, that in the study of literature issues of evaluation come up frequently.

Philosophical differences may arise with Milton's ultimate willingness to serve God by "waiting." Some readers may feel that his attitude makes sense, others may accuse him of being too passive, and there may be both praise and criticism of his devotion to God in the first place. With Piercy's poem, different ethical judgments are possible regarding the final stanza. Like the poem's speaker, some readers may feel it wrong for museums to house objects intended for practical use. Other readers may praise this practice, believing that often such objects survive only because museums preserve them. Finally, different aesthetic judgments are possible as readers decide the artistic value of Piercy's poem. Some readers may be stirred by the poem's call for "real" work; some may feel the poem too much resembles a lecture; and other readers may have mixed feelings about the poem, appreciating certain lines but not others. These different assessments of the poem would probably reflect different conceptions of what poetry in general should be like.

Sometimes you may have trouble distinguishing the three types of judgments from one another. Philosophical evaluation, ethical evaluation, and aesthetic evaluation can overlap. For example, return to Milton's endorsement of "waiting." You may conclude that his attitude is neither wise nor ethical, and for this reason you may also find it an artistic flaw in the poem. Keep in mind, however, that you can still like many aspects of a literary work even if you disagree with views you believe the author is promoting. Atheists may admire the craft of Milton's poem while refusing to share his belief in God.

If you did dispute the artistic value of Milton's poem, you would be challenging countless admirers of it. Increasingly, though, the status of Milton's poem and other literary classics is being questioned. Many scholars argue that literary studies have focused too much on white male authors. They refuse to assume that Milton's works are great and universally relevant; they criticize the long neglect of women and minority authors. Yet even as these scholars call attention to writers such as Frances Harper, other people continue to prize more well-known writers such as Milton. The result is ongoing debate about whose works should be taught in the first place.

7. *Issues of historical and cultural context.*   Because works of literature are written by people living in particular times and places, issues of **historical** and **cultural context** arise. Eventually these works may engage a wide variety of readers, including members of much-later generations and inhabitants of distant cultures. Yet these works often continue to reflect the circumstances of their creation. You can tell by the content of Frances Harper's poem "Free Labor" that she wrote it soon after the American Civil War. You may recall that Milton wrote his poem soon after the seventeenth-century English Civil War. If you did not know that fact when you first read the poem, probably much of Milton's language nevertheless struck you as belonging to an era long past. Even the word *fondly*, which is still used, had a different definition in Milton's time: Whereas most of us would now take it to mean "affectionately," for Milton it meant "foolishly."

Since Marge Piercy's language is easily understood by many people today, her poem seems much closer to the present. All the same, you can examine from a historical perspective the specific aspects of twentieth-century life Piercy mentions. You might look for answers to questions like these: To what extent, and in what places, do workers today engage in the heavy field labor she depicts? How did modern museums acquire the kinds of objects she refers to? What are the various ways that museums have exhibited these artifacts?

We provide some background for each literary work we present, thereby helping you begin to situate it historically and culturally. In Chapter 7, we explain how to keep putting literature in context, especially by doing research in the library. For now, we want to emphasize that contextualizing a work involves more than just piling up facts about its origin. In the study of literature, often issues of historical and cultural context are issues of *relevance*. The question becomes, *Which* facts about a work's creation are important for contemporary readers to know? and *How* would awareness of these facts help them understand the work better? For instance, while readers can inform themselves about Frances Harper's career as a political activist, they may disagree about the extent to which her poem should be interpreted as autobiographical.

Perhaps you do like to connect a literary work with its author's own life. Since all three poems here use the first person ("I" or "we"), you may feel that they strongly invite you to make such a link. Yet you are almost always engaging in a debatable move when you assert that a work is thoroughly autobiographical. Among other things, you risk overlooking aspects of the text that depart significantly from the author's own experiences, impressions, and beliefs. Like Milton's poem about his blindness, certain texts do seem windows into the author's life. Nevertheless, some readers would argue that Milton's poem presents just one side of him and that he actually continued to do much more than "wait." Even in Milton's case, then, the work should be distinguished from the author's life. To be sure, we are not urging you to refrain from ever connecting the two. Rather, we are pointing out that whatever links you draw may be the subject of debate.

It is also important to note that the term *history* can be defined in various ways. When you refer to a work's historical context, you need to clarify what you have in mind. After all, you may be examining one or more of the following: (1) the life of the work's author; (2) the time period in which it was written;

(3) any time period mentioned within the text; (4) its subsequent reception, including responses to it by later generations; (5) the forms in which the work has been published, which may involve changes in its spelling, punctuation, wording, and overall appearance.

8. *Issues of genre.* So far, we have been identifying categories of issues. Issues of **genre** are *about* categorization, for they involve efforts to determine what *kind* of text a particular work is. Nowadays, most people would say that the basic genres of literature are poetry, the short story, the novel, and drama. If you were asked to identify the genres of the works by Milton, Harper, and Piercy that we have been discussing, you might logically call each a poem. But you do not have to stop there. You can try to classify each poem more precisely, aiming for a term that better sums up its specific content and form. Issues of genre most often arise with such further classification. And as you come up with more exact labels for the poems, other readers may label them differently. Because Milton is obviously trying to soothe his distress over his blindness, you may see his poem as basically an act of self-consolation or therapy. Meanwhile, a number of readers may be more inclined to call his poem a sermon, believing that he is primarily concerned with strengthening his society's faith in God. Perhaps you feel that Milton's poem is both an act of self-consolation and a sermon. But even then, you must still decide whether these labels are equally appropriate. Does one convey the poem's overall drift better, or do they both convey it well? Much of the time, issues of genre are issues of priority. Readers debate not whether a certain label for a work is possible, but whether that label is the best.

9. *Issues of social policy.* Many works of literature have been attempts at social reform, exposing defects of their cultures and encouraging specific cures. A famous example is Upton Sinclair's 1906 novel *The Jungle;* by vividly depicting horrible working conditions in Chicago's stockyards, it led the meat processing industry to adopt more humane practices. Even when a work of literature is not blatantly political or seems rooted in the distant past, it may make you conscious of your own society's problems and possible solutions to them. Yet you and your classmates may propose different solutions and even disagree about what is a problem in the first place. The result is what we call issues of **social policy**.

Sometimes your position on a current issue of social policy will affect how you read a certain work. For instance, your view on whether religion should play a central role in contemporary American society may affect your response to Milton's poem. Even if current issues of social policy do not influence your original reading of a work, you can still use the work to raise such issues in your writing or in class discussion. Take Harper's poem, for example. Although it seems closely linked to America's Reconstruction period, it can serve you as a springboard for plunging into debates about how contemporary "garments" are made. A few years ago, television personality Kathie Lee Gifford was criticized because her clothing line was produced by women and children toiling in sweatshops for just a few cents an hour. In essence, many people argued that these workers were slave labor, not free labor, although the manufacturers who employed them evidently thought otherwise. Eventually Gifford herself apologized for this exploitation and, in testimony before a congressional committee, proposed ways of ending it. But Americans still have not agreed on whether and how sweatshop conditions should be abolished. Imagine a paper in which, using Harper's poem as a point of departure, you elaborate your own perspective on the Gifford case.

10. _Issues of cause and effect._ Issues of **causality** are common in literary studies. Often they arise as readers present different explanations for a certain character's behavior. Remember that even the speaker in a poem can be thought of as a character with motives worth analyzing. You can pursue questions like these: Why does the speaker of Milton's poem not hear Patience sooner? Why does Harper's speaker brood so much about slave labor in a poem titled "Free Labor"? Why does the "I" of Piercy's poem turn from describing physical activities (like harnessing, pulling, and straining) to identifying objects (Greek amphoras, Hopi vases, the pitcher)? You can also analyze characters' impact.

These questions can be rephrased to center on the author. For example, you can ask why Harper has her speaker brood about slave labor, and why Piercy has her poem shift from activities to objects. Actually, if you look back at all the questions we have brought up in discussing the various types of issues, you may see that most can be phrased as questions about the author's purposes. But keep in mind your options. You may not find it useful to focus on authorial intention in a given case. Often you will be better off sticking with one of the other types of issues we have mentioned. Or you may prefer to turn a question about authorial purpose into a question about authorial effect. For instance, how should readers react when Harper has her speaker brood about slave labor? What does Piercy accomplish when she shifts in her poem from activities to objects? You can address questions like these without sounding as if you know exactly what the author really intended.

Claims

You may not be used to calling things you say or write _claims_. But even when you utter a simple observation about the weather—for instance, "It's beginning to rain"—you are making a claim. Basically, a **claim** is a statement that is spoken or written in the hope that it will be considered true. With this definition in mind, you may start noticing claims everywhere. Most of us make lots of them every day. Furthermore, most of our claims are accepted as true by the people to whom we make them. Imagine how difficult life would be if the opposite were the case; human beings would be perpetually anxious if they distrusted almost everything they were told.

At times, though, claims do conflict with other claims. In a literature course, disagreements inevitably arise. Again, try not to let disagreements scare you. You can learn a lot from encountering views other than yours and from having to support your own. Moreover, exciting talk can occur as your class negotiates differences of opinion.

Recall that we defined an _issue_ as a question with various debatable answers. _Claims_, as we will be using the term, are the debatable answers. For examples of claims in literary studies, look back at our explanations of various kinds of issues. Along the way, we mentioned a host of claims: for instance, that Milton's "when" represents a single occasion; that Harper's speaker does not actually distinguish between slave labor and free labor; and that Piercy's definition of *real* is misguided. These claims are debatable because in each case at least one other position is possible.

Not every claim is a firm, sweeping generalization. In some instances, you may want to *qualify* a claim of yours, which involves expressing the claim in words that make it less than absolute. The terms available for qualifying a claim are numerous. You might use words such as *perhaps, maybe, seems, appears, probably,* and *most likely* to indicate that you are not reporting a definite fact. Similarly, words such as *some, many, most,* and *several* allow you to acknowledge that your claim is limited in scope, applicable to just a portion of whatever you are discussing.

In literature classes, two types of claims are especially common. To criticize Piercy's definition of *real* is to engage in **evaluation**. To identify the main ideas of her poem is to engage in **interpretation**. Conventionally, interpretation is the kind of analysis that depends on hypotheses rather than simple observation of plain fact. Throughout this book, we will refer to the practice of interpreting a work or certain aspects of it. Admittedly, sometimes you may have trouble distinguishing interpretation from evaluation. When you evaluate some feature of a work or make an overall judgment of that work, probably you are operating with a certain interpretation as well, even if you do not make that interpretation explicit. Similarly, when you interpret part of a work or the text as a whole, probably you have already decided whether the text is worth figuring out. Nevertheless, the two types of claims differ in their emphases. When you attempt to interpret a work, you are mostly analyzing it; when you attempt to evaluate the work, you are mostly judging it.

In class discussions, other students may resist a claim you make about a literary work. Naturally, you may choose to defend your view at length. But remain open to the possibility of changing your mind, either by modifying your claim somehow or by shifting completely to another one. Also, entertain the possibility that a view different from yours is just as reasonable, even if you do not share it.

In much of your writing for your course, you will be identifying an issue and making one main claim about it, which can be called your **thesis**. Then, as you attempt to support your main claim, you will make a number of smaller claims. In drafts of your paper, welcome opportunities to test the claims you make in it. Review your claims with classmates to help you determine how persuasive your thinking is. You will be left with a stronger sense of what you must do to make your paper credible.

Persuasion

As we have noted, argument is often associated with arrogant insistence. Many assume that if two people are arguing, they are each demanding to be seen as correct. At its best, however, argument involves careful efforts to persuade. When you make such an effort, you indicate that you believe your claims, even if you remain open to revising them. You indicate as well that you would like others to agree with you. Yet to attempt **persuasion** is to concede that you must support your claims if others are to value them.

The art of persuasion has been studied for centuries under the name of **rhetoric**. Today, often the term *rhetoric* is used negatively: Politicians accuse one another of indulging in "mere rhetoric," as if the term meant deceptive exaggeration. But human beings habitually resort to persuasion; hence, rhetoric deserves more esteem. Besides, only in modern times has rhetoric not been regarded as a central part of education. In ancient Greece and Rome as well as in Renaissance Europe, rhetoric was an important academic subject. It was viewed, too, as a body of thought that people could actually put to use, especially in the realm of public affairs. Much of the advice we will give you about writing looks back to this history. Over and over, we will convey to you principles drawn from the rhetorical tradition.

As you have probably discovered on many occasions, it can be hard for you to sway people who hold views different from yours. Not always will you be able to change their minds. Yet you may still convince them that your claims are at least reasonable. Moreover, the process of trying to persuade others will force you to clarify your ideas, to review why you hold them, and to analyze the people you aim to affect.

Audience

When you hear the word **audience**, perhaps you think first of people attending plays, concerts, movies, or lectures. Yet *audience* also describes readers, including the people who read your writing. Not everything you write is for other people's eyes; in this course, you may produce notes, journal entries, and even full-length drafts that only you will see. From time to time in the course, however, you will do public writing. On these occasions, you will be trying to persuade your audience to accept whatever claims you make.

These occasions will require you to consider more than just your subject matter. If you are truly to persuade your readers, you must take them into account. Unfortunately, you will not be able to find out everything about your audience beforehand. Moreover, you will have to study the ways in which your readers differ from one another. Usually, though, you will be able to identify some of their common values, experiences, and assumptions. Having this knowledge will strengthen your ability to make a case they appreciate.

In analyzing a work of literature, you may try to identify its *implied reader:* that is, the type of person that the work seems to address. Remember, too, that people may have read the work in manuscript or when it was first published. Finally, the work may have had innumerable readers since. Often we will ask you to write about a text's effect on you, and to compare your reaction with your classmates'.

Evidence

Evidence is the support that you give your claims so that others will accept them. What sort of evidence you must provide depends on what your audience requires to be persuaded. When you make claims during class discussions, your classmates and instructor might ask you follow-up questions, thereby suggesting what you must do to convince them. As a writer, you might often find yourself having to guess your readers' standards of evidence. Naturally, your guesses will be influenced by any prior experiences you have had with your audience. Moreover, you may have opportunities to review drafts with some of its members.

When you make an argument about literature, the evidence most valued by your audience is likely to be details of the work itself. Direct quotations from the text are an especially powerful means of indicating that your claims are well grounded. But when you quote, you need to avoid seeming willfully selective. If you merely quote Milton's description of himself as "useless," without acknowledging his final line ("They also serve who only stand and wait"), you may come across as distorting his poem. In general, quoting from various parts of a text will help you give the impression that you are being accurate.

If you make claims about the historical or cultural context of a work, your evidence may include facts about its original circumstances. You may be drawn to the author's own experiences and statements, believing these shed light on the text. But again, use such materials cautiously, for not always will they seem strong evidence for your claims. Even if the author of a text explicitly declared what he or she was up to in writing it, people are not obliged to accept that declaration as a guide to the finished work. Some people may feel that the author's statement of intention was deliberately misleading, while others may claim that the author failed to understand his or her own achievement.

Another kind of evidence for your arguments about literature is your **ethos**. This is a traditional term in rhetoric; it refers to the image of you that your audience gets as you attempt to persuade. Actually, there are two kinds of ethos. One is the image of you that your audience holds even before you present your analysis. Often your audience will not know much about you beforehand. In general, this kind of ethos plays a role when the speaker or writer has a prior reputation. When retired army general Colin Powell gives a speech, he can expect much of his audience to start off trusting him, since millions of Americans admire him already.

Even if you are not well known, the second kind of ethos may greatly influence how people respond to your argument. This kind is the image of you that your audience develops in hearing or reading your actual words. To secure your audience's trust, you ought to give the impression that you are calmly and methodically laying out your claims as well as your reasons for them. Making concessions to views different from yours is also a good strategy, indicating that you aim to be fair. On the other hand, if your presentation is disorganized or your tone self-righteous, you may put your audience on guard. You may come across as someone not committed to serious inquiry.

Warrants

Of all the elements of argument, **warrants** may be the least familiar to you. You have heard of search warrants and arrest warrants, documents that indicate the police are justified in searching a place or jailing a person. More generally, warrants are the beliefs that lead people to call certain things evidence for their claims. Imagine that you have just made a claim to your classmates and are now trying to support it. Imagine further that your listeners are reluctant to call your supporting information *evidence*; they want you to explain why you do so. In effect, your audience is asking you to identify your warrants: that is, the assumptions that make you think the information you have given reinforces your case. Throughout this book, we use the terms *warrants* and *assumptions* interchangeably.

Let's say you claim that, despite her denial, the speaker in Harper's poem does hear the "sad despairing cry" of a slave even when she puts on the garment made by free labor. Asked to provide evidence for your claim, you might note two things: (1) The speaker refers repeatedly to slavery throughout the rest of the poem; (2) her mention of the phrase "sad despairing cry" suggests that this sound still haunts her. But then you may be asked for your warrants, the assumptions that lead you to see your evidence as support for your claim. Some of your assumptions might be about literature itself: for instance, that repetition in a poem is significant; that the speaker of a poem may contradict herself; and that literary works are most interesting when they undercut their apparent meaning. Some of your assumptions might be about human nature: for example, that people's denials can express their unconscious obsessions. Some of your assumptions might be about specific historical periods and cultures: for instance, that slavery could not have been easily forgotten by African Americans of the 1870s, especially when white Northerners as well as white Southerners were increasingly reluctant to aid black free labor. Often literature classes are most enlightening when students discuss with one another their assumptions about literature, about human nature, and about other times and places. If your classmates differ in their assumptions, that may be because they differ in the ways they grew up, the experiences they have had, the reading they have done, and the authorities that have influenced them.

Once you state your warrants for a claim you are making, your audience may go further, asking you to identify assumptions supporting the warrants themselves. But more frequently you will have to decide how much you should mention your warrants in the first place. In class discussion, usually your classmates' and instructor's responses to your claims will indicate how much you have to spell out your assumptions. When you write, you have to rely more on your own judgment of what your audience requires. If you suspect that your readers will find your evidence unusual, you should identify your warrants at length. If, however, your readers are bound to accept your evidence, then a presentation of warrants may simply distract them. Again, reviewing drafts of your paper with potential readers will help you determine what to do.

A WRITING EXERCISE

We have noted that when you argue, you attempt to *persuade* an *audience* to accept your *claims* regarding an *issue*, by presenting *evidence* and relying on *warrants*. In addition, we have explained the italicized terms. Now we would like you to write an analysis of an argument someone has made in print. Certainly it can be an argument about literature, but you need not restrict yourself to that subject. Perhaps you will look to another discipline, analyzing an argument made in one of that field's journals or books. Perhaps you will analyze a political argument made by a newspaper or magazine columnist. Whatever the argument you choose, try to identify its issues, claims, evidence, warrants, and intended audience. State whether you find the argument persuasive, and explain why you feel about it the way you do.

LITERATURE AS ARGUMENT

Much of this book concerns arguing *about* literature. But sometimes literary works can be said to present arguments themselves. In some of the works we have included, certain characters make claims, often in debate with one another, while other works give the impression that the author is arguing for a certain position. Admittedly, not all works of literature are best seen as containing or making arguments, but occasionally, you will find that associating a literary text with argument opens up productive lines of inquiry. Moreover, as you argue about literature, arguments *within* literature can help you see how you might persuade others.

For examples of arguments within literature, turn again to Milton's poem on page 9. The poem's initial speaker, presumably Milton himself, asks "'Doth God exact day-labor, light denied?'" Although technically these words form a question, they can also be considered a claim. With them, the speaker is evidently trying to persuade his audience that God is unfair, demanding hard work from him even though he is now blind. The speaker's preceding lines can be regarded as evidence that he is using to justify his despair. He notes that though his "one talent" is to write, and though he wants to serve God by writing, he has lost his sight before his life is half over.

The speaker does not actually spell out his warrants. Consider, however, his reference to Christ's parable of the talents (Luke 19:12–27). In the ancient Middle East, a *talent* was a unit of money. In the parable, a servant is scolded by his master for hoarding the one talent that his master had given him. By telling this story, Christ implies that people should make use of the gifts afforded them by God. For the speaker in Milton's poem, the parable has a lot of authority. Evidently he feels that he should carry out its lesson. In effect, then, the parable has indeed become a warrant for him: that is, a basis for finding his blindness cause for lament.

Who, exactly, is the speaker's audience? Perhaps he is not addressing anyone in particular. Or, perhaps the speaker's mind is divided and one side of it is addressing the other. Or, perhaps the speaker is addressing God, even though he refers to God in the third person. Given that the speaker is answered by Patience, perhaps he means to address *that* figure, although Patience may actually be just a part of him rather than an altogether separate being.

At any rate, Patience takes the speaker for an audience in responding. And while Patience does not provide evidence, let alone warrants, Patience does make claims about God and His followers. Furthermore, Milton as author seems to endorse Patience's claims; apparently he is using the poem to advance them.

Besides pointing out how God is served, Milton suggests that God ought to be served, even if God lets bad things happen to good people like Milton.

Every author can be considered an audience for his or her own writing, but some authors write expressly to engage in a dialogue with themselves. Perhaps Milton wrote his poem partly to convince himself that his religion was still valid and his life still worth living. Significantly, he did not publish the poem until about twenty years later. Yet, because he did publish it eventually, at some point he must have contemplated a larger audience for it. The first readers of the poem would have been a relatively small segment of the English population: those literate and prosperous enough to have access to books of poetry. In addition, a number of the poem's first readers would have shared Milton's religious beliefs. Perhaps, however, Milton felt that even the faith of this band had to be bolstered. For one thing, not every Protestant of the time would have shared Milton's enthusiasm for the Puritan government. Recall that this regime executed the king, supposedly replacing him with the rule of God. Milton's words "His state / is kingly" can be seen as an effort to persuade readers that the Puritans did put God on England's throne.

Most works of literature do not incorporate each element of argument we have discussed. Rarely do they feature arguments that do everything: acknowledge an audience, specify an issue, articulate claims, and carefully support these claims with substantial evidence and identified warrants. When characters argue, typically they do so in dramatic situations, not the sort of circumstances that permit elaborate debate. Also, traditionally literature has been a way for authors to make their own arguments indirectly: that is, to persuade with characterization, plot, and image rather than with straightforward development of claims. Do register the "gaps" as well as the strengths of any argument you find in a literary work. If the argument seems incomplete, however, a more drawn-out argument may have made the work less compelling.

Investigating Topics of Literary Criticism

To get ideas about a literary text, try considering how it deals with **topics** that have preoccupied literary studies as a profession. Some of these topics have interested the discipline for many years. One example is work, a common subject of the poems by Milton, Harper, and Piercy. Traditionally, literary studies has also been concerned with topics such as family relations, teaching and learning, love, insiders and outsiders, acts of judgment, and mortality. Moreover, the discipline has long called attention to topics that are essentially classic conflicts: for example, innocence versus experience; free will versus fate or determinism; the individual versus society; nature versus culture; and eternity versus the passing time.

Over the last few years, however, literary studies has turned to several new concerns. For instance, quite a few literary critics now consider the ways in which literary texts are often *about* reading, writing, interpretation, and evaluation. Some other subjects that critics increasingly refer to in their analysis of literature are:

- traits that significantly shape human identity, including gender, race, ethnic background, social class, sexual orientation, cultural background, nationality, and historical context;
- how groups are represented, including stereotypes held by others;
- how people acknowledge — or fail to acknowledge — differences among human beings;
- divisions, conflicts, and multiple forces *within* the self;
- boundaries, including the processes through which these are created, preserved, and challenged;
- politics and ideology, including the various forms that power and authority can take; acts of domination, oppression, exclusion, and appropriation; and acts of subversion, resistance, and parody;
- how carnivals and other festivities challenge or preserve social order;
- distinctions between what's universal and what's historically or culturally specific;
- relations between the public and the private; the social and the personal;
- relations between the apparently central and the apparently marginal;
- relations between what's supposedly normal and what's supposedly abnormal;
- relations between "high" culture and "low" (that is, mass or popular) culture;
- economic and technological developments, as well as their effects;
- the role of performance in everyday life;
- values — ethical, aesthetic, religious, professional, and institutional;
- desire and pleasure;
- the body;
- the unconscious;
- memory, including public commemorations as well as personal memory.

If you find that a literary text touches on one of these topics, try next to determine how the work specifically addresses that topic. Perhaps you will consider the topic an element of the text's theme. In any case, remember that by itself, a topic is not the same as a theme. While a topic can usually be expressed in a word or short phrase, a theme is a whole claim or assertion that you believe the text makes.

Actually, the topics we have identified may be most worth consulting when you have just begun analyzing a literary text and are far from establishing its theme. By using these topics, you can generate preliminary questions about the text, various issues you can then explore.

To demonstrate how these topics can stimulate inquiry, we will apply some of them to the following poem, "Night Waitress." It is from the 1986 book *Ghost Money,* by the late American poet Lynda Hull (1954–1994). Hull had been developing an impressive career in literature when she died in a car accident. This poem is also about work, the speaker being the night waitress of the title.

LYNDA HULL

Night Waitress

Reflected in the plate glass, the pies
look like clouds drifting off my shoulder.
I'm telling myself my face has character,
not beauty. It's my mother's Slavic face.
She washed the floor on hands and knees   5
below the Black Madonna, praying
to her god of sorrows and visions
who's not here tonight when I lay out the plates,
small planets, the cups and moons of saucers.
At this hour the men all look   10
as if they'd never had mothers.
They do not see me. I bring the cups.
I bring the silver. There's the man
who leans over the jukebox nightly
pressing the combinations   15
of numbers. I would not stop him
if he touched me, but it's only songs
of risky love he leans into. The cook sings
with the jukebox, a moan and sizzle
into the grill. On his forehead   20
a tattooed cross furrows,
diminished when he frowns. He sings words
dragged up from the bottom of his lungs.
I want a song that rolls
through the night like a big Cadillac   25
past factories to the refineries
squatting on the bay, round and shiny
as the coffee urn warming my palm.
Sometimes when coffee cruises my mind
visiting the most remote way stations,   30
I think of my room as a calm arrival
each book and lamp in its place. The calendar
on my wall predicts no disaster
only another white square waiting
to be filled like the desire that fills   35
jail cells, the old arrest
that makes me stare out the window or want
to try every bar down the street.
When I walk out of here in the morning
my mouth is bitter with sleeplessness.   40
Men surge to the factories and I'm too tired
to look. Fingers grip lunch box handles,

belt buckles gleam, wind riffles my uniform
and it's not romantic when the sun unlids
the end of the avenue. I'm fading   45
in the morning's insinuations
collecting in the crevices of buildings,
in wrinkles, in every fault
of this frail machinery.   [1986]

A WRITING EXERCISE

After you read "Night Waitress," do a ten-minute freewrite in which you try
to identify how the poem relates to one or more of the topics mentioned on
pages 30–31. You might also find it helpful to compare this poem about work
to the poems by Milton, Harper, and Piercy on pages 9–11.

We think several of the topics now popular in literary studies are relevant to
Hull's poem. Here are just a few possibilities, along with questions that these topics can generate:

Gender.   The speaker alludes to conventional roles through which men and
women relate to each other. When the speaker declares that "at this hour the men
all look / as if they'd never had mothers," she indicates that women have often
played a maternal role for men. Furthermore, she implies that often women have
been the primary caretakers of their sons. (Notice that she makes no reference to
fathers.) What is the effect of this attention to women as mothers of men? In most
of the poem, the speaker refers to men as potential lovers. Yet even as she suggests
she would like a sexual relationship with a man, she suggests as well that she has
had trouble establishing worthwhile attachments. Why has she had such difficulty, do you think? Does the problem seem due to her personality alone, or do
you sense larger forces shaping her situation? Notice, too, that the poem refers to
the factory workers as male, while the woman who speaks is a waitress. To what
extent does American society perpetuate a gendered division of labor?

Ethnic background.   Near the start of the poem, the speaker refers to her
mother's "Slavic face" and points out that her mother served "the Black
Madonna," a religious icon popular in Central European countries like the
Czech Republic and Poland. What is the effect of these particular ethnic references? To pursue this line of inquiry, probably you will need to do research into
the Black Madonna, whether in a library or on the Internet.

Social class.   In part, considering social class means thinking about people's
ability to obtain material goods. When the speaker compares her ideal song to "a
big Cadillac," she implies that she doesn't currently possess such a luxurious car.
At the same time, she is expressing her desire for the song, not the car. Why might
the first item be more important to her right now? Social class is also a matter of

how various workplaces are related to one another. This poem evokes a restaurant, factories, refineries, and bars. How are these settings connected as parts of American society? Think, too, about how you would label the social class of the various occupations the poem mentions. What would you say is the social class of a waitress? To what classes would you assign people who work in factories and refineries? Who, for the most part, are the social classes that have to work at night?

Sexual orientation.   The speaker of "Night Waitress" seems heterosexual, an orientation often regarded as the only legitimate one. Because almost all societies have made heterosexuality the norm, a lot of people forget that it is a particular orientation and that not everyone practices it. Within literary studies, gay and lesbian critics have pointed out that a literary work may seem to deal with sexuality in general but may actually refer just to heterosexuality. Perhaps "Night Waitress" is examining heterosexuality as a specific social force. If so, how might the speaker's discontent be related to heterosexuality's influence as a particular institution? Keep in mind that you don't have to assume anything about the author's sexuality as you pursue such a question. In fact, heterosexuality may be a more important topic in Hull's poem than she intended.

Divisions, conflicts, and multiple forces within the self.   The poem's beginning indicates that the speaker experiences herself as divided. The first four lines reveal that she feels pride and disappointment in her mirror image: "telling myself my face has character, / not beauty." Later she indicates that within her mind are "remote way stations" that she visits only on occasion. Furthermore, she seems to contradict herself. Although she initially refers to her room as "a calm arrival," she goes on to describe that place negatively, as empty and confined. Early in the evening, she seems sexually attracted to the man playing the jukebox ("I would not stop him / if he touched me"), but by morning her mood is "not romantic" and she is "too tired / to look" at the male factory workers. What may be the significance of these paradoxes?

Boundaries.   In the first line the speaker is apparently looking at a window, and later, she reveals that at times she feels driven to "stare out the window" of her room. What should a reader make of these two references to such a common boundary? When the speaker observes that the men in the restaurant "do not see me," she indicates that a boundary exists between them and her. Do you think she is merely being paranoid, or do you suspect that the men are indeed ignoring her? If they *are* oblivious to her, how do you explain their behavior? Still another boundary explored in the poem is the line between night and day. What happens when the speaker crosses this line? What can night, day, and the boundary between them signify? You might also consider what the author of a literary work does with its technical boundaries. Often a poem creates boundaries in its breaks between stanzas. Yet "Night Waitress" is a continuous, unbroken text; what is the effect of Hull's making it so? At the same time, Hull doesn't always respect sentence boundaries in her lines. At several points in the poem, sentences spill over from one line to another. This poetic technique is called **enjambment**; what is its effect here?

Politics and ideology.   When, in referring to the jukebox man, the speaker declares that "I would not stop him / if he touched me," she can be taken to imply that often male customers flirt with waitresses. How might flirtation be seen as involving power, authority, and even outright domination? Do you see the poem as commenting on such things? Earlier we raised issues of social class; these can be seen as political issues, too. How would you describe a society in which some people have "a big Cadillac" and others do not?

Carnivals and other festivities.   Although the poem does not refer to a "carnival" in any sense of that word, it does mention bars, which today are regarded by many people as places of festive retreat from work. What adjectives would you use to describe the speaker when she says that sometimes she wants "to try every bar down the street"?

Distinctions between what is universal and what is historically or culturally specific.   Try to identify anything that is historically or culturally specific about this poem's setting. Certainly the word *Slavic* and the reference to the Black Madonna indicate that the speaker has a particular background. You might also note her description of the restaurant, her use of the Cadillac as a metaphor, and her mention of the "factories" and the "refineries" that are "squatting on the bay." Although a wide range of places might fit these details, the poem's setting does not seem universal. Indeed, many readers are attracted to literature *because* it deals with specific landscapes, people, and plots. Nevertheless, these same readers usually expect to get some larger, more widely applicable meanings out of literature even as they are engaged by its specific details. Are you inclined to draw general conclusions from "Night Waitress"? If so, what general meanings do you find in it? What sorts of people do you think might learn something about themselves from reading this poem?

Relations between the public and the private, the social and the personal.   The speaker of "Night Waitress" works in a very public place, a restaurant. Yet she seems to feel isolated there, trapped in her own private world. How did she come to experience public life this way, do you think? Later, she initially seems to value her room as a private retreat, calling it a "calm arrival," but then she describes it as a place so lonely that it leads her to "stare out the window or want / to try every bar down the street." How, then, would you ultimately describe the relations between the speaker's public life and her private one? In addressing this issue, probably you need to consider whether the speaker's difficulties are merely personal or reflect a larger social disorder. When, at the end of the poem, she refers to "this frail machinery," is she referring just to herself or is she suggesting that this phrase applies to her society in general? If she is indeed making a social observation, what do you sense are the "faults" in her society? Who else might be "fading"?

Relations between "high" culture and "low" culture.   Although the speaker does not identify the "songs / of risky love" playing on the jukebox, surely they are examples of what is called low, mass, or popular culture. Just as a lot of us are moved by such music when we hear it, so the jukebox player and the cook are engaged by it. In contrast, the poem itself can be considered an example of high culture. Often poetry is regarded as a serious art even by people who don't read it. In what ways, if any, does this poem conceivably resemble the songs it mentions? Given that author Lynda Hull is in essence playing with combinations of words, can we compare her with "the man / who leans over the jukebox nightly / pressing the combinations / of numbers"? (Actually, *numbers* has been a poetic term; centuries ago, it was commonly used as a synonym for the rhythms of poems.)

The role of performance in everyday life. The most conspicuous "performer" in this poem is the cook, who "sings words / dragged up from the bottom of his lungs." But in everyday life, people often perform in the sense of taking on certain roles, even disguising their real personalities. Do you see such instances of performing in this poem? If so, where? Notice that the speaker wears a uniform; can that be considered a costume she wears while performing as a waitress?

Religious values. The speaker clearly refers to religion when she recalls her mother's devotion to the Black Madonna, behavior that involved "praying / to her god of sorrows and visions." And although that god is "not here tonight," the speaker's description of waitressing has ritualistic overtones reminiscent of religious ceremonies. When she says, "I bring the cups. / I bring the silver," she could almost be describing preparations for Communion. In fact, she depicts the cook as wearing a religious emblem: "On his forehead / a tattooed cross furrows, / diminished when he frowns." What do you make of all this religious imagery? Might the speaker be trying to pursue certain religious values? Can she be reasonably described as looking for salvation?

Desire and pleasure. The speaker explicitly mentions the word *desire* when she describes the emptiness she feels in her room, a feeling of desolation "that makes me stare out the window or want / to try every bar down the street." These lines may lead you to believe that her desire is basically sexual. Yet when the speaker uses the words *I want* earlier in the poem, she expresses her wish for "a song that rolls / through the night like a big Cadillac." Here, her longing does not appear sexual in nature. Is the speaker referring to at least two kinds of desire, then? Or do you see her as afflicted with basically one kind?

The body. A notable feature of this poem is its attention to body parts. The speaker mentions her "shoulder," her "face," her mother's "face," her mother's "hands and knees," the cook's "forehead," his "lungs," her "palm," the "way stations" of her "mind," her "mouth," the factory workers' "fingers," and their "belt buckles." At the same time, the speaker never describes any particular body as a whole. What is the effect of this emphasis on mere parts? Does it connect in any way to the speaker's ultimate "fading"?

Memory. Already we have noted the speaker's reference to her mother at the start of the poem. In what way, if any, is it significant that she engages in recollection? What circumstances in her life might have prompted the speaker to look back at the past?

A WRITING EXERCISE

We have applied several topics from our list to Lynda Hull's poem "Night Waitress." Now, see how you can apply topics from the list to another poem about work. Choose one of the following four poems and try to come up with several questions about it by referring to the topics on the list. Then, select one of the questions you have formulated and freewrite for ten minutes in response to it.

The first poem, William Blake's "The Chimney Sweeper," is the oldest of the set. It appeared in Blake's 1789 book *Songs of Innocence*, each poem of which was accompanied by an engraving done by Blake (1757–1827). The other three poems are by contemporary authors. "Blackberries" is by Yusef Komunyakaa (b. 1947), who has become known for exploring various dimensions of African American experience; the poem appeared in his 1992 book *Magic City*. Next is "Singapore," by Mary Oliver (b. 1935), a Pulitzer Prize–winning American poet. This poem appeared in her 1992 book *House of Light* and was subsequently included in her 1993 collection *New and Selected Poems*. The final poem, "The Machinist, Teaching His Daughter to Play the Piano," is from B. H. Fairchild's 1997 volume *The Art of the Lathe*, which won the Kingsley Tufts Poetry Award. Although Fairchild (b. 1942) has published several books of poetry, he has also worked in factories, and much of his writing concerns industrial life.

WILLIAM BLAKE
The Chimney Sweeper

When my mother died I was very young,
And my father sold me while yet my tongue
Could scarcely cry "'weep! 'weep! 'weep! 'weep!"
So your chimneys I sweep, and in soot I sleep.

There's little Tom Dacre, who cried when his head,   5
That curled like a lamb's back, was shaved: so I said
"Hush, Tom! never mind it, for when your head's bare
You know that the soot cannot spoil your white hair."

And so he was quiet, and that very night,
As Tom was a-sleeping, he had such a sight!   10
That thousands of sweepers, Dick, Joe, Ned, and Jack,
Were all of them locked up in coffins of black.

And by came an Angel who had a bright key,
And he opened the coffins and set them all free;
Then down a green plain leaping, laughing, they run,   15
And wash in the river, and shine in the sun.

♦   ♦   ♦

Then naked and white, all their bags left behind,
They rise upon clouds and sport in the wind;
And the Angel told Tom, if he'd be a good boy,
He'd have God for his father, and never want joy.   20

And so Tom awoke; and we rose in the dark,
And got with our bags and our brushes to work.
Though the morning was cold, Tom was happy and warm;
So if all do their duty they need not fear harm.   [1789]

YUSEF KOMUNYAKAA
Blackberries

They left my hands like a printer's
Or thief's before a police blotter
& pulled me into early morning's
Terrestrial sweetness, so thick
The damp ground was consecrated   5
Where they fell among a garland of thorns.

Although I could smell old lime-covered
History, at ten I'd still hold out my hands
& berries fell into them. Eating from one
& filling a half gallon with the other,   10
I ate the mythology & dreamt
Of pies & cobbler, almost

Needful as forgiveness. My bird dog Spot
Eyed blue jays & thrashers. The mud frogs
In rich blackness, hid from daylight.   15
An hour later, beside City Limits Road
I balanced a gleaming can in each hand,
Limboed between worlds, repeating *one dollar.*

The big blue car made me sweat.
Wintertime crawled out of the windows.   20
When I leaned closer I saw the boy
& girl my age, in the wide back seat
Smirking, & it was then I remembered my fingers
Burning with thorns among berries too ripe to touch.   [1992]

MARY OLIVER
Singapore

In Singapore, in the airport,
a darkness was ripped from my eyes.
In the women's restroom, one compartment stood open.
A woman knelt there, washing something
    in the white bowl.   5

Disgust argued in my stomach
and I felt, in my pocket, for my ticket.

A poem should always have birds in it.
Kingfishers, say, with their bold eyes and gaudy wings.
Rivers are pleasant, and of course trees.   10
A waterfall, or if that's not possible, a fountain
    rising and falling.
A person wants to stand in a happy place, in a poem.

When the woman turned I could not answer her face.
Her beauty and her embarrassment struggled together, and   15
    neither could win.
She smiled and I smiled. What kind of nonsense is this?
Everybody needs a job.

Yes, a person wants to stand in a happy place, in a poem.
But first we must watch her as she stares down at her labor,   20
    which is dull enough.
She is washing the tops of the airport ashtrays, as big as
    hubcaps, with a blue rag.
Her small hands turn the metal, scrubbing and rinsing.
She does not work slowly, nor quickly, but like a river.   25
Her dark hair is like the wing of a bird.

I don't doubt for a moment that she loves her life.
And I want her to rise up from the crust and the slop
    and fly down to the river.
This probably won't happen.   30
But maybe it will.
If the world were only pain and logic, who would want it?

Of course, it isn't.
Neither do I mean anything miraculous, but only
the light that can shine out of a life. I mean   35
the way she unfolded and refolded the blue cloth,
the way her smile was only for my sake; I mean
the way this poem is filled with trees, and birds.   [1992]

B. H. FAIRCHILD

The Machinist, Teaching His Daughter to Play the Piano

The brown wrist and hand with its raw knuckles and blue nails
        packed with dirt and oil, pause in mid-air,
the fingers arched delicately,

and she mimics him, hand held just so, the wrist loose,
        then swooping down to the wrong chord.   5
She lifts her hand and tries again.

Drill collars rumble, hammering the nubbin-posts.
        The helper lifts one, turning it slowly,
then lugs it into the lathe's chuck.

The bit shears the dull iron into new metal, falling   10
        into the steady chant of lathe work,
and the machinist lights a cigarette, holding

in his upturned palms the polonaise he learned at ten,
        then later the easiest waltzes,
etudes, impossible counterpoint   15

like the voice of his daughter he overhears one night
        standing in the backyard. She is speaking
to herself but not herself, as in prayer,

the listener is some version of herself,
        and the names are pronounced carefully,   20
self-consciously: Chopin, Mozart,

Scarlatti, . . . these gestures of voice and hands
        suspended over the keyboard
that move like the lathe in its turning

toward music, the wind dragging the hoist chain, the ring   25
        of iron on iron in the holding rack.
His daughter speaks to him one night,

but not to him, rather someone created between them,
        a listener, there and not there,
a master of lathes, a student of music.   [1997]   30

| 2 |

Writing

In Chapters 3 through 6, we will discuss how to write about each of the four literary genres featured in this book. At the moment, however, we will suggest how to write about a literary work of any genre. To make our advice concrete, we will trace what one student did as she worked on a writing assignment for a course much like yours. The assignment was given to a class that had been reading and discussing several poems about work, including the poems in Chapter 1 by John Milton, Frances Harper, Marge Piercy, and Lynda Hull. Each student chose a single poem from the syllabus and wrote a 600-word argument paper on it for a general audience. We will focus on the writing process of a student named Theresa Gardella.

Ultimately, Theresa chose to write about "What Work Is," the title poem from Philip Levine's 1991 book. Like Marge Piercy, Levine (b. 1928) grew up in Detroit. Although he has long been esteemed as a poet, much of his poetry continues to recall his youth in his native city, a world of automobile plants and other forms of heavy industry. Often Levine writes about his own hard work as a laborer in Detroit factories. Even when he is not being autobiographical, his poems often examine the difficulties faced by the American working class, both of his youth and of the present.

Before examining Theresa's writing process, read Levine's "What Work Is":

PHILIP LEVINE
What Work Is

We stand in the rain in a long line
waiting at Ford Highland Park. For work.
You know what work is — if you're
old enough to read this you know what
work is, although you may not do it.   5
Forget you. This is about waiting,
shifting from one foot to another.
Feeling the light rain falling like mist

into your hair, blurring your vision
until you think you see your own brother   10
ahead of you, maybe ten places.
You rub your glasses with your fingers,
and of course it's someone else's brother,
narrower across the shoulders than
yours but with the same sad slouch, the grin   15
that does not hide the stubbornness,
the sad refusal to give in to
rain, to the hours wasted waiting,
to the knowledge that somewhere ahead
a man is waiting who will say, "No,   20
we're not hiring today," for any
reason he wants. You love your brother,
now suddenly you can hardly stand
the love flooding you for your brother,
who's not beside you or behind or   25
ahead because he's home trying to
sleep off a miserable night shift
at Cadillac so he can get up
before noon to study his German.
Works eight hours a night so he can sing   30
Wagner, the opera you hate most,
the worst music ever invented.
How long has it been since you told him
you loved him, held his wide shoulders,
opened your eyes wide and said those words,   35
and maybe kissed his cheek? You've never
done something so simple, so obvious,
not because you're too young or too dumb,
not because you're jealous or even mean
or incapable of crying in   40
the presence of another man, no,
just because you don't know what work is.   [1991]

   Once she chose to write about Levine's poem for her paper, Theresa engaged
in four sorts of activities: (1) exploring, (2) planning, (3) composing, and (4) revising. As we describe each, keep in mind that these activities need not be consecu-
tive. Theresa moved back and forth among them as she worked on her assignment.

Exploring

   As you read a literary work, you are bound to interpret and judge it. Yet not
all reading is **critical reading**, which involves carefully and self-consciously analyzing various aspects of a text, including its meanings, its effects, and what it does

with typical elements of its genre. When you read a work critically, you also note questions it raises for you—issues you might explore further in class discussion and writing. Indeed, critical reading is a process of self-reflection. During this process, you monitor your own response to the text and try to identify why you see the text the way you do.

Perhaps you assume that literature contains hidden meanings that only an elite group of readers can spot. This is a common belief, but most people are quite capable of analyzing a literary work, especially if they know certain strategies for getting ideas about it. In rhetorical theory, these strategies are called methods of invention. Here we list some that Theresa used, including a few strategies that we have mentioned already. Try out any of them that are unfamiliar to you, even as you first read a text. Again, critical reading does not require divine inspiration. The following techniques have helped many a mortal:

1. *Make predictions as you read a text, guessing how it will turn out.*   If you wind up being surprised, fine. You may gain several insights into the text, and yourself, as you reflect on the ways in which the text defies your expectations. Even if the text proceeds as you anticipated, making predictions about it is worthwhile, for at least you will have considered its possible lines of development.

2. *Read the text more than once.*   You greatly increase your chances of getting ideas about it if you do. The first time around, you may be preoccupied with following the plot or with figuring out the text's basic meaning. Only by looking at the text repeatedly may you notice several of its other aspects, including features that really stir your thoughts. Given the busy schedule of a college student, you may be tempted to read a work just once before your class discusses it. But a single reading may leave you with relatively little to say, whereas multiple readings may give you several ideas to share.

3. *Note whatever changes of mind you go through as you read and reread the text.*

4. *Describe the audience that the author apparently had in mind, and note features of the text that support your image of its implied audience.*   At the same time, consider how real readers of the text—past, present, and future—might react to it, and why they might respond so. Also reflect on your own response to the text, noting anything in your own life that affects your reading of it.

5. *Read at least part of the text aloud, even if you are alone.*   Doing this will give you a better sense of how the text manipulates language.

6. *Consciously focus on the text's content and on its form.*   If you can focus on both content and form at the same time, fine, but many readers have trouble paying attention to the two simultaneously. In this case, deliberately alternate your focus first on content, then on form. This way you increase your chances of noticing things that the text is saying and doing.

7. *Consult a dictionary when you come across words in the text that you do not understand.*   Keep in mind that a text may make a familiar word ambiguous,

leaving you with the impression that the author is attaching more than one meaning to it. An example might be Levine's use of the word *work*, which seems to take on various definitions as his poem proceeds. Furthermore, a text may define a commonly used word in a way unfamiliar to you. As we noted earlier, an example would be Milton's use of the word *fondly*, which in his time meant "foolishly," not "affectionately." If you suspect that a writer is using a common word in what for you is an uncommon way, turn to a dictionary to check the word's possible meanings.

8. *Note patterns within the text.* At the same time, pay attention to elements of the text that appear to threaten its unity, for instance, apparent contradictions or digressions.

9. *Try to identify the text's most important word, image, or scene.* At the same time, consider how to justify your choice.

10. *Identify moments where the text makes a significant shift in meaning, imagery, tone, plot, narrator, or point of view.* These moments may very well occur at typographic breaks in the text. In a poem, for example, significant changes may occur when one stanza ends and another begins. Similarly, a play may change significantly as it moves from scene to scene. Short stories and essays may also engage in important shifts as they go from paragraph to paragraph. But you may find turning points anywhere in the text, so do not look solely at its obvious moments of transition.

11. *Mark passages in the text that strike you as especially memorable.* These passages would include any that you might quote in a paper about the text.

12. *Aim to complicate the views you take of characters in the text.* If you tend to see a character as thoroughly mistaken, evil, or "sick," look for potentially redeeming qualities of that person. Similarly, if you tend to see a character as thoroughly good, look for qualities that suggest the person is less than perfect. Furthermore, consider whether you or the author are inclined to stereotype people. Note, too, any ways in which the characters fail to fit stereotypes.

13. *Raise questions about the text even as you read.* For help, you can turn to our list of ten different types of issues (pp. 17–24). In effect, the list indicates some aspects of the text that might be especially worth pondering. Recall that these include the following:

- facts obscured or absent in the text
- the text's theme
- possible definitions of key words in the text
- the symbols it employs
- its patterns
- evaluations that might be made in response to it
- its historical and cultural context
- its genre
- its relevance to current political debates
- causes and effects of its characters' behavior; the author's aims and effects

14. Note whether and how the text addresses topics of particular interest to professional literary critics today. (For a discussion of such topics, refer to the last section of Chapter 1, pp. 30–36.

15. Think about the writer's alternatives: things the writer could have done and yet didn't do. Then, imagine that the writer had pursued these alternatives. How would the effect of the text have been different?

16. Consider whether and how the text itself features elements of argument. (Refer back to pp. 15–28 in Chapter 1.)

17. Compare the text with others on the same subject. So far, we have encouraged you to compare various poems about work. Going beyond the world of literature, you might compare whatever text you are focusing on to certain films, television shows, songs, advertisements, and articles in newspapers and magazines.

18. Discuss the text with your instructor, your classmates, and other people you know. If differences emerge between their views and yours, try to identify the exact issues at hand, as well as the possible reasons for those differences. Perhaps you will talk about the text with people who have not read it at all. If so, note the questions these people have about the text. Note, too, what you find yourself emphasizing as you describe the text to them.

You can also develop and pull together your thoughts about a text by informally writing about it. And the sooner you plunge into the rhythms of composing, the more comfortable you will feel producing a full-fledged paper. Your informal, preliminary writing can take various shapes. The following are just some of the things you might do.

1. Make notes in the text itself. A common method is to mark key passages, either by underlining these passages or running a highlighter over them. Both ways of marking are popular because they help readers recall main features of the text. But use these techniques moderately if you use them at all, for marking lots of passages will leave you unable to distinguish the really important parts of the text. Also, try "talking back" to the text in its margins. Next to particular passages, you might jot down words of your own, indicating any feelings and questions you have about those parts. On any page of the text, you might circle related words and then draw lines between these words to emphasize their connection. If a word or an idea shows up on numerous pages, you might circle it each time. Furthermore, try cross-referencing, by listing on at least one page the numbers of all those pages where the word or idea appears.

2. As you read the text, occasionally look away from it and jot down anything in it you recall. This memory exercise lets you review your developing impressions of the text. When you turn back to its actual words, you may find that you have distorted or overlooked aspects of it that you should take into account.

3. At various moments in your reading, freewrite about the text for ten minutes or so. Spontaneously explore your preliminary thoughts and feelings about it, as well as any personal experiences the text leads you to recall. One logical moment to do freewriting is when you have finished reading the text. But you do not have to wait until then; as you read, you might pause occasionally to freewrite. This way, you give yourself an opportunity to develop and review your thoughts about the text early on.

4. *Create what composition theorist Ann Berthoff calls a "dialectical notebook."* It involves using pages of your regular notebook in a particular way. On each page, draw a line down the middle to create two columns. In the left column, list various details of the text: specifically, words, images, characters, and events that strike you. Then, in the right column, jot down for each detail one or more sentences indicating *why* you were drawn to it. Take as many pages as you need to record and reflect on your observations. You can also use the two-column format to carry out a dialogue with yourself about the text. This is an especially good way to ponder aspects of the text that you find confusing, mysterious, or complex.

5. *Play with the text by revising it.* Doing so will make you more aware of options that the author rejected and give you a better sense of the moves that the author chose to make. Specifically, you might rearrange parts of the text, add to it, change some of its words, or shift its narrative point of view. After you revise the text, compare your alternative version with the original, considering especially differences in their effects.

A WRITING EXERCISE

Do at least ten minutes of freewriting about Levine's poem. Note questions you have about the poem that might be worth addressing in a more formal paper. Also compare Levine's poem on work to Milton's, Harper's, Piercy's, or Hull's poem on the subject. What similarities do you find? What differences?

The first time Theresa read Levine's poem, she started out predicting that it would define *work*. After all, its title is "What Work Is." Soon, though, she felt her expectation thwarted. For one thing, the speaker claims "you know what work is," as if the word does not need to be defined. Then, the speaker proceeds to declare that the poem is not even about work, but rather about "waiting." Theresa did not know how to interpret this change of subject. Her confusion was only heightened at the end of the poem, where the speaker contradicts the poem's beginning by asserting "you don't know what work is." After her first reading of the poem, Theresa came away from it puzzled.

At the same time, Theresa was excited because she felt that she had discovered at least one issue that she could write her paper about. As we noted, Theresa found herself grappling specifically with an issue of definition. She suspected that if she wrote her paper on this poem, she would analyze how it defines the word *work*, especially in relation to the word *waiting*.

Theresa realized, though, that first she had to pinpoint the text's patterns. Therefore, she began noting words that the poem uses more than once. After personal reflection, consultation with her teacher, and a meeting with a small group of classmates, Theresa had compiled a substantial list of words: *work, stand, know, waiting, rain, long, love, sad, ahead, man, wide, not,* and *because.* She also saw that the statement "you know what work is" occurs twice. Furthermore, Theresa noticed that certain words in the poem closely echo each other: *know / knowledge, say / said, shifting / shift.* Some of the poem's words represent related concepts: for instance, the "light rain falling like mist" can be connected to *flooding* and *crying.* A second example occurs in the last sentence, where the words *never, not, incapable, no,* and *don't* all emphasize negativity.

Not until she had read the poem aloud several times did Theresa become aware that it also features patterns of **alliteration**. In alliteration, certain words near one another begin with the same consonant. Here are some examples in Levine's poem:

forget, foot, feeling, falling, fingers

someone, shoulders, same sad slouch, stubbornness, sad

wasted, waiting (twice), wants (also: some*w*here)

brother, beside, behind

works, worst, wide, words

never, not (twice)

Yet Theresa knew that she had to do more than trace patterns. After all, she was thrown by the poem's shifts, its apparent discontinuities. So she also tried to pinpoint these breaks. As we reported, she was extremely conscious of the speaker's shift from the word *work* to *waiting* near the start. She was quite aware, too, that the poem's final line clashes with its earlier statement that "you know what work is." But upon reflection she felt that the biggest change occurs in the middle of the poem. There, with the words "you love your brother," the poem thoroughly departs from the scene of people waiting for a job, and it comes to focus instead on brotherly love.

As Theresa reread the poem several times, she looked for words that, in one way or another, helped connect its two halves. Again, she recognized as a form of connection the poem's imagery of falling water (*rain, flooding,* and *crying*), which runs throughout the text. She became aware that certain words in the poem have a dual frame of reference. They mean one thing in the context of the men's waiting in line and another, quite different thing when applied to the brothers' relationship. An example is the phrase "sad refusal." Clearly this phrase expresses the determination of the sleeping brother not to let life defeat him. Yet it could also apply to the statement made by the company's representative to the men waiting in line. By saying "'No, / we're not hiring today,'" the representative engages in a "sad refusal," though his listeners are the ones left sad. Similarly, while the word *stand* first appears as a label for what the men in line do, later it appears in connection with the brothers' bond ("now suddenly you can hardly stand / the love flooding you for your brother"). The same thing happens with the words *shifting* and *shift:* The first describes behavior in the line, but the second refers to the work of the sleeping brother. Note, too, what happens with the word *long*. At first it refers to the length of the line, but later it refers to the brothers' personal history ("How long has it been since you told him / you loved him").

Together, these double reference words led Theresa to consider what the poem is doing with the subject of time. She perceived the men waiting in line as oriented toward the future: They hope to be employed. But later the speaker accuses the brother in line of waiting too long to tell his brother he loves him. *This* waiting, Theresa saw, is not a matter of looking to the future. Rather, it is a failure to acknowledge the past: specifically, all the years that have passed before the brother in line can express fraternal affection.

Theresa was beginning to envision a paper in which she made claims about how the poem relates waiting to past, present, and future. As yet, though, she had not decided exactly what her main claim would be. Nor had she determined how her paper would examine the poem's references to work. In addition, Theresa still had some questions about the text itself. The following is an excerpt from freewriting she did at this point:

I'm still not sure who the "you" is. In the fourth line, the "you" seems to be the reader. Then the speaker says "Forget you." But then the poem keeps referring to "you," and this "you" seems to be not the reader but someone waiting in the line. Maybe it's the speaker himself. Anyway, I'm confused.

I also wonder if the poem is autobiographical. It might be about Levine's own experience of waiting in a job line and thinking about his relationship with his brother. The references to car factories make me think the city is Detroit, and that's where Levine grew up. He might be both the speaker and the "you" that the speaker addresses for most of the poem. But does this mean the poem takes place in the past? Levine is now a well-known poet, so I doubt that he's currently looking for a job. Since he was born in 1928, maybe the poem is set around 1950, when he would have been in his twenties.

Of course, there are unemployed people today, so I don't have any trouble relating the poem to the present even if it does take place years ago. Plus I guess it doesn't really matter whether the poem is about Levine himself. Other people still have to relate to it if it's going to succeed as a poem. I can identify with the

"you." I've applied for lots of jobs, and I haven't
always gotten them. And I've waited in lots of lines.
Just a few weeks ago, I waited in a long line at this
school to register for courses. Plus I know that sometimes I haven't thought about my family the way that I
should have. It's true that I haven't been as desperate
as the men in line in the poem seem to be. But I can
still empathize with them pretty much.

   In class, our instructor said that a lot of literary
critics today see literary works as being about reading
and writing. I hadn't looked at literature that way
before, but the idea is interesting to me, and I've been
thinking about it the more I read Levine's poem. I wonder
if the poem is to some extent about Levine's experience
in writing it, or our experience in reading it, or both.
I mean, besides using the word "shifting," the poem
itself shifts in focus. And the poem itself seems to me
like a long line that I'm moving through, waiting to get
the meaning. Maybe Levine wants me to think about the
work I am doing in reading his poem. Maybe he wants me to
see this work as involving reflection on human relationships, like the relationship between the brothers,
instead of just being a matter of waiting for the meaning
to emerge. Plus I think "foot" is a term in poetry. If I
remember right, it's a unit of measurement. A line in a
poem is a certain number of feet. But am I reading too
much into Levine's poem at this point?

Freewriting enabled Theresa to raise several issues. At the same time, she
wondered if she had to resolve them completely before writing her paper. She
knew that the paper would have to address at least some of her questions about
the poem, but she also knew that the paper could not deal with everything that
puzzled her. When you first get an assignment like hers, you may fear that you
will have nothing to say. But you will come up with a lot of material if, like
Theresa, you take time for exploration. As we have suggested, it's a process of
examining potential subjects through writing, discussion, and just plain thinking.
One of your challenges will then be to choose among the various issues you have
formulated. Like Theresa, you will need to decide which issues to pursue and
which to drop.

Planning

Planning for an assignment like Theresa's involves five main activities:

1. choosing the text you will analyze;
2. identifying your audience;
3. identifying the main issue, claim, and evidence you will present;
4. identifying particular challenges you will face and warrants you will use; and
5. determining how you will organize your argument.

Theresa considered several poems before choosing one for her paper. She settled on Levine's for five reasons. First, it was a text that left her with plenty of questions. Second, she believed that these questions could be issues for other readers. Third, she felt increasingly able to _argue_ about the poem—that is, to make and support claims about it. Fourth, she believed that she could adequately analyze the poem within the assignment's word limit. Finally, Levine's poem interested her the most, largely because she found it the most complex and thought-provoking.

Faced with the same assignment, you might choose another poem than Theresa did. Still, the principles that she followed are useful. Think about them whenever you are free to decide which texts you will write about. With some assignments, of course, you may need a while to decide which text is best for you. And later, after you have made your decision, you may want to make a switch. For example, you may find yourself changing your mind once you have done a complete draft. Frustrated by the text you have chosen, you may realize that another inspires you more. If so, consider making a substitution. Naturally, you will feel more able to switch if you have ample time left to write the paper, so avoid waiting to start your paper just before it is due.

To know what your readers will see as an issue, and to make your claims about it persuasive to them, you need to develop an audience profile. Perhaps your instructor will specify your audience, even invite you to write for classmates. Most often, though, instructors ask students to write for a "general" audience, the readership that Theresa was asked to address. Assume that a general audience is one that will want evidence for your claims. While this audience will obviously include your instructor, let it also include your classmates, since in class discussions they will be an audience for you whenever you speak. Besides, your class may engage in peer review, with students giving one another feedback on their drafts.

If your audience is indeed supposed to be a general group of readers, what can you assume about their prior knowledge? You may not be sure. Above all, you may wonder how familiar your readers already are with the text you are analyzing. Perhaps your teacher will resolve your uncertainty, telling you exactly how much your audience knows about the text. Then again, you may be left to guess. Should you presume that your audience is totally unfamiliar with the text? This approach is risky, for it may lead you to spend a lot of your paper merely summarizing the text rather than analyzing it. A better move is to write as if your audience is at least a bit more knowledgeable. Here is a good rule of thumb: Assume that your audience has, in fact, read the text, but that you need to recall for this group any features of the text that are crucial to your argument. Although probably your paper will still include summary, the amount you provide will be limited, and your own ideas will be more prominent.

Perhaps your instructor will ask you occasionally to write for a specific audience whom you have imagined. Even when not required, such an exercise can be fun and thought-provoking for you as you plan a paper. Think about how you might refer to Harper's poem "Free Labor" if, like Kathie Lee Gifford, you testified to Congress about the garment industry's current reliance on poorly paid sweatshop workers. Theresa's teacher asked her what she would say if she were giving a speech about Levine's poem to the United Auto Workers convention. This question left Theresa with mixed feelings. To her, Levine's poem chiefly concerns the work of preserving human relationships. But she suspected that auto workers would scoff if she emphasized this topic more than their jobs. Moreover, she sensed that Levine is not mocking people's wish to be employed. What he *is* doing, she concluded, is encouraging his readers to *extend* their usual definition of work so that it includes the labor involved in building human relationships.

When you have written papers for previous classes, you may have been most concerned with coming up with a thesis. Maybe you did not encounter the term *issue* at all. But good planning for a paper does entail identifying the main issue you will address. Once you have sensed what that issue is, try phrasing it as a question. If the answer would be obvious to your readers, be cautious, for you really do not have an issue if the problem you are raising can be easily resolved.

Also, try to identify what *kind* of issue you will focus on. For help, look at our list of the various types (pp. 17–24). Theresa realized that her main issue could be one of pattern. The question might be, Are the two halves of Levine's poem actually related, or is the second a definite break from the first? But Theresa felt more comfortable making the issue one of definition. Even then, however, she could think of at least three possible questions:

How does Levine's poem define *work*?

How does the poem define *waiting*?

How does the poem define *work* and *waiting* in relation to each other?

Ultimately, Theresa decided to write a paper that raised and addressed the third question. To her, it was the most stimulating, and just as important, she felt able to answer it well. Perhaps you have grown comfortable with the term *thesis* and want to keep using it. Fine. Bear in mind, though, that your thesis is your main *claim*. And when you put your main issue as a question, then your main claim is your answer to that question. Sometimes you will come up with question and answer simultaneously. Once in a while, you may even settle on your answer first, not being certain yet how to word the question. Whatever the case, planning for your paper involves articulating both the question (your issue) and the answer (your main claim). Try actually writing both down, making sure to phrase your main issue as a question and your main claim as the answer. Theresa's main issue was, How does the poem define *work* and *waiting* in relation to each other? After much thought, she expressed her main claim this way:

```
The poem first defines work as physical labor, and wait-
ing as the process of searching for a job. Eventually,
the poem defines work as emotional labor in human rela-
tionships, and it implies that often people unfortunately
"wait" in the sense of letting a lot of time pass before
they tell members of their family that they love them.
```

Audiences usually want evidence, and as we noted earlier, most arguments you make about literature will need to cite details of the work itself. In particular, direct quotation is usually an effective move. Theresa planned to elaborate her claim by bringing up several of Levine's own words, especially those that change meaning as the poem shifts from physical work to emotional work. Remember you need to avoid seeming willfully selective when you quote. Theresa knew that for her argument to be plausible, she would have to quote from both halves of Levine's text.

Theresa recognized that she would be facing other challenges. One of them involved the *you* of the poem. Although Theresa had decided that it does not matter exactly who this *you* is, she knew that some of her readers might feel otherwise. Therefore, she planned to include a paragraph that explained why they should not be concerned. Another challenge involved the key terms of Theresa's argument. She knew that the poem does not actually use the word *work* to describe emotional labor. Nor does the poem actually use the word *waiting* in referring to the *you's* neglect of his brother. Basically, she would be arguing that the poem redefines these two words by *implication*. To make her view credible, she would have to refer extensively to the words that the poem does use.

Often, to think about particular challenges of your paper is to think about your warrants. Remember that warrants are assumptions; they are what lead you to call certain things evidence for your claims. Theresa knew that one of her warrants was an assumption about Levine himself: namely, that he was not just being crazy when he ended his poem by contradicting the statement "you know what work is." Rarely will your paper need to admit all the warrants you are relying on. Most of the time, your task will be to guess which warrants your readers do want stated. Theresa felt there was at least one warrant she would have to spell out: her belief that a poem may redefine terms implicitly rather than explicitly.

To make sure their texts seem organized, most writers first do an **outline**, a list of their key points in the order they will appear. Outlines are indeed a good idea, but bear in mind that there are various kinds. One popular type, which you may already know, is the **sentence outline**. As the name implies, it lists the writer's key points in sentence form. Its advantages are obvious: This kind of outline forces you to develop a detailed picture of your argument's major steps, and it leaves you with sentences you can then incorporate into your paper. Unfortunately, sentence outlines tend to discourage flexibility. Because they demand much thought and energy, you may hesitate to revise them, even if you come to feel your paper would work better with a new structure.

A second, equally familiar outline is the **topic outline**, a list in which the writer uses a few words to signify the main subjects that he or she will discuss. Because it is sketchy, this kind of outline allows writers to go back and change plans if necessary. Nevertheless, a topic outline may fail to provide all the guidance a writer needs.

We find a third type useful: a **rhetorical purpose outline**. As with the first two, you list the major sections of your paper. Next, you briefly indicate two things for each section: the effect you want it to have on your audience, and how you will achieve that effect. Here is the rhetorical purpose outline that Theresa devised for her paper.

INTRODUCTION

The audience needs to know the text I'll discusss.	I'll identify Levine's poem.
The audience must know my main issue.	I'll show how the poem is confusing about how it defines and relates work and waiting.
The audience must know my main claim.	I'll claim that although the poem first defines work as physical labor and waiting as the process of searching for a job, eventually it defines work as emotional labor in human relationships, and it implies that often people unfortunately wait in the sense of letting a lot of time pass before they tell their family that they love them.

CONCESSION

The audience must be reassured that it doesn't matter that I haven't figured out who the "you" is.	I'll admit that I'm not certain about the identity of the "you," but I'll point out that my issue and my main claim can be valid no matter who the "you" is.

ANALYSIS OF THE POEM'S FIRST HALF

The audience needs to be sure of how the poem defines work and waiting in its first half.	I'll briefly review how the first half defines these terms, perhaps quoting briefly but relying mostly on paraphrase.

ANALYSIS OF THE POEM'S SECOND HALF

The audience needs to see that the second half of the poem defines work and waiting differently from how the first half defines them.	I'll quote and paraphrase specific lines that point to work as emotional labor and waiting as a failure to acknowledge the family.
The audience needs to feel the poem is suggesting that people should take seriously these new definitions.	I'll point out that the whole movement of the poem is toward these definitions.

IDENTIFICATION OF RELATED WORDS
WHOSE MEANING IS TRANSFORMED

The audience may want further evidence that the poem transforms the meaning of work and waiting as it proceeds.	I'll show how related words also get redefined as the poem moves from its first half to its second. Specifically, I'll discuss the words standing, shifting, long, and sad refusal.

CONCLUSION

The audience may need to be clearer about how important the second definitions of work and waiting are in relation to the first.	I'll say that while Levine evidently feels that people haven't paid enough attention to the second set of meanings, he isn't necessarily calling for them to throw out the first set.

For your own rhetorical purpose outlines, you may want to use phrases rather than sentences. If you do use sentences, as Theresa did, you do not have to write all that many. Note that Theresa wrote relatively few as she stated the effects she would aim for and her strategies for achieving those effects. Thus, she was not tremendously invested in preserving her original outline. She felt free to change it if it failed to prove helpful.

Composing

Not always is **composing** distinguishable from exploring, planning, and revising. As you prepare for your paper, you may jot down words or whole sentences. Once you begin a draft, you may alter that draft in several ways before you complete it. You may be especially prone to making changes in drafts if you use a computer, for word processing enables you to jump around in your text, revisiting and revising what you have written.

Still, most writers feel that doing a draft is an activity in its own right, and a major one at that. The next four chapters present various tips for writing about specific genres, and the appendix discusses writing research papers. Meanwhile, here are some tips to help you with composing in general.

Title

You may be inclined to let your **title** be the same as that of the text you discuss. Were you to write about Levine's poem, then, you would be calling your own paper "What Work Is." But often such mimicry backfires. For one thing, it may lead your readers to think that you are unoriginal and perhaps even lazy. Also, you risk confusing your audience, since your paper would actually be about Levine's poem rather than being the poem itself. So, take the time to come up with a title of your own. Certainly it may announce the text you will focus on, but let it do more. In particular, use your title to indicate the main claim you will be making. With just a few words, you can preview the argument to come.

Style

Perhaps you have been told to "sound like yourself" when you write. Yet that can be a difficult demand (especially if you are not sure what your "self" is really like). Above all, the **style** you choose depends on your audience and purpose. In writing an argument for a general audience, probably you would do best to avoid the extremes of pomposity and breezy informality. Try to stick with words you know well, and if you do want to use some that are only hazily familiar to you, check their dictionary definitions first.

At some point in our lives, probably all of us have been warned not to use *I* in our writing. In the course you are taking, however, you may be asked to write about your experiences. If so, you will find *I* hard to avoid. Whether to use it does become a real question when you get assignments like Theresa's, which require you chiefly to make an argument about a text. Since you are supposed to focus on that text, your readers may be disconcerted if you keep referring to yourself. Even so, you need not assume that your personal life is irrelevant to the task. Your opening paragraph might refer to your personal encounters with the text, as a way of establishing the issue you will discuss. A personal anecdote might serve as a forceful conclusion to your paper. Moreover, before you reach the conclusion, you might orient your readers to the structure of your paper by using certain expressions that feature the word *I*: for example, *As I suggested earlier, As I have noted, As I will argue later*. In general, you may be justified in saying *I* at certain moments. When tempted to use this pronoun, though, consider whether it really is your best move.

In a paper, the expressions *I think* and *I feel* are rarely effective. Often writers resort to such phrasing because they sense they are offering nothing more than their own opinion. The audience may view such expressions as indications of a weak argument or limited evidence. You might make the claim more persuasive by avoiding *I think* and *I feel* and by qualifying it through words such as *probably, possibly, maybe*, and *perhaps*. If you believe that you have little evidence for a claim you want to make, take time out from writing and go back to exploring your ideas. If you can, come up with additional means of support.

Arguments about literature are most compelling when supported by quotations, but be careful not to quote excessively. If you constantly repeat other people's words, providing few of your own, your readers will hardly get a sense of you as an author. Moreover, a paper full of quotation marks is hard to read. Make sure to quote selectively, remembering that sometimes you can simply paraphrase. When you do quote, try to cite only the words you need. You do not have to reproduce a whole line or sentence if one word is enough to support your point.

When summarizing what happens in a literary work, be careful not to shift tenses as you go along. Your reader may be confused if you shift back and forth between past and present. We suggest that you stick primarily to the present tense, which is the tense that literary critics customarily employ. For example, instead of saying that the men *waited* in line, say that they *wait* in line.

Introduction

Many writers aim to impress their audience right away. You may be tempted, then, to begin your paper with a grand philosophical statement, hoping your readers will find such an **introduction** profound. Often, however, this approach results in broad, obvious generalities. Here are some examples:

Society doesn't always appreciate the work that everyone does.

Over the centuries, there has been a lot of literature, and much of it has been about work.

Philip Levine is a great poet writing today.

As writing theorist William Coles points out, statements like these are mere "throat-clearing." They may lead your audience to think that you are delaying, not introducing, your real argument. Rather than beginning your paper with such statements, try mentioning the specific text you will analyze. Get started making assertions about that text.

Usually, your introduction will identify the main issue that you will discuss. Perhaps you will be able to assume that your audience is already aware of this issue and sees it as important. Theresa felt that her audience would wonder, as she did, how Levine relates *working* and *waiting*. Sometimes, however, your introduction will need to set out your issue at greater length. It will need to identify the issue as a significant question with no obvious answer.

A classic way to establish the importance of an issue is to show that other critics have grappled with it or wrongly ignored it. You may, however, get assignments in your course that do not push you to consider what previous critics have said. An alternative method of establishing your issue's significance is personal anecdote. By describing how the issue came to matter to you, you may persuade your readers to see it as mattering to them. If you do not want to be autobiographical, you have at least one other option. You can show that if your issue is left unaddressed, your readers will remain puzzled by other key aspects of the text you are discussing.

Development

When you write a paper, naturally you want the parts of each sentence to hang together. But make sure, too, that each sentence connects clearly to the one before and the one after. Smooth transitions from one paragraph to the next encourage your reader to follow the **development** of your argument. Certain words can help you signal relations between sentences. Here are just a few examples. Each could appear at the beginning of a sentence, where it would indicate how that sentence relates to the one before.

- Numerical order: *first, second, third,* etc.
- Temporal order: *then, next, earlier, previously, before, later, subsequently, afterward*
- Addition: *also, in addition to, furthermore, moreover, another*
- Degree: *more/less important, more/less often*
- Effect: *thus, therefore, as a result, consequently, hence, so*
- Opposition: *but, yet, however, nevertheless, still, even so, by contrast, on the contrary, conversely, on the other hand*
- Exemplarity: *for example, for instance*
- Emphasis: *indeed, in fact*
- Restatement: *that is, in other words*
- Specificity: *specifically, more precisely, in particular*

Do not fall into the habit of relying on *and* as a connective. As a means of linking sentences or of bridging ideas within them, *and* may seem a safe choice; besides being a common word, it looks too little to cause trouble. Nevertheless, as a connective *and* is often vague, failing to show how words actually relate. Note the following sentence:

The "you" has not shown enough brotherly love, and he does not really "know what work is."

The word *and* does little to fuse the sentence's two halves. A more precise way to connect the halves would be with language that shows their relation to be cause and effect:

> The "you" has not shown enough brotherly love; *therefore*, he does not really "know what work is."

Some people might disagree with this statement, claiming the relation is actually effect and cause:

> The "you" has not shown enough brotherly love, *because* he does not really "know what work is."

Whatever the merits of these two revisions, both are more coherent than the sentence using *and*, which hardly conveys relation at all. Also, if your paper constantly uses *and* or any other particular word, your prose may come across as monotonous.

The word *and* often becomes a prime means of transition in papers that mostly just summarize plots of texts. Presumably, though, your goal in a paper is to *analyze* whatever text you are discussing, not simply outline it. If you see that you are using *and* a lot in your writing, consider the possibility that you are, in fact, summarizing more than analyzing. In our experience, writers are most apt to lapse into plot summary toward the middle of their paper. At that point, they may grow tired of developing and keeping track of their own ideas. The easiest thing to do then is to coast, simply paraphrasing their chosen text line by line. Pause in your writing from time to time to see if you have lapsed into this practice. Remember that you can analyze details of a text without sticking to their original order.

How coherent a paper seems depends in part on the length of its paragraphs. Usually, a paragraph should be at least three sentences long. When readers confront one very short paragraph after another, they are apt to feel that they are seeing random, fragmented observations rather than a well-organized argument. Of course, paragraphs can also be too long. Readers have trouble following the structure of one that runs a full page. If you find yourself writing a lengthy paragraph, stop and check to see if there is any place in it where starting a new paragraph makes sense.

Emphasis

Many people assume that academic writing consists of long, dense statements. Furthermore, they assume that such prose is virtually unreadable. Whether or not they are right about the kind of writing favored in college, your own readers may get tired and lost if each of your sentences seems endless. On the other hand, your writing may strike your readers as choppy if each sentence contains just a few words. Usually, your papers will be most effective if you vary the lengths of your sentence for **emphasis**. In any paper you write for your course, aim for a mixture of sentence lengths, blending long, medium, and short.

But in any of your sentences, use only the amount of words you need to make your point. For example, do not resort to sixteen words when eight will suffice. Your readers are likely to become impatient, even bored, if your prose seems padded. Also, they may doubt your credibility, suspecting that you are pretending to have more ideas than you do.

Perhaps you fear that if you economize with your language, all your sentences will wind up short. But a concise sentence is not always brief; a sentence can be long and yet tightly edited, with every word in it deserving a place. Another possible fear has to do with writer's block. You may worry that you will have trouble getting words down if you must justify every single one of them. A good solution is to postpone editing for a while, perhaps even waiting until you have finished a draft. Simply remember that at some point you should review whatever you have written, looking for words you might trim.

Your sentences will have more impact if you use active rather than passive verbs. To grasp the difference, read the following two sentences:

> At the end, the "you" is accused by the speaker of the poem of not knowing "what work is."

> At the end, the speaker of the poem accuses the "you" of not knowing "what work is."

Certainly both sentences are grammatical. The second, however, is more concise and dynamic. That is because it uses the active form of the verb *to accuse* and indicates right away the agent performing the action. The first sentence uses the passive form, *is accused by*. The word *is* can serve as a tip-off: Passive verbs always feature some version of *to be*.

Passive verbs are not always bad. Sometimes a sentence will work better if it uses one. We can even envision a situation where our first sample sentence would perhaps make more sense. Imagine that up to this point, the writer has repeatedly referred to the "you." Imagine, too, that the writer had left off mentioning the speaker several paragraphs back. By making the "you" the grammatical subject of the sentence, the writer can maintain consistency, whereas suddenly switching to "the speaker" might throw readers off. Usually, however, passive verbs are unnecessary and counterproductive. Make them an exception, not the rule.

Usually, a sentence will seem better paced if you keep the main subject and verb close together. When several words come between subject and verb, readers may have trouble following along. This pair of sentences illustrates what we mean:

> The word *long*, first brought up in the opening line, reappears with a different meaning in the poem's second half.

> First brought up in the opening line, the word *long* reappears with a different meaning in the poem's second half.

Neither sentence is bad. But the first forces the reader to slow down right in the middle, since it puts several words between subject and verb. By keeping them together, the second sentence flows more.

Sentences are easier to read when they include at most one negative expression: words such as *not, never, don't,* and *won't.* On the other hand, a sentence is often hard to follow when it features several negatives. Look at the following pair of examples:

Not saying that physical work is never good, the speaker simply will not let the "you" get away with not doing emotional work.

Not criticizing physical work, the speaker simply suggests that the "you" should also do emotional work.

While the first sentence is grammatically correct and makes a logical point, its blizzard of negatives will confuse many readers. The second sentence makes basically the same point, but because it minimizes negatives, it is easier to read.

A point can have greater or less emphasis depending on where you place it. If you want to call attention to a paragraph's main idea, try beginning the paragraph with it. In any case, most likely your readers will assume that a paragraph's opening sentence is important. Usually they will pay special attention to its last sentence, too. Therefore, try not to fill either of these slots with relatively trivial points. Also, remember that you may obscure an important idea if you put it in the middle of a paragraph. There, the idea will have trouble getting the prominence it deserves.

Conclusion

You can always end your paper by summarizing the argument you have made. In fact, many readers will welcome a recap. Yet a conclusion that merely restates your argument risks boring your audience. Therefore, try to keep any final summary brief, using your **conclusion** to do additional things.

For example, the conclusion is a good place to make concessions. Even if you have already indicated ways in which people may reasonably disagree with you, you may use the close of your paper to acknowledge that you have no monopoly on truth. Your conclusion is also an opportunity for you to evaluate the text you have been discussing or to identify questions that the text still leaves in your mind. Consider as well the possibility of using your conclusion to bring up some personal experience that relates to the text. Yet another option is to have your conclusion identify implications of your argument that you have not so far announced: How might people apply your method of analysis to other texts? What, in effect, have you suggested about how people should live? What image have you given of the author that you have been discussing?

You might also end your paper by indicating further research you would like to do. Admittedly, this sort of conclusion is more typical of the sciences and social sciences. Literary critics tend to conclude their arguments as if there is nothing more they need to investigate. But if you do suggest you have more work to do, your readers may admire you for remaining curious and ambitious.

Sample Student Paper: First Draft

The following is Theresa's first complete draft of her paper. Eventually she revised this draft after a group of her classmates reviewed it, and she reflected further on it herself. For the moment, though, read this first version and decide what you would have said to her about it.

Theresa Gardella

Professor Schwartz

English 102

10 March ----

The Shifting Definitions of <u>Work</u> and

<u>Waiting</u> in Philip Levine's "What Work Is"

The title of Philip Levine's poem "What Work Is" suggests that the poem will clearly define <u>work</u>. But as it
goes on, it gets confusing about this subject. Early on,
the speaker says, "You know what work is." By contrast,
at the end the speaker says, "You don't know what work
is." Another puzzling thing is that the speaker says
early on that despite the poem's title, "this is about
waiting." So, after I first read the poem, I wondered how
it was defining <u>work</u> and <u>waiting</u>. I also wondered how it
was relating these two words. After thinking a lot about
the poem, I want to claim now that it redefines both
words as it moves along. First, it refers to work as
physical labor and to waiting as the process of searching
for a job. Eventually it defines work as emotional labor
in human relationships, and it implies that often people
wait, in the sense of letting a lot of time pass, before
they tell members of their family that they love them.
The first kind of waiting looks to the future. The second
kind of waiting is in part a failure to take sufficient
account of someone else in the present, the "you"'s
brother sleeping at home. This second kind of waiting is
also a failure to acknowledge the past, the amount of
time that the "you" has let go by before telling his
brother that he loves him.

Before going further, I must confess that I am still
not sure who the "you" of the poem is. My first impression was that the "you" is the reader, since the speaker
says "if you're / old enough to read this you know what /
work is, although you may not do it." But pretty soon
after this statement, the "you" apparently becomes one of
the people waiting in line for work at Ford Highland

Park, "Feeling the light rain falling like mist / into
your hair." As the poem goes on, the "you" seems to get
even more specific. The speaker says things like "you
love your brother" and "you've never / done something so
simple, so obvious." In addition, the "you" has a brother
who works at an auto plant, studies German, and sings
opera. When the speaker concludes by saying "you don't
know what work is," I am still left wondering if this is
the same "you" who did know what work is back at the
start. Moreover, I wonder if at least one of the "you"'s
in the poem is really the speaker. Yet even though I
still cannot decide the identity of the "you," the poem
redefines work and waiting in any case, and that is what
I will claim in this paper. My argument applies whether
or not any of us can be sure who the "you" is.

   In the first half of the poem, the speaker clearly
refers to work as physical labor. The men being described are standing in line at an auto plant, Ford Highland Park, hoping to get a job there. The men's time in
this line seems to be "hours wasted waiting," though,
because the plant representative is probably going to say
"'No, / we're not hiring today.'" Although that representative is himself "waiting" to make his response, the
poem has so far been emphasizing the waiting process of
the unemployed men who hope that the plant will hire
them.

   The second half of the poem does have an additional
reference to work as physical labor. The "you"'s brother
"works eight hours a night so he can sing / Wagner." But
in this half the speaker tends to emphasize the work
involved in expressing love for the rest of one's family.
The speaker suggests that the "you" has let too much time
go by before telling his brother "you loved him." The
"you" apparently does love his brother. Moreover, expressing love for him would evidently be a "simple" and
"obvious" thing to do. But the speaker says to the "you"

that "you don't know what work is." In part, this could mean work as physical labor again. The speaker would thus be saying that the "you" hasn't expressed brotherly love because he hasn't thought enough about the physical hardships that his brother has endured. Nevertheless, the more important meaning of <u>work</u> here seems to be emotional labor. The speaker would thus be saying that the "you" doesn't understand that expressing love for his brother is a form of work he hasn't thought about and that he really should do, instead of concentrating on his own search for a job.

I admit that the second half of the poem does not actually mention the word <u>waiting</u>. But because the speaker has said earlier that "this is about waiting," the reader should feel encouraged to think that the word applies to the second half of the poem as much as to the first half. No longer does the speaker refer, though, to waiting in the sense of standing in line for a job. When the speaker asks the "how long has it been" question, it seems as if this question involves waiting in the sense of the "you"'s taking too long to show the brotherly love he feels.

The shifts in definition of <u>work</u> and <u>waiting</u> that I am talking about are reinforced by shifts in the meanings of other words as the poem moves from its first half to its second. In the first half, the people looking for physical labor "stand" in line for it. In the second half, emotional labor is suggested by the words "you can hardly stand / the love flooding you for your brother." Also, while in the first half the unemployed are "shifting" as they wait, the second half brings up feelings by mentioning the brother's "miserable night shift." Similarly, although it is the line of unemployed people that's "long" in the first half, the second half of the poem suggests a "long" time has gone by since the "you" last showed his love for his brother.

A clear switching point in the poem is the phrase
"sad refusal." This phrase could easily fit what the
plant's representative will probably say to the men waiting in line for a job. He will engage in a sad refusal in
the sense of denying them a job, though it is the men
rather than the representative who will be made sad by
this announcement. Yet as currently used in the poem, the
phrase "sad refusal" refers to the attitude of the
"you"'s brother. He is going to press on with his ambi-
tions no matter what. As I have said, the second half of
the poem focuses on the emotional labor that the "you"
should engage in as far as his brother is concerned. The
speaker evidently wants the "you" to acknowledge more his
brother's spirit. So, the "you" too has engaged in a sad
refusal in the sense that he has been unwilling to show
his brother love.

Even though the poem comes to emphasize emotional
work, that does not mean it is saying people should forget about doing physical work and consider it pointless.
The speaker suggests that the "you" should pay more
attention to his brother in part because the brother
labors so hard. Overall, the poem is not telling us to
dismiss physical work. Instead, it is urging us to realize that emotional work is at least as important.

Revising

Most first drafts are far from perfect. Even experienced professional writers
often have to revise their work. Besides making changes on their own, many of
them solicit feedback from others. In various workplaces, writing is collaborative,
with coauthors exchanging ideas as they try to improve a piece. Remain open to
the possibility that your draft needs changes, perhaps several. Of course, you are
more apt to revise extensively if you have given yourself enough time. Conversely,
you will not feel able to change much of your paper if it is due the next day. You
will also limit your ability to revise if you work only with your original manuscript,
scribbling possible changes between the lines. This practice amounts to conser-
vatism, for it encourages you to keep passages that really ought to be overhauled.

You may have trouble, however, improving a draft if you are checking many
things in it at once. Therefore, read the draft repeatedly, looking at a different
aspect of it each time. A good way to begin is to outline the paper you have writ-

ten and then compare that outline with your original one. If the two outlines differ, your draft may or may not need adjusting; perhaps you were wise to swerve from your original plan. In any case, you should ponder your departures from that plan, considering whether they were for the best.

If, like Theresa, you are writing an argument paper, here are some topics and questions you might apply as you review your first draft. Obviously some of these considerations overlap. Nevertheless, take them in turn rather than all at once.

Logic

- Will my audience see that the issue I am focusing on is indeed an issue?
- Will the audience be able to follow the logic of my argument?
- Is the logic as persuasive as it might be? Is there more evidence I can provide? Do I need to identify more of my warrants?
- Have I addressed all of my audience's potential concerns?

Organization

- Does my introduction identify the issue that I will focus on? Does it state my main claim?
- Will my audience be able to detect and follow the stages of my argument?
- Does the order of my paragraphs seem purposeful rather than arbitrary?
- Have I done all I can to signal connections within and between sentences? Within and between paragraphs?
- Have I avoided getting bogged down in mere summary?
- Will my conclusion satisfy readers? Does it leave any key questions dangling?

Clarity

- Does my title offer a good preview of my argument?
- Will each of my sentences be immediately clear?
- Am I sure how to define each word that I have used?

Emphasis

- Have I put key points in prominent places?
- Have I worded each sentence for maximum impact? In particular, is each sentence as concise as possible? Do I use active verbs whenever I can?

Style

- Are my tone and level of vocabulary appropriate?
- Will my audience think me fair-minded? Should I make any more concessions?
- Do I use any mannerisms that may distract my readers?

- Have I used any expressions that may annoy or offend?
- Is there anything else I can do to make my paper readable and interesting?

Grammar

- Is each of my sentences grammatically correct?
- Have I punctuated properly?

Physical Appearance

- Have I followed the proper format for quotations, notes, and bibliography?
- Are there any typographical errors?

We list these considerations from most to least important. When revising a draft, think first about matters of logic, organization, and clarity. There is little point in fixing the grammar of particular sentences if you are going to drop them later because they fail to advance your argument.

As we noted, a group of Theresa's classmates discussed her draft. Most of these students seemed to like her overall argument, including her main issue and claim. Having been similarly confused by Levine's poem, they appreciated the light that Theresa shed on it. They were especially impressed by her evidence, since she repeatedly drew on Levine's actual text. Nevertheless, the group made several comments about Theresa's paper that she took as suggestions for improvement. Ultimately, she decided that several changes were in order, the three main ones being these:

- Many of her sentences could be more concise. This problem is common to first drafts; often writers cannot detect all the wordiness in a draft until they finish it and then review it. Theresa saw in particular that she could cut down on the number of self-references ("I") and that she did not have to mention "the speaker" as much as she had.
- She should move the material in her second paragraph to her conclusion, where her concession about not knowing the "you"'s identity would make for an appropriate ending. Several students in her group liked this concession but found it distracting in the second paragraph, for two reasons: (1) Its apologetic tone prevented Theresa from developing authority for her argument; (2) the first and second paragraphs together featured the first person ("I") so much that readers might feel their attention being taken away from Levine's poem.
- She could hint that some of the words in the poem also refer to what Levine is doing. In particular, Levine writes "lines" and makes "shifts" in meaning. Theresa had been reluctant to relate the poem to its author. While such connections interested her, she feared they would greatly complicate her paper, sending her reader off in all sorts of directions. Now she saw that she could add at least a brief reference to Levine's own "shifts" in the poem.

Sample Student Paper: Revised Draft

Here is the new version of her paper that Theresa wrote. Again, decide what you think of it.

Theresa Gardella

Professor Schwartz

English 102

21 April ----

The Shifting Definitions of <u>Work</u> and

<u>Waiting</u> in Philip Levine's "What Work Is"

Philip Levine's title "What Work Is" suggests that his poem will clearly define <u>work</u>. Yet it gets confusing about this subject. Early on, the speaker says, "You know what work is." But the poem concludes with the statement, "You don't know what work is." Also puzzling is that the speaker says early on that, despite the poem's title, "this is about waiting." So, how <u>does</u> the poem define and relate these two words, <u>work</u> and <u>waiting</u>? In fact, it redefines both words as it moves along. First, it refers to work as physical labor and to waiting as the process of searching for a job. Eventually, though, it defines work as emotional labor in human relationships. Moreover, the poem implies that often people wait a long time to tell members of their family that they love them. The first kind of waiting looks to the future. The second kind of waiting is in part a failure to acknowledge some- one else in the present: the "you"'s brother sleeping at home. This kind of waiting is also a failure to acknowl- edge the past: the amount of time that the "you" has allowed to pass before telling his brother he loves him.

The first half of the poem refers to work as physical labor as it describes the men standing in line. They hope to get a job at an auto plant, Ford Highland Park. This period of time seems to be "hours wasted waiting," though, because the plant representative is probably going to say, "'No / we're not hiring today.'" Although that representative is himself waiting to make his response, the poem has so far emphasized the other men's waiting for employment.

The second half of the poem makes an additional reference to work as physical. The "you"'s brother "works eight hours a night so he can sing / Wagner." But in this half, the poem turns to emphasizing the work involved in expressing love of family. The speaker suggests that the "you" has let too much time go by before telling his brother "you loved him." The "you" apparently does love his brother. Moreover, expressing love for him would evidently be a "simple" and "obvious" thing to do. Nevertheless, the speaker says to the "you" that "you don't know what work is." In part, this could mean work as physical labor again. The speaker would thus be saying that the "you" has not expressed brotherly love because he's thought too little about his brother's physical hardships. Yet the more important meaning of work here seems to be emotional labor. The speaker would thus be saying that the "you" does not understand that expressing love for his brother is work. In addition, the speaker would be pushing the "you" to think more about this work and to do it, rather than just search for a job.

Admittedly, the second half of the poem does not mention the word <u>waiting</u>. But because the speaker has said earlier that "this is about waiting," we should see the word <u>waiting</u> as probably applying to the second half too. No longer does the poem refer, though, to waiting as standing in line for a job. The "how long has it been" question suggests that the word <u>waiting</u> now means taking too long to show love for one's family. In this case, the "you" has neglected his brother.

Other words in the poem change meaning, too, thus reinforcing what happens with <u>work</u> and <u>waiting</u>. Ironically, one of these shifts involves the word <u>shift</u> itself. While in the first half the unemployed are "shifting" as they wait for physical work, the second half brings in emotions by mentioning the brother's "miserable

night shift." Another change is with the word <u>stand</u>. In
the first half, the people looking for physical labor
"stand" in line for it. The second half brings up emotional labor as it mentions that "you can hardly stand /
the love flooding you for your brother." Similarly,
although "long" first describes the line of unemployed
people, in the second half it refers to the "you"'s emotional life, through the "how long has it been" question.

A clear switching point in the poem is "sad refusal."
This phrase could fit what the plant's representative will
probably say to the men waiting for a job. He will engage
in a sad refusal by denying them a job, though it is they
rather than he who will be made sad by this announcement.
As actually used in the poem, "sad refusal" describes the
attitude of the "you"'s brother, who is going to pursue
his goals despite his hardships. A third possible meaning
comes in the poem's second half, where the speaker evidently wants the "you" to acknowledge more his brother's
spirit. The "you," too, has engaged in a sad refusal in
the sense that he has been unwilling to show his brother
love.

I must confess that I am still not sure who the "you"
of the poem is. Perhaps he is the reader, since the
speaker says "if you're / old enough to read this you
know what / work is, although you may not do it." But
pretty soon after this statement, the "you" apparently
becomes one of the people waiting in line for work at
Ford Highland Park, "feeling the light rain falling like
mist / into your hair." As the poem goes on, the "you"
seems to get even more specific. The speaker says things
like "you love your brother" and "you've never /
done something so simple, so obvious." In addition, the "you"
has a brother who works at an auto plant, studies German,
and sings opera. When the speaker concludes by saying
"you don't know what work is," I am still left wondering
if this is the same "you" who did know what work is back
at the start. Moreover, I wonder if at least one of the

```
"you"'s in the poem is really the speaker. Yet whatever
the "you"'s identity, the poem redefines work and waiting
in the ways I have pointed out.

    Even though the poem comes to emphasize emotional
work, the poem is not necessarily dismissing physical
work as pointless. The speaker even seems to admire the
brother because of the physical work he does. Overall,
the poem is not criticizing either kind of work, but
rather stressing that emotional work is at least as
important as the physical kind.
```

To us, Theresa's revision heightens the impact of her paper. In particular, she has trimmed several sentences while preserving their points. While some references to "I" remain, they do not prove distracting; rather, they end the paper on a warm personal note. All the same, we would hesitate to call this revision the definitive version of Theresa's paper. Maybe you have thought of things she could do to make it even more effective. In presenting her two drafts, we mainly want to emphasize the importance of revision. We hope, too, that you will remember our specific tips as you work on your own writing.

3

Writing about Stories

Short stories can be said to resemble novels. Above all, both are works of fiction. Yet the difference in length matters. As William Trevor, a veteran writer of short stories, has observed, short fiction is "the art of the glimpse; it deals in echoes and reverberations; craftily it withholds information. Novels tell all. Short stories tell as little as they dare." Maybe Trevor overstates the situation when he claims that novels reveal everything. All sorts of texts feature what literary theorist Wolfgang Iser calls "gaps." Still, Trevor is right to emphasize that short stories usually tell much less than novels do. They demand that you understand and evaluate characters on the basis of just a few details and events. In this respect, short stories resemble poems. Both tend to rely on compression rather than expansion, seeking to affect their audience with a sharply limited number of words.

Short stories' focused use of language can make the experience of reading them wonderfully intense. Furthermore, you may end up considering important human issues as you try to interpret the "glimpses" they provide. Precisely because short stories "tell as little as they dare," they offer you much to ponder as you proceed to write about them.

In discussing that writing process, we will refer often to the two stories that follow. Both stories tell of a healthy person's encounter with someone physically suffering. The first story, "A Visit of Charity," is by a pioneer of the modern American short story, Eudora Welty (b. 1909), who still lives in her hometown of Jackson, Mississippi. This particular piece appeared in Welty's first collection, *A Curtain of Green and Other Stories*, published in 1941. The second story, "The Gift of Sweat," is by a much younger American, Rebecca Brown (b. 1956). It is the lead-off piece of her 1994 book *The Gifts of the Body*, a sequence of short stories narrated by a woman who does housekeeping for people with AIDS — a kind of service work that Brown, too, has done.

EUDORA WELTY
A Visit of Charity

It was mid-morning—a very cold, bright day. Holding a potted plant before her, a girl of fourteen jumped off the bus in front of the Old Ladies' Home, on the outskirts of town. She wore a red coat, and her straight yellow hair was hanging down loose from the pointed white cap all the little girls were wearing that year. She stopped for a moment beside one of the prickly dark shrubs with which the city had beautified the Home, and then proceeded slowly toward the building, which was of whitewashed brick and reflected the winter sunlight like a block of ice. As she walked vaguely up the steps she shifted the small pot from hand to hand; then she had to set it down and remove her mittens before she could open the heavy door.

"I'm a Campfire Girl. . . . I have to pay a visit to some old lady," she told the nurse at the desk. This was a woman in a white uniform who looked as if she were cold; she had close-cut hair which stood up on the very top of her head exactly like a sea wave. Marian, the little girl, did not tell her that this visit would give her a minimum of only three points in her score.

"Acquainted with any of our residents?" asked the nurse. She lifted one eyebrow and spoke like a man.

"With any old ladies? No—but—that is, any of them will do," Marian stammered. With her free hand she pushed her hair behind her ears, as she did when it was time to study Science.

The nurse shrugged and rose. "You have a nice *multiflora cineraria*° there," she remarked as she walked ahead down the hall of closed doors to pick out an old lady.   5

There was loose, bulging linoleum on the floor. Marian felt as if she were walking on the waves, but the nurse paid no attention to it. There was a smell in the hall like the interior of a clock. Everything was silent until, behind one of the doors, an old lady of some kind cleared her throat like a sheep bleating. This decided the nurse. Stopping in her tracks, she first extended her arm, bent her elbow, and leaned forward from the hips—all to examine the watch strapped to her wrist; then she gave a loud double-rap on the door.

"There are two in each room," the nurse remarked over her shoulder.

"Two what?" asked Marian without thinking. The sound like a sheep's bleating almost made her turn around and run back.

One old woman was pulling the door open in short, gradual jerks, and when she saw the nurse a strange smile forced her old face dangerously awry. Marian, suddenly propelled by the strong, impatient arm of the nurse, saw next the side-face of another old woman, even older, who was lying flat in bed with a cap on and a counterpane° drawn up to her chin.

---

multiflora cineraria: A house plant with brightly colored flowers and heart-shaped leaves.
counterpane: Bedspread.

"Visitor," said the nurse, and after one more shove she was off up the hall.   10
Marian stood tongue-tied; both hands held the potted plant. The old woman, still with that terrible, square smile (which was a smile of welcome) stamped on her bony face, was waiting. . . . Perhaps she said something. The old woman in bed said nothing at all, and she did not look around.

Suddenly Marian saw a hand, quick as a bird claw, reach up in the air and pluck the white cap off her head. At the same time, another claw to match drew her all the way into the room, and the next moment the door closed behind her.

"My, my, my," said the old lady at her side.

Marian stood enclosed by a bed, a washstand and a chair; the tiny room had altogether too much furniture. Everything smelled wet — even the bare floor. She held on to the back of the chair, which was wicker and felt soft and damp. Her heart beat more and more slowly, her hands got colder and colder, and she could not hear whether the old women were saying anything or not. She could not see them very clearly. How dark it was! The window shade was down, and the only door was shut. Marian looked at the ceiling. . . . It was like being caught in a robbers' cave, just before one was murdered.

"Did you come to be our little girl for a while?" the first robber asked.   15

Then something was snatched from Marian's hand — the little potted plant.

"Flowers!" screamed the old woman. She stood holding the pot in an undecided way. "Pretty flowers," she added.

Then the old woman in bed cleared her throat and spoke. "They are not pretty," she said, still without looking around, but very distinctly.

Marian suddenly pitched against the chair and sat down in it.

"Pretty flowers," the first old woman insisted. "Pretty — pretty . . ."   20

Marian wished she had the little pot back for just a moment — she had forgotten to look at the plant herself before giving it away. What did it look like?

"Stinkweeds," said the other old woman sharply. She had a bunchy white forehead and red eyes like a sheep. Now she turned them toward Marian. The fogginess seemed to rise in her throat again, and she bleated, "Who — are — you?"

To her surprise, Marian could not remember her name. "I'm a Campfire Girl," she said finally.

"Watch out for the germs," said the old woman like a sheep, not addressing anyone.

"One came out last month to see us," said the first old woman.   25

A sheep or a germ? wondered Marian dreamily, holding on to the chair.

"Did not!" cried the other old woman.

"Did so! Read to us out of the Bible, and we enjoyed it!" screamed the first.

"Who enjoyed it!" said the woman in bed. Her mouth was unexpectedly small and sorrowful, like a pet's.

"We enjoyed it," insisted the other. "You enjoyed it — I enjoyed it."   30

"We all enjoyed it," said Marian, without realizing that she had said a word.

The first old woman had just finished putting the potted plant high, high on the top of the wardrobe, where it could hardly be seen from below. Marian wondered how she had ever succeeded in placing it there, how she could ever have reached so high.

"You mustn't pay any attention to old Addie," she now said to the little girl. "She's ailing today."

"Will you shut your mouth?" said the woman in bed. "I am not."

"You're a story." 35

"I can't stay but a minute—really, I can't," said Marian suddenly. She looked down at the wet floor and thought that if she were sick in here they would have to let her go.

With much to-do the first old woman sat down in a rocking chair—still another piece of furniture!—and began to rock. With the fingers of one hand she touched a very dirty cameo pin on her chest. "What do you do at school?" she asked.

"I don't know . . ." said Marian. She tried to think but she could not.

"Oh, but the flowers are beautiful," the old woman whispered. She seemed to rock faster and faster; Marian did not see how anyone could rock so fast.

"Ugly," said the woman in bed. 40

"If we bring flowers—" Marian began, and then fell silent. She had almost said that if Campfire Girls brought flowers to the Old Ladies' Home, the visit would count one extra point, and if they took a Bible with them on the bus and read it to the old ladies, it counted double. But the old woman had not listened, anyway; she was rocking and watching the other one, who watched back from the bed.

"Poor Addie is ailing. She has to take medicine—see?" she said, pointing a horny finger at a row of bottles on the table, and rocking so high that her black comfort shoes lifted off the floor like a little child's.

"I am no more sick than you are," said the woman in bed.

"Oh, yes you are!"

"I just got more sense than you have, that's all," said the other old woman, 45 nodding her head.

"That's only the contrary way she talks when *you all* come," said the first old lady with sudden intimacy. She stopped the rocker with a neat pat of her feet and leaned toward Marian. Her hand reached over—it felt like a petunia leaf, clinging and just a little sticky.

"Will you hush! Will you hush!" cried the other one.

Marian leaned back rigidly in her chair.

"When I was a little girl like you, I went to school and all," said the old woman in the same intimate, menacing voice. "Not here—another town . . ."

"Hush!" said the sick woman. "You never went to school. You never came 50 and you never went. You never were anything—only here. You never were born! You don't know anything. Your head is empty, your heart and hands and your old black purse are all empty, even that little old box that you brought with you you brought empty—you showed it to me. And yet you talk, talk, talk, talk, talk all the time until I think I'm losing my mind! Who are you? You're a stranger—a perfect stranger! Don't you know you're a stranger? Is it possible that they have actually done a thing like this to anyone—sent them in a stranger to talk, and rock, and tell away her whole long rigmarole? Do they seriously suppose that I'll be able to keep it up, day in, day out, night in, night out, living in the same room with a terrible old woman—forever?"

Marian saw the old woman's eyes grow bright and turn toward her. This old woman was looking at her with despair and calculation in her face. Her small lips suddenly dropped apart, and exposed a half circle of false teeth with tan gums.

"Come here, I want to tell you something," she whispered. "Come here!"

Marian was trembling, and her heart nearly stopped beating altogether for a moment.

"Now, now, Addie," said the first old woman. "That's not polite. Do you know what's really the matter with old Addie today?" She, too, looked at Marian; one of her eyelids dropped low.

"The matter?" the child repeated stupidly. "What's the matter with her?"   55

"Why, she's mad because it's her birthday!" said the first old woman, beginning to rock again and giving a little crow as though she had answered her own riddle.

"It is not, it is not!" screamed the old woman in bed. "It is not my birthday, no one knows when that is but myself, and will you please be quiet and say nothing more, or I'll go straight out of my mind!" She turned her eyes toward Marian again, and presently she said in the soft, foggy voice, "When the worst comes to the worst, I ring this bell, and the nurse comes." One of her hands was drawn out from under the patched counterpane — a thin little hand with enormous black freckles. With a finger which would not hold still she pointed to a little bell on the table among the bottles.

"How old are you?" Marian breathed. Now she could see the old woman in bed very closely and plainly, and very abruptly, from all sides, as in dreams. She wondered about her — she wondered for a moment as though there was nothing else in the world to wonder about. It was the first time such a thing had happened to Marian.

"I won't tell!"

The old face on the pillow, where Marian was bending over it, slowly gath-   60
ered and collapsed. Soft whimpers came out of the small open mouth. It was a sheep that she sounded like — a little lamb. Marian's face drew very close, the yellow hair hung forward.

"She's crying!" She turned a bright, burning face up to the first old woman.

"That's Addie for you," the old woman said spitefully.

Marian jumped up and moved toward the door. For the second time, the claw almost touched her hair, but it was not quick enough. The little girl put her cap on.

"Well, it was a real visit," said the old woman, following Marian through the doorway and all the way out into the hall. Then from behind she suddenly clutched the child with her sharp little fingers. In an affected, high-pitched whine she cried, "Oh, little girl, have you a penny to spare for a poor old woman that's not got anything of her own? We don't have a thing in the world — not a penny for candy — not a thing! Little girl, just a nickel — a penny —"

Marian pulled violently against the old hands for a moment before she was   65
free. Then she ran down the hall, without looking behind her and without looking at the nurse, who was reading *Field & Stream* at her desk. The nurse, after another triple motion to consult her wrist watch, asked automatically the question put to visitors in all institutions: "Won't you stay and have dinner with *us?*"

Marian never replied. She pushed the heavy door open into the cold air and ran down the steps.

Under the prickly shrub she stooped and quickly, without being seen, retrieved a red apple she had hidden there.

Her yellow hair under the white cap, her scarlet coat, her bare knees all flashed in the sunlight as she ran to meet the big bus rocketing through the street.

"Wait for me!" she shouted. As though at an imperial command, the bus ground to a stop.

She jumped on and took a big bite out of the apple.   [1941]   70

REBECCA BROWN

The Gift of Sweat

I went to Rick's every Tuesday and Thursday morning. I usually called before I went to see if he wanted me to pick up anything for him on the way. He never used to ask me for anything until once when I hadn't had breakfast and I stopped at this place a couple blocks from him, the Hostess with the Mostest, to get a cinnamon roll and I got two, one for him. I didn't really think he'd eat it because he was so organic. He had this incredible garden on the side of the apartment with tomatoes and zucchinis and carrots and he used to do all his own baking. I also got two large coffees with milk. I could have eaten it all if he didn't want his. But when I got to his place and asked him if he'd had breakfast and showed him what I'd brought, he squealed. He said those cinnamon rolls were his absolute favorite things in the world and he used to go to the Hostess on Sunday mornings. He said he'd try to be there when they were fresh out of the oven and get the best ones, the ones from the center of the pan, which are the stickiest and softest. It was something he used to do for himself on Sunday, which was not his favorite day.

So after that when I called him before I went over and asked if he wanted anything, he'd still say no thanks, and then I would say, "How about the usual," meaning the rolls and coffee, and he'd say he'd love it.

So one morning when I called and asked him if he wanted "the usual" and he said he didn't, I was surprised.

He said, "Not today!" He sounded really chirpy. "Just get your sweet self over here. I got a surprise for you."

I said OK and that I'd see him in a few. I made a quick cup of coffee and   5 downed the end of last night's pizza and went over. I was at his place in half an hour.

I always knocked on the door. When he was there he'd always shout, "Hello! Just a minute!" and come let me in. It took him a while to get to the door but he liked being able to answer it himself, he liked still living in his own place. If he wasn't at home I let myself in and read the note he would have left me — that he had an appointment or something, or if there was some special thing he wanted

me to do. Then I would clean or do chores. I used to like being there alone sometimes. I could do surprises for him, like leave him notes under his pillow or
rearrange his wind-up toys so they were kissing or other silly things. Rick loved
surprises.

But this one morning when I knocked on the door it took him a long time to
answer. Then I heard him trying to shout, but he sounded small. "Can you let
yourself in?"

I unlocked the door and went in. He was in the living room on the futon. It was
usually up like a couch to sit on, but it was flat like a bed and he was lying on it.

I went over and sat on the floor by the futon. He was lying on his side, facing
away from me, curled up. His knees were near his chest.

"Rick?" I said. I put my hand on his back. 10

He didn't move, but said, "Hi," very quietly.

"What's going on?" I said.

He made a noise like a little animal.

"You want me to call your doc?"

He swallowed a couple of times. Then he said, "I called UCS. Margaret is 15
coming over to take me to the hospital."

"Good," I said, "she'll be here soon."

"Yeah," he said. Then he made that animal noise again. He was holding his
stomach. "I meant to call you back," he said, "to tell you you didn't need to come
over today."

"That's OK, Rick. I'm glad I'm here. I'm glad I'm with you right now."

"I didn't feel bad when you called." He sounded apologetic. "It was so
sudden."

"Your stomach?" 20

He tried to nod. "Uh-huh. But everywhere some."

He was holding the corner of his quilt, squeezing it.

"I was about to get in the shower. I wanted to be all clean before you came
over. It was so sudden."

"Oh, Rick," I said, "I'm sorry you hurt so much."

"Thank you." 25

"Is there anything I can do before Margaret gets here?"

"No." He swallowed again. I could smell his breath. "No thank you."

Then his mouth got tight and he squeezed the quilt corner, then he was
pulsing it, then more like stabs. He started to shake. "I'm cold," he said.

I pulled the quilt over most of him. It had a pattern of moon and stars. "I'm
gonna go get another blanket," I said.

"Don't go," he said really fast. "Please don't go." 30

"OK," I said, "I'll stay here."

"I'm so cold," he said again.

I touched his back. It was sweaty and hot.

I got onto the futon. I slid on very carefully so I wouldn't jolt him. I lay on my
side behind him. I could feel him shaking. I put my left arm around his middle. I
slipped my right hand under his head and touched his forehead. It was wet and
hot. I held my hand on his forehead a couple of seconds to cool it. Then I petted

his forehead and up through his hair. His hair was wet too. I combed my fingers through his wet hair to his ponytail. I said, "Poor Rick. Poor Ricky."

He was still shaking. I pulled my body close to him so his butt was in my lap   35
and my breasts and stomach were against his back. I pressed against him to warm him. He pulled my hand onto his stomach. I opened my hand so my palm was flat across him, my fingers spread. He held his hand on top of mine, squeezing it like the quilt. I could feel the sweat of his hand on the back of mine, and of his stomach, through his shirt, against my palm. I could feel his pulse all through him; it was fast.

I tightened my arms around him as if I could press the sickness out.

After a while he started to shake less. He was still sweating and I could feel more wet on the side of his face from crying.

When Margaret came we wrapped his coat around him and helped him, one on either side of him, to the car. Rick hunched and kept making noises. I helped him get in and closed the door behind him while Margaret got in the driver's side. While she was fumbling for her keys I ran around to her and asked her, "You want me to come with you?"

She said, "You don't need to. We'll be OK."

Rick didn't say anything.   40

I leaned in and said, "Your place will be all clean when you come back home, Rick."

He tried to smile.

"I'll call you later," said Margaret. She put her hand up and touched the side of my face. "You're wet," she told me.

I touched my face. It was wet. "I'll talk to you later," I said to her.

"I'll see you later, Rick," I said.   45

He nodded but didn't say anything. His face was splotched. Margaret found her keys and started the car.

I went back into his apartment. When I closed the door behind me I could smell it. It was a slight smell, sour, but also partly sweet. It was the smell of Rick's sweat.

I started cleaning. I usually started in the kitchen, but as soon as I set foot in there and saw the kitchen table I couldn't. I turned around and stood in the hall a second and held my breath. After a while I let it out.

I did everything else first. I stripped the bed and put a load of laundry in. I vacuumed and dusted. I dusted all his fairy gear, his stones and incense burners and little statues and altars. I straightened clothes in his closet he hadn't worn in ages. I untangled ties and necklaces. I put cassettes back in their cases and reshelved them. I took out the trash. I did it all fast because I wanted to get everything done, but I also wished I could stretch it out and still be doing it and be here when he came home as if he would come home soon.

I cleaned the bathroom. I shook cleanser in the shower and sink and cleaned   50
them. I sprayed Windex on the mirror. When I was wiping it off I saw myself. My face was splotched. My t-shirt had a dark spot. I put my hands to it and sniffed them. They smelled like me, but also him. It was Rick's sweat. I put my hands up

to my face and I could smell him in my hands. I put my face in my hands and closed my eyes. I stood there like that a while then I went to the kitchen.

What was on the kitchen table was this: his two favorite coffee mugs, his and what used to be Barry's. There was a Melitta over one full of ground coffee, all ready to go. There were two dessert plates with a pair of cinnamon rolls from the Hostess, the soft sticky ones from the center of the pan.

I thought of Rick going down there, how long it took him to get down the street, how early he had to go to get the best ones. I thought of him planning a nice surprise, of him trying to do what he couldn't.

Rick told me once how one of the things he missed most was Sunday breakfast in bed. Every Saturday night he and Barry would watch a movie on the VCR in the living room. They'd pull the futon out like a bed and watch it from there and pretend they were at a bed-and-breakfast on vacation. Rick would make something fabulous and they'd eat it together. That was when he was still trying to help Barry eat. After Barry died Rick started going to the Hostess, especially on Sundays, because he had to get out of the apartment. He used to go to the Hostess all the time until it got to be too much for him. That's about the time I started coming over.

I sat at the table he'd laid for us. I put my elbows on the table and folded my hands. I closed my eyes and lowered my head and put my forehead in my hands. I tried to think how Rick would think, I tried to imagine Barry.

After a while I opened my eyes. He'd laid the table hopefully. I took the food   55
he meant for me, I ate.   [1994]

A WRITING EXERCISE

Once you have read the two stories, write your reaction to them off the top of your head, spending at least ten minutes on each. For each story, note any personal experience affecting your response as well as one or more questions that you have about the story even after you have finished reading it. Remember that question-posing is a good way to prepare for a formal paper on the story, enabling you to identify issues worth writing about at length.

A Student's Personal Response to the Stories

Monica Albertson was enrolled in a class that read and discussed both Welty's "A Visit of Charity" and Brown's "The Gift of Sweat." Here is some freewriting she did about each story:

```
I'm not sure which character I should be sympathizing
with in Welty's story. Right away I disliked the girl
because she wasn't really interested in seeing the old
women. I don't know why the story is called "A Visit of
Charity," since she just wanted to get more points. And
yet I have to admit that when I was younger I was sort of
like her. I remember one time that my church youth group
```

had to sing Christmas carols at an old folks' home, and I
was uneasy about having to meet all these ancient men and
women I didn't know, some of whom could barely walk or
talk. It's funny, because I was always comfortable around
my grandparents, but I have to confess that being around
all those old people at once spooked me a little. I
smiled a lot at them and joined in the singing and helped
hand out candy canes afterward. But I couldn't wait to
leave. Once I did, I felt proud of myself for going
there, but I guess I also felt a little guilty because I
didn't really want to be there at all. So, maybe I'm
being hypocritical when I criticize the girl in Welty's
story for insensitivity. Anyway, I expected that Welty
would present in a good light any old women that Marian
encountered, just to emphasize that Marian was being
unkind and that it's really sad for people to have to
live in a retirement home (or senior citizens center or
whatever they're calling such places nowadays). And yet
the two old women she meets are cranky and unpleasant.
Even the receptionist doesn't come off all that good. If
I were Marian, I probably would have left even sooner
than she did! Maybe Welty didn't want us to sympathize
with anyone in the story, and maybe that's OK. I tend to
want a story to make at least some of the characters sym-
pathetic, but maybe it's unfair of me to demand that.
Still, I'm wondering if I'm not appreciating Welty's
characters enough. When the two old women argue, should
we side with one of them, or are we supposed to be bothered by them both? Are we supposed to think any better of
the girl by the time she leaves? The apple she eats immediately made me think of the Adam and Eve story, but I
don't know what I'm supposed to do with that parallel.

On the other hand, I was very moved by the scene in
Brown's story when the narrator holds the sick man like
she's his mother and she's comforting her child. It made
me think of times when I myself was sick in bed and my
mother would come in and put cold compresses on my

burning forehead and do other things like that. Also I
really admire the narrator for being willing to do house-
work for someone with AIDS and for treasuring his sweat.
I can imagine plenty of people would worry about catching
AIDS from Rick that way. I have to admit that even I
would be anxious about touching any of his bodily fluids.
I guess Brown thinks that's an unreasonable fear. Maybe
I would react to this story differently if I knew someone who had AIDS, but I don't, or I think I don't. I did
know a couple of gay kids in high school but just to say
hi to.

One question I found myself asking is why the narrator doesn't tell us right away what's in the kitchen. Why
keep the breakfast a secret for a while? Instead of
telling us about it, she takes a deep breath and goes and
does the cleaning. She must have been having some important thoughts while cleaning but I couldn't figure out
what they were. (I still admire her, though, for cleaning
Rick's home when she probably didn't have to.) Not until
later does she tell us about the breakfast and then she
finally starts eating it. Is she at first just too
depressed by his collapse to enjoy what he's prepared and
tell us about it? Or, does she feel guilty because he
exhausted himself doing all this for her? Another question I have concerns the title. The title is "The Gift of
Sweat," and I can certainly see that the narrator values
Rick's sweat, but the main gift in the story seems to be
the breakfast he's prepared. So is the title misleading?
By the way, I thought it interesting that the breakfast
was basically just cinnamon rolls. Many people would consider those junk food. For me, rolls like that are too
rich to eat at any time of day. In the morning I'm a Special K fan if I eat anything at all. But there seems to
be something holy about Rick's breakfast. In fact, when
the narrator eats it, I thought of Communion. But maybe
that's just the Catholic in me. If I were in danger of
dying maybe I would just go for junk food too!

Before Monica could produce a full-fledged paper on either Welty's story or Brown's, she had to do more writing and thinking. Yet, simply by jotting down some memories and questions that the stories raised for her, she provided herself with the seeds of a paper. Compare your thoughts to hers. To what extent did you react to these stories as Monica did? In what ways, if any, did your responses differ from hers? What would you say to her if she were your classmate, especially as she proceeded to write a more developed argument based on her first impressions?

The Elements of Short Fiction

Whether discussing them in class or writing about them, you will improve your ability to analyze stories like Welty's and Brown's if you grow familiar with typical elements of short fiction. These elements include plot and structure, point of view, characterization, setting, imagery, language, and theme.

Plot and Structure

For many readers, the most important element in any work of fiction is **plot**. As they turn the pages of a short story, their main question is, "What will happen next?" In reading Welty's story, quite possibly you wanted to know how Marian's visit to the rest home would turn out. In reading Brown's story, most likely you hoped to learn why Rick was unable to let the narrator into his home. Furthermore, if a friend unfamiliar with Welty's and Brown's stories asked you what each was about, probably you would begin by summarizing their plots.

A WRITING EXERCISE

In one or two sentences, summarize what you take to be the plot of Welty's story. Then, read the following three summaries of her plot, which were written by three other students. Finally, list a few similarities and differences you notice as you compare the three summaries with one another and with yours.

> *Jerry's summary:* A girl visits an Old Ladies' Home just so she can add some points to her record as a Campfire Girl. Much to her dismay, she encounters two roommates who fight a lot with each other, and their unpleasantness eventually causes her to flee.

> *Carla's summary:* A young girl named Marian who starts off basically interested in only herself is forced to consider the suffering of old people when she spends time with two old women at a retirement home. Eventually she leaves in fear and disgust, but as she leaves she eats an apple, which implies that she is no longer as innocent as she was and that she is maybe a little more prepared to acknowledge what goes on in the wider world.

> *Matt's summary:* A really insensitive girl meets two old women, and though in many respects she is put off by both of them, she can't help being intrigued by the one who is sick in bed. Maybe she becomes more aware of mortality at this point, but if so she has trouble facing it, and in the end runs away.

To an extent, the students point out different things. For instance, only Carla mentions the apple, and only Matt observes that Marian is momentarily interested in the bedridden woman. Also, these two students are more willing than Jerry is to speculate about Marian's final state of mind. At the same time, Carla's summary ends on a slightly more upbeat note than Matt's. She emphasizes that Marian has perhaps become more open-minded, while Matt concludes by pointing out that Marian nevertheless flees.

Any summary of Welty's story will be somewhat personal. It is bound to reflect the reader's own sense of who the story's main characters are, which of their actions are significant, how these actions are connected, and what principles these actions illustrate. Were you to compare summaries with Jerry, Carla, and Matt in class, each of you might learn much from discussing experiences and beliefs that influenced your accounts.

Even so, you do not have to treat every summary of Welty's story as merely subjective. Probably some accounts of it are more attentive than others to actual details of Welty's text. If a reader declared that Marian loves visiting the Old Ladies' Home, many other readers would rightfully disagree, pointing out that Marian dashes off. If you discussed Welty's story with Jerry, Carla, and Matt, the four of you would probably consider which summary of it is best. Furthermore, probably each of you would argue for your respective candidates by pointing to specific passages in Welty's text. Ultimately, you might still prefer your own summary. On the other hand, you might wind up adopting someone else's, or you might want to combine aspects of various summaries you have read.

Jerry's, Carla's, and Matt's summaries do have some features in common, indicating that there are certain basic things for you to consider when you examine a short story's plot. For example, plots usually center on human beings, who can be seen as engaging in actions, as being acted upon, or both. In recounting the plot of Welty's story, each of the three students focuses on Marian. Furthermore, each describes her as acting (she "encounters," "flees," "spends time," "leaves," "eats," "meets," "runs away") *and* as being affected by other forces (the "unpleasantness" of the old women "causes her to flee"; she is "forced to consider" their pain; she is "put off" as well as "intrigued"). Also, most short stories put characters into a high-pressure situation, whether for dark or comic effect. To earn the merit points she desires, Marian has to contend with the feuding roommates.

Besides physical events, a short story may involve psychological developments. Each student here points to mental changes in Welty's heroine. According to Jerry, Marian experiences "dismay." According to Carla, she "starts off basically interested in only herself" but perhaps becomes "a little more prepared to acknowledge what goes on in the wider world." According to Matt, she starts off "really insensitive," perhaps grows "more aware of mortality," yet then "has trouble facing it." Many stories do show characters undergoing complete or partial conversions. Meanwhile, a number of stories include characters who stick to their beliefs but gain a new perspective on them.

Jerry, Carla, and Matt connect Marian's visit to the rest home with her subsequent behavior. Like most plot summaries, in other words, theirs bring up relations of cause and effect. The novelist and short-story writer E. M. Forster refers to cause and effect in his famous definition of plot. To Forster, a plot is not simply one incident after another, such as "the king died and then the queen died." Rather, it is a situation or a whole chain of events in which there are reasons *why* characters behave as they do. Forster's example: "The king died, and then the queen died of grief."

Writers of short stories do not always make cause and effect immediately clear. Another possible plot, Forster suggests, is "The queen died, no one knew why, until it was discovered that it was through grief at the death of the king." In this scenario, all of the characters lack information about the queen's true psychology for a while, and perhaps the reader is in the dark as well. Indeed, many short stories leave the reader ignorant for a spell. For instance, only near the conclusion of her story does Welty reveal that prior to entering the rest home, Marian had put an apple under the shrub. Why does the author withhold this key fact from you? Perhaps Welty was silent about the apple because, had she reported it right away, its echoes of Eve might have overshadowed your interpretation of the story as you read. Worth considering are issues of effect: what the characters' behavior makes you think of them and what impact the author's strategies have on you.

When you summarize a story's plot, you may be inclined to put events in chronological order. But remember that short stories are not always linear. Often they depart from strict chronology, moving back and forth in time. Consider the following opening sentences, both of which deal with a funeral ceremony. The first is from "A Rose for Emily," a famous story written in 1931 by the classic American author William Faulkner. The second is from "Killings," a more recent story (1979) by the contemporary writer Andre Dubus.

> When Miss Emily Grierson died, our whole town went to her funeral: the men through a sort of respectful affection for a fallen monument, the women mostly out of curiosity to see the inside of her house, which no one save an old manservant—a combined gardener and cook—had seen in at least ten years.

> On the August morning when Matt Fowler buried his youngest son, Frank, who had lived for twenty-one years, eight months, and four days, Matt's older son, Steve, turned to him as the family left the grave and walked between their friends, and said: "I should kill him."

Probably Faulkner's opening makes you wonder why Emily Grierson kept people out of her house. Probably Dubus's opening makes you wonder how Frank died and whom Steve means by "him." Eventually the authors do answer these questions by moving their stories back in time. Faulkner presents episodes in Emily's life, returning only at the end of the story to the time after her death. Dubus spends much of his story's first half on flashbacks that inform you about Frank's murder; then, Dubus returns to the present and shows Matt's effort to avenge his son. Many literary critics use the term **discourse** for a text's actual ordering of events. Chronologically, Emily Grierson's funeral comes near the end of Faulkner's short story. Yet it appears at the beginning of his discourse. Chronologically, Frank's funeral is sandwiched between several events. Yet it is the start of Dubus's discourse.

Alice Adams, author of many short stories, offers a more detailed outline of their typical **structure**. She has proposed the formula ABDCE: These letters stand for **action, background, development, climax,** and **ending**. More precisely, Adams has said that she sometimes begins a story with an action, follows that action with some background information, and then moves the plot forward in time through a major turning point and toward some sort of resolution. Not all writers of short stories follow this scheme. In fact, Adams does not always stick to it. Certainly a lot of short stories combine her background and development stages, moving the plot along while offering details of their characters' pasts. And sometimes a story will have several turning points rather than a single distinct climax. But if you keep Adams's formula in mind, if only as a common way to construct short stories, you will be better prepared to recognize how a story departs from chronological order.

The first paragraph of Welty's story seems to be centered on *action*. Marian arrives at the Old Ladies' Home and prepares to enter it. Even so, Welty provides some basic information in this paragraph, describing Marian and the rest home as if the reader is unfamiliar with both. Yet only in the second paragraph do you learn Marian's name and the purpose of her visit. Therefore, Welty can be said to obey Adams's formula, beginning with *action* and then moving to *background*. Note, however, that the second paragraph features *development* as well. By explaining to the receptionist who she is and why she is there, Marian takes a step closer to the central event, her meeting with the two roommates. The remainder of the story keeps moving forward in time.

Brown's story "The Gift of Sweat" begins with two paragraphs mostly devoted to background. They tell you about the arrangements between the narrator and Rick prior to the particular day that will be the story's focus. With the opening words of her third paragraph — "So one morning when I called" — Brown signals that she has spent the previous two on background material. Now, she implies, she will turn to developing the story's main situation.

What about *climax*, Adams's fourth term? Traditionally, the climax of a story has been defined as a peak moment of drama appearing near the end. Also, it is usually thought of as a point when at least one character commits a significant act, experiences a significant change, makes a significant discovery, learns a significant lesson, or perhaps does all these things. With Welty's story, you could argue that the climax is when Marian asks Addie her age, meets with refusal, sees Addie crying, and tries to bolt. Certainly this is a dramatic moment, involving intense display of emotion resulting in Marian's departure. But Welty indicates, too, that Marian here experiences inner change. When she looks on Addie "as though there was nothing else in the world to wonder about," this is "the first time such a thing had happened to Marian."

Adams's term *ending* may seem unnecessary. Why would anyone have to be reminded that stories end? Yet a story's climax may engage readers so much that they overlook whatever follows. If the climax of Welty's story is Marian's conversation with tearful Addie, then the ending is basically in four parts: the plea that Addie's roommate makes to Marian as she is leaving; Marian's final encounter with the receptionist; Marian's retrieval of the apple; and her escape on the bus, where she bites into the apple. Keep in mind that the ending of a story may relate somehow to its beginning. The ending of Welty's "A Visit of Charity," for instance, brings the story full circle. Whereas at the start Marian gets off a bus, hides the apple, and meets the receptionist, at the conclusion she rushes by the receptionist, recovers the apple, and boards another bus. However a story ends, ask yourself if any of the characters has changed at some point between start and finish. Does the conclusion of the story indicate that at least one person has developed in some way, or does it leave you with the feeling of lives frozen since the start? As Welty's story ends, readers may have various opinions about Marian. Some may find that she has not been changed all that much by her visit to the home, while others may feel that it has helped her mature.

A common organizational device in short stories is **repetition**. It takes various forms. First, a story may repeat certain words; in Brown's story, for example, the narrator repeatedly refers to sweat. Second, a story may involve repeated actions. In Welty's story, the two roommates repeatedly argue; Marian travels by bus at beginning and end; and the receptionist consults her wristwatch both when Marian arrives and when she leaves. Third, a story may echo previous events. In Brown's story, the narrator mentions her earlier visits to Rick and his past trips to the Hostess. Of course, in various ways a story's current situation will be new. In Brown's story, Rick's present condition makes his trek to the Hostess a big step for him, and he winds up in pain.

Point of View

A short story may be told from a particular character's perspective or **point of view**. Probably you have noticed that Brown's story is written in the **first person**; it is narrated by someone using the pronoun *I*. With every first-person story, you have to decide how much to accept the narrator's point of view, keeping in mind that the narrator may be psychologically complex. How objective does the narrator seem in depicting other people and events? In what ways, if any, do the narrator's perceptions seem influenced by his or her personal experiences, circumstances, feelings, values, and beliefs? Does the narrator seem to have changed in any way since the events recalled? How reasonable do the narrator's judgments seem? At what moments, if any, do you find yourself disagreeing with the narrator's view of things?

Not every short story is narrated by an identifiable person. Many of them are told by what has been traditionally called an **omniscient narrator**. The word *omniscient* means "all-knowing" and is often used as an adjective for God. An omniscient narrator is usually a seemingly all-knowing, objective voice. This is the kind of voice operating in the first paragraph of Welty's story. There, Marian is described in an authoritatively matter-of-fact tone that appears detached from her: "Holding a potted plant before her, a girl of fourteen jumped off the bus in front of the Old Ladies' Home." Keep in mind, though, that a story may primarily rely on an omniscient narrator and yet at some points seem immersed in a character's perspective. This, too, is the case with Welty's story. Consider the following passage about Marian:

Everything smelled wet — even the bare floor. She held on to the back of the chair, which was wicker and felt soft and damp. Her heart beat more and more slowly, her hands got colder and colder, and she could not hear whether the old women were saying anything or not. She could not see them very clearly. How dark it was! The window shade was down, and the only door was shut. Marian looked at the ceiling. . . . It was like being caught in a robbers' cave, just before one was murdered.

The passage remains in the third person, referring to "she" rather than to "I." Nevertheless, the passage seems intimately in touch with Marian's physical sensations. Indeed, the sentence "How dark it was!" seems something that Marian would say to herself. Similarly, the analogy to the robbers' cave may be Marian's own personal perception, and as such, the analogy may reveal more about her own state of mind than about the room. Many literary critics use the term **free indirect style** for moments like this, when a narrator otherwise omniscient conveys a particular character's viewpoint by resorting to the character's own language.

First-person singular narration and omniscient narration are not the only methods for telling a story. For instance, William Faulkner's "A Rose for Emily" is narrated by "we," the first-person plural. Even more striking is the technique used by the contemporary American author Pam Houston in her 1989 short story "How to Talk to a Hunter." The story seems to be narrated from an unnamed woman's point of view, but she avoids the word *I* and instead consistently refers to *you*. While Houston's method is unusual, it serves as a reminder that short stories can be told in all sorts of ways.

Throughout this book, we encourage you to analyze an author's strategies by considering the options that he or she faced. You may better understand a short story's point of view if you think about the available alternatives. For example, how would you have reacted to Welty's story if it had focused on Addie's perceptions more than on Marian's? With Brown's story, how would you have felt if the narrator had been omniscient?

A WRITING EXERCISE

Choose a passage from Welty's or Brown's story and rewrite it from another point of view. Then exchange your rewritten passage with a classmate's response to this assignment. Finally, write a paragraph analyzing your classmate's revision. Specifically, compare the revision with the original passage that your classmate chose, noting any differences in effect.

Characters

Although we have been discussing plots, we have also referred to the people caught up in them. Any analysis you do of a short story will reflect your understanding and evaluation of its **characters**. Rarely does the author of a story provide you with extended, enormously detailed biographies. Rather, you see the story's characters at select moments of their lives. To quote William Trevor again, the short story is "the art of the glimpse."

A WRITING EXERCISE

Choose any character from the two stories featured here. Then, off the top of your head, jot down at least five adjectives you think apply to that character. Next, exchange lists with a classmate, even if the list you get in return deals with another character. When you look at your classmate's list, circle the adjective that surprises you most. Finally, write a brief essay in which you consider how applicable that adjective is. Do you agree with your classmate that it suits the character he or she chose? Why, or why not?

You may want to judge characters according to how easily you can identify with them. Yet there is little reason for you to read works that merely reinforce your prejudices. Furthermore, you may overlook the potential richness of a story if you insist that its characters fit your usual standards of behavior. An author can teach you much by introducing you to the complexity of people you might automatically praise or condemn in real life. If you tend to admire home-care providers, Brown's portrayal of one can be thought-provoking for you, since this particular provider is not sure what to do with the breakfast that Rick has set out in his kitchen. You may be tempted to dismiss the roommates in Welty's story as unpleasant, even "sick"; in any case, take the story as an opportunity to explore *why* women in a rest home may express discontent.

One thing to consider about the characters in a story is what each basically desires. At the beginning of Welty's story, for example, Marian is hardly visiting the Old Ladies' Home out of "charity," despite that word's presence in the story's title. Rather, Marian hopes to earn points as a Campfire Girl. Again, characters in a story may change, so consider whether the particular characters you are examining alter their thinking. Perhaps you feel that Marian's visit broadens her vision of life; then again, perhaps you conclude that she remains much the same.

Reading a short story involves relating its characters to one another. In part, you will be determining their relative importance in the story. When a particular character seems to be the story's focus, he or she is referred to as the story's **protagonist**. Many readers would say that Marian is the protagonist of Welty's story and that the home-care worker is the protagonist of Brown's. When a protagonist is in notable conflict with another character, the latter is referred to as the **antagonist**. Brown's story seems to lack an antagonist, unless you want to argue that the AIDS virus is one. What about Welty's story? Do you find any antagonists there?

Even a seemingly minor character can perform some noteworthy function in a story. Take Brown's character Margaret, who is apparently the narrator's supervisor. On the surface, Margaret seems much less important to the story than the narrator and Rick do. For one thing, Margaret's appearance is brief: She arrives, she exchanges some words with the narrator, and then she drives off with Rick. Before she goes, though, Margaret points out that the narrator is sweaty, and thus she makes the reader aware of this fact. Furthermore, Brown uses Margaret to put the narrator in a psychologically complex situation. Once Margaret takes Rick away, the narrator must figure out how to express her concern for him, which she ultimately does by thoroughly cleaning his home. On the whole, Margaret is more a plot device than a fully developed personality. Nevertheless, she merits study if only as an example of author Brown's craft.

In many short stories, characters are allies or enemies. But as the story proceeds, they may alter their relationships, forging new bonds or developing new conflicts. Although Welty's Marian initially finds both roommates unpleasant, she grows more conscious of the tension *between* them, and then for a moment she sympathizes with Addie. It is possible, too, for one character to be ambivalent about another, feeling both drawn and opposed to that person. One might argue, for example, that the two roommates in Welty's story have a love-hate relationship, needing each other's company even as they bicker. As perhaps you have found in your own experience, human relationships are often far from simple. Works of literature can prove especially interesting when they suggest as much.

What power and influence people can achieve have often depended on particular traits of theirs. These include their gender, social class, race, ethnic background, nationality, sexual orientation, and the kind of work they do. Because these attributes can greatly affect a person's life, pay attention to them if an author refers to them in describing a character. For instance, in Brown's story, the narrator indicates her gender as she recalls how she lay down with pain-stricken Rick: "I pulled my body close to him so his butt was in my lap and my breasts and stomach were against his back." But would the story be significantly different if she were a man? Perhaps. Certainly it is interesting that she has become a caretaker of what was formerly the home of a male couple. Also, note that the physical position described in the quoted passage is that of mother with fetus. In fact, just before the passage, the narrator addresses Rick as if he were her child, changing his name to "Ricky." Remember, too, that for many people, Mother is the original Hostess with the Mostest! Still, you may feel that we are making too much of gender here. If so, what would you point to in arguing that view?

Typically, characters express views of one another, and you have to decide how accurate these are. Some characters will seem wise observers of humanity. Others will strike you as making distorted statements about the world, revealing little more than their own biases and quirks. And some characters will seem to fall in the middle, coming across as partly objective and partly subjective. On occasion, you and your classmates may find yourselves debating which category a particular character fits. One interesting case is Welty's character Addie. Look again at the speech in which she berates her roommate:

> "Hush!" said the sick woman. "You never went to school. You never came and you never went. You never were anything—only here. You never were born! You don't know anything. Your head is empty, your heart and hands and your old black purse are all empty, even that little old box that you brought with you you brought empty—you showed it to me. And yet you talk, talk, talk, talk, talk all the time until I think I'm losing my mind! Who are you? You're a stranger—a perfect stranger! Don't you know you're a stranger? Is it possible that they have actually done a thing like this to

anyone — sent them in a stranger to talk, and rock, and tell away her whole
long rigmarole? Do they seriously suppose that I'll be able to keep it up, day
in, day out, night in, night out, living in the same room with a terrible old
woman — forever?"

Some may argue that this speech is merely an unreasonable rant, indicating
Addie's dour mood rather than her roommate's true nature. (For one thing, contrary to Addie's declaration, the roommate must have been born!) Yet it can also
be argued that Addie shrewdly diagnoses her situation. Perhaps statements like
"you never were born," "your head is empty," and "you're a stranger" are true in a
metaphorical sense.

Setting

Usually a short story enables readers to examine how people behave in concrete circumstances. The characters are located in a particular place or **setting**.
Moreover, they are shown at particular moments in their personal histories.
Sometimes the story goes further, referring to them as living at a certain point in
world history.

As the word *sometimes* implies, short stories do vary in the precision with
which they identify their settings. At one extreme is "Another Way to Die" by the
contemporary Japanese writer Haruki Murakami. This story's place and time are
sharply defined: The action occurs in a Manchurian zoo in August 1945, when
the Russian army was about to seize the region from its Japanese occupiers. On
the other hand, the setting of Welty's "A Visit of Charity" is less exact. The story's
main scene is clearly a nursing home for women, but the text does not refer explicitly to a particular region or era. Even when a story's setting is rather vague, however, certain details of the text may seem historically or geographically specific.
Brown's story says rather little about Rick's apartment and events in the larger
world, but since he has AIDS, the time frame is probably no earlier than the 1980s.

Short stories differ as well in the importance of their setting. Sometimes location serves as a mere backdrop to the plot, while at other times it is a looming
presence. This second possibility is especially true of stories in which people journey to places they have not seen before. When Welty's character Marian visits the
Old Ladies' Home, readers get her vivid impressions of it. Even when a story's setting is ordinary to the characters and to you, it may become filled with drama and
meaning as the plot develops. For most people, kitchens are mundane places, but
in Brown's story a kitchen becomes a scene of significant action. There, Brown's
narrator must decide whether to accept the hospitality for which Rick has endan-
gered his health.

Stories may focus on one site and yet show it changing over time. This is the
case with William Faulkner's "A Rose for Emily," in which Emily's town comes to
view her differently over the years. Of course, a story may take place in more than
one setting, and when it does, the differences between its various sites may be
notable. In New Zealander Katherine Mansfield's story "The Garden-Party," the
young protagonist struggles to understand the sharp contrast between two events
she witnesses: the garden party of the title, which is on her family's estate, and

another family's mourning for a dead workman, which occurs in a nearby house. Even apparently minor shifts of location may prove important. Although Welty's story focuses chiefly on the Old Ladies' Home, it also shows you the world beyond that building when Marian eats her apple and flees. Perhaps Marian's escape is an illusion in the sense that old age awaits her, too. At the moment, though, Marian evidently sees this outside world as a refuge from the old and infirm.

One way of analyzing characters is to consider how they accommodate themselves — or fail to accommodate themselves — to their surroundings. The two roommates in Welty's story are evidently frustrated with living in the Old Ladies' Home, and they take out this frustration on each other. In Brown's story, the narrator's cleaning of Rick's home may leave you with mixed feelings. When, in his absence, she strips his bed, washes his laundry, vacuums his floor, dusts his objects, straightens his clothes, stores his cassettes, removes his garbage, and scrubs his bathroom, she is certainly caring for him. At the same time, her actions signify that he has lost all privacy. Though it is his own apartment, she has taken charge.

A WRITING EXERCISE

To become more aware of how setting may function in a short story, write a two- to three-page description of a setting you associate with someone you know. Choose a particular room, building, or landscape in which you have seen that person. In your description, use details of the setting to reveal something about his or her life.

Imagery

Just like poems, short stories often use **imagery** to convey meaning. Sometimes a character in the story may interpret a particular image just the way you do. Some stories, though, include images that you and the characters may analyze quite differently. One example is the apple in Welty's story. Whereas Marian probably views the apple as just something to eat, many readers would make other associations with it, thinking in particular of the apple that Adam and Eve ate from the Tree of Knowledge in Eden. By the end of Welty's story, perhaps Marian has indeed become like Adam and Eve, in that she has lost her innocence and grown more aware that human beings age. At any rate, many readers would call Marian's apple a **symbol**. Traditionally, that is the term for an image seen as representing some concept or concepts. Again, probably Marian herself does not view her apple as symbolic; indeed, characters within stories rarely use the word *symbol* at all.

Images may appear in the form of metaphors or other figures of speech. For example, when Marian enters the Old Ladies' Home, she experiences "a smell in the hall like the interior of a clock." Welty soon builds on the clock image as she describes the receptionist checking her wristwatch, an action that this character repeats near the end. Welty's whole story can be said to deal with time and its effects, both on the old and on the young.

Images in short stories usually appeal to the reader's visual sense. Most often, they are things you can picture in your mind. Yet stories are not limited to rendering visual impressions. They may refer and appeal to other senses, too. In Brown's story, the narrator is struck by how Rick's sweat smells. Similarly, Welty's young heroine notes the odor of the hall.

A WRITING EXERCISE

Write a brief essay in which you analyze how a particular advertisement uses imagery. The ad may come from any medium, including a newspaper, a magazine, television, or radio. What specific associations do you make with the ad's imagery? Why do you think the advertiser used it? Would you say that this use of imagery is successful? Why, or why not?

Language

Everything about short stories we have discussed so far concerns **language**. After all, works of literature are constructed entirely out of words. Here, however, we call your attention to three specific uses of language in stories: their title, their predominant style, and their dialogue.

A story's title may be just as important as any words in the text. Not always will the relevance of the title be immediately clear to you. Usually you have to read a story all the way through before you can sense fully how its title applies. In any case, play with the title in your mind, considering its various possible meanings and implications.

A WRITING EXERCISE

Write a brief essay in which you examine how Welty's title relates to her story or Brown's title relates to hers. Consider the writer's alternatives. If you choose to discuss Welty's "A Visit of Charity," you may find it helpful to think about this famous passage from the New Testament: "And now abideth faith, hope, charity, these three; but the greatest of these is charity" (1 Corinthians 13:13). You may also want to look up the word *charity* in a dictionary.

Not all short stories have a uniform **style**. Some feature various tones, dialects, vocabularies, and levels of formality. Stories that do have a predominant style are often narrated in the first person, thus giving the impression of a presiding "voice." Brown's story "The Gift of Sweat," with its matter-of-fact, conversational tone, comes across as an anecdote that someone is relating to a friend.

Dialogue may serve more than one purpose in a short story. By reporting various things, characters may provide you with necessary background for the plot. In Welty's story, it's only from the roommates' fragmentary remarks that Marian — and the reader — can learn anything about their lives up until now. Also, by saying certain things to one another, characters may advance the plot. When, in Brown's story, suffering Rick says to the narrator "please don't go," she winds up in a physical intimacy with him that they may not have had together before. Actually, dialogue can be thought of as action in itself. Try to identify the particular kinds of acts that characters perform when they speak. For instance, Rick's "please don't go" can be labeled a plea. When Welty's character Addie addresses her roommate in the speech we quoted earlier, she makes accusations.

Dialogue may function as well to reveal shifts in characters' relations with one another. Through much of Welty's story, Addie's roommate is rather brusque with Marian; as Marian starts to leave, however, she acts like a beggar toward her: "Oh, little girl, have you a penny to spare for a poor old woman that's not got anything of her own?" Whether or not this performance is a mere pose, it suggests that the woman now hopes to get more out of Marian than she has gotten so far.

Theme

We have already discussed the term **theme** on pages 17–19. There, we identified issues of theme as one kind of issue that comes up in literary studies. At the same time, we suggested that term *theme* applies to various literary genres, not just short stories. Later, in Chapters 4, 5, and 6, we examine theme in connection with essays, poems, and plays. Here, though, we will consider theme as an element of short fiction. In doing so, we will be reviewing some points from our earlier discussion, applying them now to the two stories you have just read.

Recall that we defined the theme of a work as the main claim it seems to make. Furthermore, we identified it as an assertion, proposition, or statement rather than as a single word. "Charity" is obviously a *topic* of Welty's story, but because it is just one word, it is not an adequate expression of the story's *theme*. The following exercise invites you to consider just what that theme may be.

A WRITING EXERCISE

Here are several statements that readers have declared to be Welty's theme. Rank them, placing at the top the one you think most accurate and moving down to the one you think least accurate. Then, in two or three pages, explain your reasoning, referring to each statement at least once. Propose your own statement of the theme if none of these strikes you as adequate.

1. Be nice to old people, for many of them have it tough.
2. None of us can escape the passage of time.
3. Searching for merit points is incompatible with a true spirit of charity.
4. Everyone has to give up dreams of innocence and paradise, just as Adam and Eve did.
5. Although we are tempted to repress our awareness of mortality, we should maintain that awareness.
6. We should all behave charitably toward one another.
7. We can tell how charitable we are by the way we treat people we find strange or irritable.

8. Old age homes need to be made more pleasant, both for the residents and for their visitors.

9. Whenever we become strongly aware of mortality, we tend to repress that awareness, thus robbing ourselves of any benefit we may gain from it.

10. Young people are capable of showing interest in others, if only for a moment, but for better or worse they're basically self-centered.

Think about the other points we made when we discussed theme in Chapter 1. To see how these apply to short fiction, we can start by relating each point to the stories by Welty and Brown.

1. Try to state a text's theme as a midlevel generalization.   If you were to put it in very broad terms, your audience would see it as fitting a great many works besides the one you have read. If you went to the opposite extreme, tying the theme completely to specific details of the text, your audience might think the theme irrelevant to their own lives.

The phrase "the moral of the story" suggests that a story can usually be reduced to a single message, often a principle of ethics or religion. Plenty of examples can be cited to support this suggestion. In the New Testament, for instance, Christ tells stories — they are called *parables* — to convey some of His key ideas. In any number of cultures today, stories are used to teach children elements of good conduct. Moreover, people often determine the significance of a real-life event by building a story from it and by drawing a moral from it at the same time. These two processes conspicuously dovetailed when England's Princess Diana was killed in a car crash. Given that she died fleeing photographers, many people saw her entire life story as that of a woman hounded by media. The moral was simultaneous and clear: Thou shalt honor the right to privacy.

When you read short stories, you may be inclined to define their themes as broad generalizations, along the lines of "Thou shalt honor the right to privacy." For instance, the theme of Brown's "The Gift of Sweat" can probably be phrased as "We should do whatever we can for sick people." But that statement hardly conveys the specific flavor of Brown's text. After all, it can be used to sum up any number of stories, including Welty's. A story is often most interesting when it *complicates* some widely held idea that it seemed ready to endorse. As we have noted, it is possible to lose sight of a story's theme by placing too much emphasis on minor details in the text. Such would be the case if you declared Brown's theme to be "You're nice if you clean for a man with AIDS, but you show true sensitivity to him if you accept breakfast when he prepares it for you, even if that task makes him sicker." The more common temptation, however, is to turn a story's theme into an all-too-general cliché.

Therefore, a useful exercise is to start with a very general thematic statement but then make it increasingly specific. For a test case, refer again to our quite general version of Brown's theme: "We should do whatever we can for sick people." Your next step would be to identify the specific spin that Brown's story puts on this idea. How does her story differ from others on this theme? Note, for instance, that Brown's narrator evidently wants to help sick people right from the beginning of the story, whereas other stories might trace how a character gradually becomes committed to charity. Also, not every story about helping sick people would emphasize sweat and cleaning as Brown's does. With these two observations and others in mind, try now to restate our version of Brown's theme so that it seems more in touch with the specific details of her text.

2. *The theme of a text may be related to its title.*   It may also be expressed by some statement made within the text. But often various parts of the text merit consideration as you try to determine its theme.

In our discussion of a short story's language, we called attention to the potential significance of its title. The title may serve as a guide to the story's theme. What clues, if any, do you find in Welty's title "A Visit of Charity" and Brown's title "The Gift of Sweat"? Of course, determining a story's theme entails going beyond the title. You have to read, and usually reread, the entire text. In doing so, you may come across a statement that seems a candidate for the theme because it is a philosophical generalization. Nevertheless, take the time to consider whether the story's essence is indeed captured by this statement alone.

3. *You can state a text's theme either as an observation or as a recommendation.*   Each way of putting it evokes a certain image of the text's author. When you state the theme as an **observation**, you depict the author as a psychologist, a philosopher, or some other kind of analyst. When you state the theme as a **recommendation**—which often involves your using the word *should*—you depict the author as a teacher, preacher, manager, or coach. That is, the author comes across as telling readers what to do.

As we have noted, stories are often used to teach lessons. Moreover, often the lessons are recommendations for action, capable of being phrased as "Do X" or "Do not do X." The alternative is to make a generalization about some state of affairs. When you try to express a particular story's theme, which of these two options should you follow? There are several things to consider in making your decision. First is your personal comfort: Do you feel at ease with both ways of stating the theme, or is one of these ways more to your taste? Also worth pondering is the impression you want to give of the author. Do you want to portray this person as a maker of recommendations, or do you want to assign the author a more modest role? Because Brown has helped people with AIDS, you may want to state the theme of her story as a prescription for physical and spiritual health. Yet maybe Brown is out to remind her audience that health-care providers have human frailties; hence, expressing her theme as an observation may be the more appropriate move.

4. *Consider stating a text's theme as a problem.*   That way, you are more apt to convey the complexity and drama of the text.

We have suggested that short stories often pivot around conflicts between people and conflicts within people. Perhaps the most interesting stories are ones that pose conflicts not easily resolved. Probably you will be more faithful to such a text if you phrase its theme as a problem. In the case of Brown's story, for example, you might state the theme as follows: "When we try to help people, we may find ourselves resisting the gifts they want to give us, because our guilt over their suffering interferes with our ability to accept things they do for us."

5. *Rather than refer to* the *theme of a text, you might refer to* a *theme of the text, implying that the text has more than one.*   You would still be suggesting that you have identified a central idea of the text. Subsequently, you might have to defend your claim.

Unlike the average novel, the typical short story pivots around only a few ideas. Yet you need not insist that the story you are analyzing has a single theme; in fact, even the shortest piece of short fiction may have a number of them. Besides, your audience is apt to think you nicely open-minded if you suggest that the theme you have discovered is not the only one. We believe, for example, that Brown's story has at least two themes. One is that people with AIDS deserve more understanding, appreciation, and attention than many of them now get. A second theme is that care of the ill may involve more than helping them keep their life "clean"; it may also mean sharing their "sweat," by making bodily contact with them and accepting whatever they achieve in their pain. Although we are label-ing each of these ideas *a* theme of Brown's story rather than *the* theme of it, we are still making strong claims. To use the term *theme* at all implies that we are identifying key principles of the text. You might disagree with our claims about Brown's themes, and if you did, we would have to support our position in order to change your mind.

Perhaps the biggest challenge you will face in writing about short stories is to avoid long stretches of plot summary. Selected details of the plot will often serve as key evidence for you. You will need to describe such moments from the story you are discussing, even if your audience has already read it. But your readers are apt to be frustrated if you just repeat plot at length. They will feel that they may as well turn back to the story itself rather than linger with your rehash. Your paper is worth your readers' time only if you provide insights of your own, *analyzing* the story rather than just *summarizing* it.

To understand what analysis of a short story involves, let's return to Monica Albertson, the student whose freewriting you read earlier. Monica was assigned to write an argument paper about Welty's or Brown's story for an audience consist-ing of her classmates as well as her instructor. Monica knew that she was more interested in writing about Brown's story. But she realized as well that for her paper to be effective, she had to come up with an issue worth addressing, a claim about that issue, and evidence for that claim. Moreover, she had to be prepared to identify the warrants or assumptions behind her evidence.

For most writing assignments, settling on an issue will be your most impor-tant preliminary step. Without a driving question, you will have difficulty produc-ing fresh, organized, and sustained analysis. To identify an issue concerning "The Gift of Sweat," Monica reviewed her freewriting, noting questions she had already raised there about Brown's text. She saw that her questions revolved around the story's narrator. Specifically, this character's behavior posed for Mon-ica issues of cause and effect. Monica wondered (1) why the narrator does not immediately reveal what is in the kitchen; (2) why the narrator cleans Rick's home instead of eating the breakfast right away; and (3) why the narrator's self-examination in the bathroom leads her finally to enter the kitchen, describe the breakfast, and eat it. In addition, Monica wondered about the significance of the story's title, "The Gift of Sweat," since the most important "gift" in the story seems to be food rather than sweat. This apparent contradiction can be phrased, too, as a cause-and-effect issue: Why does Brown call her story "The Gift of Sweat" if she ultimately emphasizes the gift of a breakfast? or, What is the effect of Brown's giving the story the title she does, especially when the story ultimately highlights a gift of breakfast? (Note that the second way of putting the question does not require Monica to determine the author's intentions, as the first does.)

Obviously Monica had several possible issues, as well as several possible ways of phrasing them. Therefore, she next considered whether any of these issues deserved priority. Looking at each issue she had raised, she thought about how much it interested her, how important it seemed to the story, and how easily she could address it within a 600-word paper. She also considered whether any of her issues could be combined. Ultimately, Monica settled on the following question as the focus of her analysis: Why does Rick's sweat lead the narrator to return to the kitchen and eat the breakfast that Rick has prepared? This question blended some of the issues that Monica had already raised, and again, it can be seen as an issue of cause and effect.

Monica chose to pursue this question after reviewing the options that Brown had in writing "The Gift of Sweat." In particular, Monica realized that Brown could have had something other than Rick's sweat be the catalyst for the narrator's ultimate acceptance of Rick's breakfast. Indeed, as Monica's class had discussed, many people fear the sweat of someone with AIDS, for they unreasonably believe they can catch the virus through superficial contact with an infected person. Given this widespread conviction, Brown's decision to have her narrator value Rick's sweat struck Monica as quite an intriguing move.

When you write a paper about a short story, your audience will expect a focused and coherent analysis. Therefore, you may have to be selective, omitting some of your ideas about the story as you emphasize others. As her freewriting reveals, Monica sensed religious symbolism in the meal that concludes "The Gift of Sweat." Yet she was not sure whether she had enough evidence to support this line of inquiry and felt it would seem a digression from her argument about the narrator's behavior. As you will see, Monica's final draft refers only slightly to religion, although she remained quite interested in this possible dimension of Brown's story.

A paper about a short story need not explicitly mention the elements of short fiction we have identified. Nevertheless, thinking of these elements can help you plan such a paper, providing you with some preliminary terms for your analysis. Monica came to see that her paper would be very much about a particular character in Brown's story, the home-care provider, who is both narrator and protagonist. Specifically, Monica's paper would be concerned with how this character behaves during the story's climax and ending. Clearly the paper would deal as well with imagery in the story: in particular, the image of Rick's sweat. Monica realized, too, that she would be touching on the story's theme, especially if she presented her main claim as a lesson that the story's narrator learns. But Monica was wary of reducing the story to one particular point, as thematic claims risk doing. Therefore, as you will see in the final version of her paper, Monica decided to make her main claim a cause-and-effect statement explaining the narrator's behavior.

When you plan a paper about a short story, keep in mind that you are more apt to persuade your readers if you include quotations from the text you discuss. Before you attempt a complete draft, copy down in your notebook any words from the story that might figure in your analysis. Monica, for example, was pretty sure that her paper analyzing the narrator's behavior in "The Gift of Sweat" would incorporate this statement made by the narrator just before the story ends: "I tried to think how Rick would think, I tried to imagine Barry." Yet, as with plot summary, quoting should be kept within limits, so that the paper seems an original argument about the story instead of a mere recycling of it. Monica was tempted to quote the three paragraphs from Brown's story that describe the narrator's cleaning of Rick's home. Eventually, though, Monica realized that so much quoting would seem excessive and that writing a brief reference to the cleaning in her own words would probably suffice.

Sample Student Paper: Final Draft

Here is Monica's final draft of her paper about "The Gift of Sweat." As you read it, keep in mind that it emerged only after she had done several preliminary drafts, in consultation with some of her classmates as well as her instructor. Although Monica's paper is a good example of how to write about a short story, most drafts can stand to be revised further. What do you think Monica has done well in her paper? If she planned to do yet another version, what suggestions would you make?

```
Monica Albertson

Professor Harvey

English 102

5 May ----

            "The Gift of Sweat" as a Story about

                   Learning to Identify

     The narrator of Rebecca Brown's story "The Gift of

Sweat" evidently does housekeeping for people with AIDS,

including Rick, the other major character. On one of her

regular Sunday visits to Rick's home, the narrator finds

him lying in pain. But basically all she can do is cuddle

him. After Rick is taken off to the hospital, the narra-

tor looks into his kitchen and sees that he has bought
```

cinnamon rolls for the two of them. At first she is
unwilling to enter the kitchen, yet later she does decide
to go there and eat the breakfast. The narrator reaches
this decision when she becomes more aware of Rick's sweat
on her. In fact, she actually seems to appreciate his
sweat. But many readers may wonder why it is a positive
influence on the narrator, especially since many people
in real life would try to avoid the sweat of a person
with AIDS, wrongly believing they might get infected. The
narrator's thinking is not as puzzling, though, as it may
first appear. Rick's sweat on her body enables her to
identify with him, in the sense that it brings home to
her the willpower he has shown despite his condition.
Once his sweat reminds her that he is more than just a
victim, she can more easily accept his offering of the
breakfast.

For most of the story, the narrator seems mainly
interested in helping. Probably this desire to help is
what led her to become a caregiver for people with AIDS
in the first place. When she discovers Rick in pain, she
is frustrated that she can only do a little to relieve
his suffering. As she cuddles him, she yearns to have
something like the power of Christ, who could heal sick
people just by touching them: "I tightened my arms around
him as if I could press the sickness out." Probably the
narrator feels frustrated, too, when her supervisor Margaret takes Rick off to the hospital without her. She
needs to feel needed. In the words of a poem by Marge
Piercy, she wants "to be of use."

The narrator's desire to help is a big influence on
her when she first spots the breakfast that Rick has set
up in his kitchen. Her response is avoidance: She backs
away from the kitchen and doesn't even tell the reader
what she has seen. Probably this response results in part
from the guilt she feels over Rick's having risked his
health to get the rolls. But the narrator's interest in
helping Rick also seems to be a factor. Apparently she is

so committed to assisting Rick that she has difficulty
accepting what he has bought and prepared for her. Maybe
she even prefers to look upon Rick as helpless and therefore in constant need of her help. You can tell that she
is really into helping because instead of eating the
breakfast, she throws herself into cleaning the rest of
Rick's home.

The narrator's change of mind occurs after she has
cleaned Rick's bathroom. At that point, she becomes very
conscious of the sweat that Rick has left on her: "I put
my hands up to my face and I could smell him in my hands.
I put my face in my hands and closed my eyes." Here she
is not just seeing his sweat but also inhaling it. Probably one reason she values it is that it provides her with
a trace of Rick's presence even after he has gone off to
the hospital. But in addition, the sweat enables her to
identify with Rick. Most likely she has trouble distinguishing his sweat from hers in the first place. She
seems, however, to be engaging in an even stronger
identification with him when she reports that her hands
"smelled like me, but also him."

Readers are still left with the question of what this
identification really means as well as why it leads the
narrator to accept Rick's breakfast at last. The nature of
this identification becomes clearer once the narrator
reenters Rick's kitchen. For the first time in the story,
she makes a big effort to view his life from <u>his</u> perspective rather than from hers. In fact, near the very end of
the story, she reports that "I tried to think how Rick
would think, I tried to imagine Barry." Barry was Rick's
companion, who is now dead (apparently from AIDS). In the
story's last few pages, the narrator recalls how Rick tried
to help Barry, just as she has tried to help Rick: "Rick
would make something fabulous and they'd eat it together.
That was when he was still trying to help Barry eat." The
narrator also recognizes the effort that Rick showed that
very morning in shopping for the cinnamon rolls: "I thought

of Rick going down there, how long it took him to get down the street, how early he had to go to get the best ones." Although this shopping expedition does not really involve helping, it demonstrates that Rick wants to be more than just a receiver of help. When the narrator observes that his expedition is a case of "him trying to do what he couldn't," some readers may think that she still views him as basically helpless. But at this point she is clearly emphasizing the effort he has shown, rather than the pain that his effort has caused him.

Overall, Rick's sweat has changed the narrator's image of Rick. She is now able to imagine both Rick and her as helpers, or as people who try to be as active and generous as helpers are. Previously, the narrator's conception of Rick as helpless made her feel bad about eating his breakfast. When the scene in the bathroom changes her image of Rick, she is able to accept the breakfast, for she now sees it as indicating his generosity and determination.

It is significant that the narrator uses the same gesture on two occasions: when she notices Rick's sweat on her in the bathroom, and when she is finally about to eat his breakfast. Both times, she closes her eyes and puts her face in her hands. The repetition of this image encourages readers to connect the narrator's awareness of Rick's sweat with her decision to eat. One is cause and the other is effect. Furthermore, the gesture resembles the saying of grace before a meal. This impression is especially appropriate when the narrator accepts the gift of Rick's breakfast. But, as the title of the story indicates, Rick sweat is also a gift for the narrator, although not exactly in the same sense. The breakfast is a gift because it is something of value that Rick has offered the narrator free of charge. On the other hand, Rick's sweat is a gift because, through it, the narrator grows able to appreciate Rick's perspective and therefore his offer of the breakfast.

4

Writing about Poems

Some students are put off by poetry, perhaps because their early experiences with it were discouraging. They imagine poems have deep hidden meanings that they can't uncover. Maybe their high-school English teacher always had the right interpretation, and they rarely did. This need not be the case. Poetry can be accessible to all readers.

The problem is often a confusion about the nature of poetry, since poetry is more compressed than prose. It focuses more on connotative, emotional, or associative meanings and conveys meaning more through suggestion, indirection, and the use of metaphor, symbol, and imagery than prose does. Poetry seldom hands us a specific meaning. Poetic texts suggest certain possibilities, but the reader completes the transaction. Part of the meaning comes from the writer, part from the text itself, and part from the reader. Even if students are the same age, race, religion, and ethnicity, they are not exact duplicates of each other. All of them have their own experiences, their own family histories, their own emotional lives. If thirty people are reading a poem about conformity or responsibility, all thirty will have varying views about these concepts, even though there will probably be commonalities. (Our culture is so saturated with media images that it is nearly impossible to avoid some overlap in responses.)

In a good class discussion, then, we should be aware that even though we might be members of the same culture, each of us reads from a unique perspective, a perspective that might also shift from time to time. If a woman reads a poem about childbirth, her identity as a female will seem more relevant than if she were reading a poem about death, a more universal experience. In other words, how we read a poem and how significant and meaningful the poem is for us depends both on the content of the poem and our specific circumstances. Suppose you read a poem about dating at age fourteen; you would likely have very different responses rereading it at nineteen, twenty-five, and fifty. We read poems through our experiences. As we gain new experiences, our readings change.

That is one reason why it is important to respond in writing to your first reading. You want to be able to separate your first thoughts from those of your classmates; they too will be bringing their own experiences, values, and ideas to the discussion. In the give-and-take of open discussion, it may be difficult to remember what you first said. Of course, the point of a classroom discussion is not simply to defend your initial response, for then you would be denying yourself the benefit of other people's ideas. A good discussion should open up the poem, allow you to see it from multiple viewpoints, and enable you to expand your perspective, to see how others make sense of the world.

This rich mixture of the poet's text, the reader's response, and discussion among several readers can create new possibilities of meaning. Even more than fiction or drama, poetry encourages creative readings that can be simultaneously true to the text and to the reader. A lively class discussion can uncover a dozen or more plausible interpretations of a poem, each backed up with valid evidence both from the poem and the reader's experience. You may try to persuade others that your views about the poem are correct; others may do the same to you. This negotiation is at the heart of a liberal, democratic education. In fact, maybe the most respected and repeated notion about being well-educated is the ability to empathize with another's point of view, to see as another sees. Reading, discussing, and writing about poetry can help you become a person who can both create meaning and understand and appreciate how others do. This is one important way literature matters.

We have chosen three poems by Robert Frost (1874–1963) that have mattered to millions of readers. Frost writes beautiful, apparently simple poems, ones that rhyme, have compelling images, and tell accessible stories of American country life. Yet there is something deeper and more complex in these classics. The surface meaning of these poems seems clear enough, but below the surface they are tantalizing and purposefully ambiguous — "indeterminate" poems that seem to mean many things, depending on the values and experiences readers bring with them to their reading.

ROBERT FROST

Stopping by Woods on a Snowy Evening

Whose woods these are I think I know.
His house is in the village, though;
He will not see me stopping here
To watch his woods fill up with snow.

My little horse must think it queer   5
To stop without a farmhouse near
Between the woods and frozen lake
The darkest evening of the year.

He gives his harness bells a shake
To ask if there is some mistake.   10
The only other sound's the sweep
Of easy wind and downy flake.

◆   ◆   ◆

The woods are lovely, dark and deep,
But I have promises to keep,
And miles to go before I sleep,   15
And miles to go before I sleep.   [1923]

ROBERT FROST

The Road Not Taken

Two roads diverged in a yellow wood,
And sorry I could not travel both
And be one traveler, long I stood
And looked down one as far as I could
To where it bent in the undergrowth;   5

Then took the other, as just as fair,
And having perhaps the better claim,
Because it was grassy and wanted wear;
Though as for that the passing there
Had worn them really about the same,   10

And both that morning equally lay
In leaves no step had trodden black.
Oh, I kept the first for another day!
Yet knowing how way leads on to way,
I doubted if I should ever come back.   15

I shall be telling this with a sigh
Somewhere ages and ages hence:
Two roads diverged in a wood, and I—
I took the one less traveled by,
And that has made all the difference.   [1916]   20

ROBERT FROST

Mending Wall

Something there is that doesn't love a wall,
That sends the frozen-ground-swell under it,
And spills the upper boulders in the sun;
And makes gaps even two can pass abreast.
The work of hunters is another thing: 5
I have come after them and made repair
Where they have left not one stone on a stone,
But they would have the rabbit out of hiding,

To please the yelping dogs. The gaps I mean,
No one has seen them made or heard them made,   10
But at spring mending-time we find them there.
I let my neighbor know beyond the hill;
And on a day we meet to walk the line
And set the wall between us once again.
We keep the wall between us as we go.   15
To each the boulders that have fallen to each.
And some are loaves and some so nearly balls
We have to use a spell to make them balance:
"Stay where you are until our backs are turned!"
We wear our fingers rough with handling them.   20
Oh, just another kind of outdoor game,
One on a side. It comes to little more:
There where it is we do not need the wall:
He is all pine and I am apple orchard.
My apple trees will never get across   25
And eat the cones under his pines, I tell him.
He only says, "Good fences make good neighbors."
Spring is the mischief in me, and I wonder
If I could put a notion in his head:
"*Why* do they make good neighbors? Isn't it   30
Where there are cows? But here there are no cows.
Before I built a wall I'd ask to know
What I was walling in or walling out,
And to whom I was like to give offense.
Something there is that doesn't love a wall,   35
That wants it down." I could say "Elves" to him,
But it's not elves exactly, and I'd rather
He said it for himself. I see him there
Bringing a stone grasped firmly by the top
In each hand, like an old-stone savage armed.   40
He moves in darkness as it seems to me,
Not of woods only and the shade of trees.
He will not go behind his father's saying,
And he likes having thought of it so well
He says again, "Good fences make good neighbors."   [1914]   45

A WRITING EXERCISE

"Stopping by Woods on a Snowy Evening," "The Road Not Taken," and "Mending Wall" are perhaps Frost's most popular poems. Read each selection twice and then record your impression of what the poems seem to be about. Include any personal associations that seem relevant. Are there noticeable similarities and differences among the three? Try to freewrite steadily for about ten to twelve minutes. The exercise is an exploratory technique to help you plan an essay on these three poems. As with all exploring, being self-reflective, raising questions, and noting the context of the issues and their relevance to your life are all useful things to include.

Students' Personal Responses to the Poems

Here we have several students' responses to Frost's three poems. As a way to add different voices to the discussion, compare what you have written with what they have written.

Mary Ellen Chin, eighteen years old, writes:

> In "The Road Not Taken" Robert Frost is very pleased that he went down the road less traveled because that has made him much happier in his later life. He doesn't want to look back. He sighs out of relief that he doesn't have to worry about past decisions. In "Stopping by Woods on a Snowy Evening" Frost is also looking to the future and to his responsibilities and duties. He appreciates the beauty of nature but is not one to dillydally. He is a hard worker and doesn't require much sleep. In "Mending Wall" Frost is willing to help his old neighbor rebuild the wall but doesn't really care for it. He would rather it were down. The old man is fairly ignorant and just wants it up because his father did. As in the other two poems, Frost here is practical and not obsessed by the past.

Twenty-four-year-old Mitchell Ellerby writes:

> I see the speaker in "The Road Not Taken" as a sad man, one who has made a mistake, probably a big one like marrying the wrong person or maybe leaving the right one. This is a poem about bad choices and the regret that often follows in its wake. I think he really tried to judge what was the right thing to do --"and looked down one as far as I could" --but just blew it. Now it's too late and he sighs out of futility for taking the wrong road. "Stopping by Woods on a Snowy Evening" seems the

direct result of his sorrow. He says it's the "darkest evening of the year," which is a statement about his soul not the light. The whole wintry scene is the condition of his frozen heart. I think he is having such a bad time that he might walk into the woods and simply curl up and disappear from the pain. The woods are "lovely" because they offer an immediate way out of his life. But he can't go through with it. It seems he has made promises to somebody, maybe a wife or a young child. In a sad poem, this is his one saving grace. But even that doesn't improve his mood as he plods on, wearily hoping finally for sleep or death. "Mending Wall" is about the emotional barriers that people keep between them. The speaker knows this is a bad idea right away when he says "something there is that doesn't love a wall." Later on he demands to know why walls are good, but his neighbor just repeats a cliché about good fences making good neighbors. But because he calls him an "old-stone savage," I figure he really thinks such a saying is primitive. I don't know if Robert Frost wanted these poems to be read together, but if you put "Mending Wall" first, then the other two follow. What I'm saying is that if you build walls between people or if you cut yourself off from others, then you will feel depressed, you will think you have made bad choices, taken wrong turns. And if you really feel isolated, you might even contemplate suicide in the woods.

Tom Mason, age nineteen, writes:

I think "The Road Not Taken" describes something we all go through, making choices that will affect us later. I know I should have made another decision instead of going to college. Quite literally, I wanted to take the road less traveled and go on a bike tour through Europe. Everybody was going to college, even my friends who hated school--just because their parents wanted them to. Actually, I like school, but I have lived my whole life in this little town in southern Maryland. I've

never seen the world. I haven't even been to New York.
I wanted to take a year off, but I got so much grief that
I was forced to back down. And that has made all the
difference. What I wanted to do was sit by beautiful
spots in the Alps like the speaker in "Stopping by Woods
on a Snowy Evening." That must be very satisfying. He
feels one with nature, with the lovely woods. I think he
is ready to come back to civilization, just like I would
have been after my interlude in an exotic and far-off
land. In "Mending Wall" the speaker doesn't like walls. I
agree and one way to understand our neighbors is to
travel, to understand other cultures. How else can we
really understand each other? I'm afraid if I stay in my
little town, I'll become like that savage who can only
quote his father. Like the elves, I want the walls to
come down, but I'm surrounded by conformists.

Forty-year-old Sophia De Puy writes:

Robert Frost seems to be a confused person or maybe
just ambivalent about what he really wants to do or what
he thinks. In "The Road Not Taken," he wants to "travel
both" roads; he wants to have it both ways. The line "had
worn them really about the same" suggests to me there
really wasn't a big difference in the choice. He does say
both are equal, so what's the big deal? Why does he say
going down one path has made all the difference? Actually
when you think about it, that's an odd thing to say since
we never know what might have happened. Would I have been
happier or more satisfied if I had gone to college instead
of getting married to my high-school boyfriend? That made
a difference, but then all our thousands of decisions
make some kind of difference. I really wonder about that
"sigh." Is it regret, satisfaction, or resignation? Does
Frost know? He also seems confused in "Stopping by Woods
on a Snowy Evening." There seems to be a temptation to
retreat from the world on the one hand and a commitment
to participate in the world's duties and promises on the

other. I have sometimes felt like giving up too, but I
endured. I think he has mixed feelings. He thinks the
woods (which I see as death) are lovely but he weakly
decides to continue. In "Mending Wall" he is also not sure
if he wants the wall up or not. It looks like he wants it
down, but then why does he ask his neighbor to repair it
with him? Why does he mend the wall unless he thinks walls
really do work? Frost is like many of my friends: not too
sure which way to go, what position to take.

A WRITING EXERCISE

Choose one poem by Frost, and reread the responses by Mary Ellen, Mitchell, Tom, and Sophia. Next, write a brief paragraph or two comparing your response to theirs. You may want to list significant points of agreement and disagreement before attempting to write the comparison.

Out of dozens of students, we picked these four because they provide an interesting range of responses to what at first appear to be three fairly straightforward poems. But poetry is so condensed and so energized that even seemingly simple poems allow readers to read between the lines and to fill in gaps in a variety of ways. More than likely, Frost did not specifically mean "The Road Not Taken" to refer to a bike trip to Europe as Mitchell Ellerby describes it. But this is fine. Mitchell filled in the gaps from his own experience. Unless you take the poem quite literally, Frost's two roads could be just about any choice we have to make.

What choices did the poem remind you of? How about the speaker's reason for stopping? To commune with nature, to take a break from a hard day's work, or to contemplate suicide? How would you fill in that gap? And what is the speaker of "Mending Wall" really interested in doing with the walls? Did you interpret that image as a literal wall or fence? As a less-tangible barrier like a border? Or did you, like Mitchell, figure the wall is a metaphor for our refusal to understand others and our tendency to avoid showing our private emotions, our deeper selves? These are questions to which there are no definitive answers. Definitive answers are not what poetry is about.

Each of the four students begins his or her understanding of these three poems with reasonable, often perceptive, observations. They move from these to write interesting explorations. To move ahead in the writing process from exploring to planning, it is useful to briefly review some elements of poetry. Of course, no element of poetry exists by itself; each works together. Our four students tended to focus on the thematic element of poetry. This is a good start since this anthology is arranged thematically, but the consideration of other elements can enhance their analysis.

The Elements of Poetry

Speaker and Tone

The voice we hear in a poem could be the poet's, but it is better to think of the **speaker** as a sort of poetic construction: perhaps a **persona** (mask) for the poet, or perhaps a complete fiction. The speaker's **tone** or attitude is sometimes difficult to discern. It could be ironic or sentimental, joyful or morose, or a combination. In "The Road Not Taken," for example, determining the speaker's tone hinges on how you hear certain words, especially an ambiguous word like *sigh*. We know of one critic who believes the speaker is closely aligned with Frost in complaining that most people want their poetry to have a catchy, bumper-sticker conclusion. Even though the poem doesn't really say one road is "less traveled by," the speaker resigns himself to telling people he did choose the unusual and "that has made all the difference." This is a different reading than most and suggests how a simple word like *sigh* can be interpreted in different ways. It also indicates how the theme of the poem is connected to the speaker's voice and tone. If you read this poem as a celebration of choice, then the tone of *sigh* is probably positive. If you think the speaker's attitude is negative, then you most likely hear a *sigh* of sadness.

A WRITING EXERCISE

Each of the poems has a first-person narrator, a speaker with whom a reader must reckon to make sense of the poem's meaning. Try to characterize the "I" of each poem. You may want to consider, for example, the attitude of the speaker in "Stopping by Woods on a Snowy Evening." What is the speaker's attitude toward the woods? Toward promises? How does the speaker in "The Road Not Taken" seem to feel about his decision? What is the attitude of the speaker in "Mending Wall" toward the neighbor? Toward the wall?

Diction and Syntax

In "Stopping by Woods on a Snowy Evening," the speaker uses ordinary concrete words, not the flowery and abstract poetic **diction** many people associate with poetry. Except perhaps for "downy flake," the words here are almost conversational. The same seems true for "The Road Not Taken." But these words gain power and grace in their simplicity. Arranging exact words in a meticulously constructed order is a most demanding aspect of poetry. Frost's genius is to do so with such apparent ease. It is his words that make a poem memorable, even more so than his ideas. The words in Frost's line "The woods are lovely, dark and deep" seem just right. The **denotations** (literal meanings) of these words work fine, but their **connotations** (associations, emotional overtones, suggestions) help create both a sense of serenity and the possibility of an ultimate withdrawal.

Frost's colloquial diction also helps to create the personality of the speaker (and the poet) as a country sage, one who does not need "highfalutin" diction to see clearly and deeply. But Frost's poems are crafted works of art. Like a professional basketball player driving to the hoop or a dancer executing a perfect leap, Frost makes it look gracefully easy. Take the first line of "Stopping by Woods," for example; Frost achieves added emphasis and rhythm here by inverting the usual **syntax**, or word order. By comparison, the usual subject/verb/object pattern ("I think I know whose woods these are") sounds flat. By inverting the usual word order, Frost subtly shifts our attention to the woods, not to the speaker's thinking.

A WRITING EXERCISE

All of these poems use simple language to denote apparently simple actions: stopping by woods at night, choosing a road, building a wall. Reread them with an eye to where connotations may take you or where unusual syntax might signal ambiguity or complexity. (In "Mending Wall," for example, what connotations do you associate with "savage," "darkness," and "good neighbors"?) List a few of these points and freewrite on them for ten minutes to see where your own free associations may take you.

Figures of Speech

When we use **figures of speech,** we mean something other than the words' literal meaning. In "Mending Wall" Frost writes that the stones from the wall are "loaves." This direct comparison is a **metaphor**. Had he said it more indirectly using *like* or *as*—for example, "like loaves"—it would be a **simile**. Aristotle claimed that metaphor is a poet's intuitive grasp of the way unlike things are similar. Is a simile a clearer, less suggestive way to imply sameness? Frost says his neighbor in "Mending Wall" is "like an old-stone savage armed." Might it have been too direct to claim that his neighbor is a savage? What do you think the difference is between "like a savage" and is "an old-stone savage"? Metaphors are suggestive, and it is still possible to read that line positively—if, for example, you (like the French Romantic philosopher Jean-Jacques Rousseau) believe in the dignity of "the noble savage." Frost's metaphor in the next line, "he moves in darkness," does, however, seem to suggest the conventional Western meaning of the savage as ignorant. Metaphors and similes enhance poetry's multiple possibilities.

A **symbol** is also a suggestive device. Symbols stand for more than themselves, for something beyond the specific words used. What, after all, does the wall stand for in "Mending Wall"? The context of its use in the poem helps the reader determine what the wall might stand for. The numerous details of Frost's poem suggest some kind of abstract barrier, but the specific possibilities are still open. Readers of "Mending Wall" mention that the wall could be anything from lack of intimacy to fear of strangers to the Berlin Wall. When Frost wrote "Mending Wall," he could have been thinking of novelist Henry James's claim that symbols cast long shadows.

Sometimes poets create more elaborate symbolic apparatus. In "The Road Not Taken," the road can be symbolic of conformity, but the idea of choice is played out in such detail that critics call this an **allegory**, or sustained symbolism. A popular film with clear allegorical implication is *Star Wars* (1977) where Luke Skywalker (goodness) triumphs over Darth Vader (evil) on his journey toward self-fulfillment. Using Obi-Wan (wisdom) to achieve the Force (morality), Luke rescues Princess Leia (purity), and so on. Both symbolism and allegory intimately extend and reinforce the meaning and significance of poetry.

Do you find any of these poems allegorical? (For example, how might the woods, the frozen lake, the darkest evening, the promises, and the miles be seen as allegorical in "Stopping by Woods on a Snowy Evening"?) Do the poems resist being read as allegories? In a couple of pages, make the case for whether any, or all, of the poems can be considered allegorical.

Sound

The English poet Alexander Pope hoped that poetry's **sound** could become "an echo to [its] sense," that what the ear hears would reinforce what the mind understands. To many people, **rhyme** is the most recognizable aspect of poetry. The matching of final vowel and consonant sounds can make a poem trite or interesting. The now-familiar rhyming of "moon" and "June" with "swoon" suggests a poet that will settle for a cliché rather than do the hard work of being fresh. Rhyme, of course, is pleasing to the ear and makes the poem easier to remember, but it also gives the poem psychological force.

In the first stanza of "Stopping by Woods," lines 1, 2, and 4 use **perfect rhyme;** they sound exactly alike. Note, too, that the unrhymed third line rhymes with the first line of the next stanza ("here" with "queer"). This is also true in the second stanza when "lake" rhymes with "shake" in the first line of stanza three. And later the "ee" sound in *sweep* rhymes with that in "deep." Such patterns, called **rhyme schemes,** are indicated with letters. The first **quatrain** (four-line stanza) would be marked *aaba*, the second *bbcb*, the third *ccdc*, the last *dddd*. Why do you think Frost ends with the repeated **couplet** (two lines)?

This is more than a clever way to interconnect the four stanzas because both ear and mind are pleased when they move forward to a new sound and then back for a moment to an old one. When we read "he gives his harness bells a *shake*," we remember "lake" from the previous stanza. When we hear "the woods are lovely, dark and *deep*," we also remember "sweep." Does such forward and backward movement suggest a tension, an ambivalence? In the student essay that follows this section, Sophia De Puy makes just this point, arguing that the speaker's anxiety is echoed in the poem.

The pleasure of reading "Stopping by Woods" is also enhanced by both **alliteration** and **assonance.** Alliteration is the repetition of consonant sounds; a closely related device, assonance repeats vowel sounds. Notice in the third stanza how Frost duplicates the "ee" sound in "sweep" in both "easy" and "downy." Can you find a duplicate for the "ow" in "downy"? Also notice the alliterative "s" sound in "some," "sound," and "sweep." Can you find other "s" sounds? Do these sounds help establish a mood?

One of the best ways to understand how a poem "works" is to rewrite it—or part of it—using a different rhyme scheme, or different rhyme words, while trying to keep the poem as close as possible to its original meaning. Try this with "Stopping by Woods on a Snowy Evening" or "The Road Not Taken." Or try to capture the meaning of "Mending Wall" in a short poem with a simple rhyme scheme.

Rhythm and Meter

Rhythm in poetry refers to the beat, a series of stresses, pauses, and accents. We are powerfully attuned to rhythm, whether it is our own heartbeat or the throb of the bass guitar in a rock band. When we pronounce a word, we give more **stress** (breath, emphasis) to some syllables than to others. When these stresses occur at a regular interval over, say, a line of poetry, we refer to it as **meter**. When we scan a line of poetry, we try to mark its stresses and pauses. We use ´ to indicate a stressed syllable and ˘ for an unstressed one. The basic measuring unit for these stressed and unstressed syllables in English is the **foot**. There are four usual feet: *iambic, trochaic, anapestic,* and *dactylic.* An **iamb** is an unstressed syllable followed by a stressed one, as in "the woods." Reversed we have a **trochee**, as in "tiger." An **anapest** contains three syllables that are unstressed, then unstressed, then stressed, as in "When the blue / wave rolls nightly / on deep Galilee." The reverse, the **dactyl,** can be heard in the Mother Goose rhyme, "Pussy cat, / pussy cat / where have you / been?" Look again at the last stanza of "Stopping by Woods on a Snowy Evening." When we read it out loud, we hear a fairly regular beat of iambs:

> The woods / are love / ly, dark / and deep
>
> But I / have pro / mises / to keep
>
> And miles / to go / before / I sleep
>
> And miles / to go / before / I sleep

Depending on the number of feet, we give lines various names. If a line contains one foot, it is a **monometer**; two is a **dimeter**; three a **trimeter**; four a **tetrameter**; five a **pentameter**; six a **hexameter**; seven a **heptameter**; and eight an **octometer**. So Frost's last stanza is mostly iambic tetrameter. (Line 14 is a variation.) Most lines in Shakespeare's sonnets are iambic pentameter, or five iambs.

Note how Frost alters line 14 slightly for variety. He also employs **end stops** and **enjambment** for emphasis. When a line ends with a period we are meant to pause (end stop), but in line 3, for example, we are supposed to pause only briefly, continuing on until we get to the period in line 4 (enjambment). These poetic techniques improve the sound and flow of the poem and enhance the thoughts and feelings that give poetry its depth and meaningfulness.

A WRITING EXERCISE

Right on the page, mark out the rhythm and meter of "The Road Not Taken," using the system of marks we just presented. Then describe the predominant rhythm and meter. Alternatively, map out the rhythm and meter of the poem you wrote for the preceding exercise.

Theme

Some readers are fond of extracting **theme statements** from poems, claiming, for example, that the theme of "Stopping by Woods" is about the need to struggle on or that "Mending Wall" champions nonconformity over tradition. In a sense these thematic observations are plausible enough, but they are limiting and misleading. "Stopping by Woods" certainly has something to do with the tension between retreat and responsibility, but the significance for each reader might be much more specific, having to do with drug addiction or suicidal impulses, with joyful acceptance of duty or a need for aesthetic beauty. Reducing a complex, ambiguous poem to a bald statement robs the poem of its evocative power, its mystery, and its art.

Some critics stress the response of readers; others care only for what the text itself says; still others are concerned with the social and cultural implications of the poem's meaning. There are psychoanalytic readers who see poems as reflections of the psychological health or illness of the poet; source-hunting or intertextual readers want to find references and hints of other literary works hidden deep within the poem. Feminist readers may find sexism, Marxists may find economic injustice, and gay and lesbian readers may find heterosexual bias. Readers can and will find in texts a whole range of issues. Perhaps we find what we are looking for, or we find what matters most to us.

This does not mean that we should think of committed readers as biased or as distorting the text to fulfill their own agenda, although biased or distorted readings are not rare. In a literature course, readers are entitled to read poems according to their own lights as long as they follow the general conventions of academic discourse. That is, if you can make a reasonable case that "Stopping by Woods" is about, say, the inability of animals ("My little horse must think it queer") to appreciate the aesthetic beauty of nature, then you should marshal your evidence both from the text and from your own experience and put your energy into writing an essay that is clear, informed, and persuasive.

A WRITING EXERCISE

State in sentence form two possible themes for each of the three poems. Then exchange your sentences with a classmate. Choose one of your classmate's sentences and freewrite on it for five minutes, exploring how the sentence captures the theme of the poem. Finally, exchange your freewriting and discuss. Did you find the same themes? What are significant differences?

Sample Student Paper: Revised Draft

After her initial response, Sophia De Puy planned her essay on Frost and wrote her first draft. When the class worked in small groups, she received feedback from her group about what she was doing well and how to improve her essay. She also met with her instructor, who made some suggestions about revising her focus.

Sophia wrote the following revision that combines her own subjective response with explication and analysis.

Sophia De Puy

Professor Frye

English 102

21 April ----

Robert Frost's Uncertainties:

A Reading of Three Poems

Hardly anything makes us feel better about life than to read a novel or see a film where good wins over evil, where the hero knows what he or she is doing, where the choices are clear and certain, the path cleared of ambiguity. Maybe it goes without saying that we draw comfort from these narratives because they are so unlike the stories we actually live. In my own life, I am well acquainted with uncertainty. I used to dream that when I entered my twenties--then my thirties--my decisions, indeed my life, would clarify itself. I was confused but thought that later on I would know which choice was right.

As a high-school senior, I was in love with the captain of the track team, a handsome and virile javelin thrower. He disliked school but was great at repairing foreign cars. He wanted us to get married, to open our own specialty garage, and to start a family. My parents wanted me to go to college and be a nurse. I was torn, confused, uncertain but finally did marry. That was twenty years ago. Today I have two sons in college. Unfortunately, my husband died two years ago; fortunately, he left us a good deal of money. So I have decided to go back and start again. I have been moderately happy, mostly. But did I make the right decision? I don't know. Do we ever know? Do we have the nerve to look back and admit our befuddlement at life's choices? I think some writers do.

I was particularly taken with this enigma of choice when I read Robert Frost's "The Road Not Taken."

Interesting, I thought, that he focuses on the mysterious, the unknowable road he doesn't take. Frost's speaker echoed my own thoughts about "what if." When I was twenty and nursing my first son on Saturday nights, I would fantasize about what I would be doing if I had gone to college with my girlfriends: Drinking at some wild frat party? Talking about our hopes and dreams or our anxieties and frustrations in a fashionable café with would-be poets? The path I didn't take seemed romantic and exciting. Like Frost's speaker, I was "sorry I could not travel both / And be one traveler." I too stood for a long time trying to decide if I had taken the best path. Only I could answer, but I didn't know. I was both in love and longing for the freedom of my youth. My husband had wanted real life to happen. I wanted to be two travelers.

Frost's speaker has a choice to make between "two roads." I could speculate about what they might be, but I think it's best to fill in that gap with my own experience. When he says he looked down one road "as far as [he] could," I was reminded that I too tried to imagine my future having children, married to a blue-collar man, staying in my neighborhood. Should I venture forth into the world, go away to college, delay marriage? I took "the other" road just like Frost's speaker. The usual interpretation of this poem seems to turn on a misreading of lines 9, 10, and 11. But Frost seems quite lucid here:

> Though as for that the passing there
> Had worn them really about the same,
> And both that morning equally lay . . .

Isn't it clear that both roads, both choices were equally attractive? This isn't a matter of being a conformist or a rebel, or a farmer or a poet, it's just one of life's many conundrums: Which choice is best? Should I go to school or get married? I didn't know, and neither did Frost. He says he "kept the first for another day,"

which is, of course, technically impossible. True, I am
now going to college--but at forty, not eighteen. You
can never go back, simply because you have changed, have
grown. Somehow I don't see myself pledging for Delta
whatever or worrying if I have a date for Saturday night.

This brings me to the mysterious and controversial
last stanza. I read the "sigh" as the speaker's resignation at having to imply in the last two lines that he is
contented that he made the right decision by taking the
"one less traveled by." But as I suggested, Frost's
speaker claims earlier both roads were worn "about the
same." Is he somehow going along with those people who
demand simple, clear answers, people who want poets to be
all wise? I know for a long while I used to say how glad
I was that I got married and had two great children. But
secretly I was never that sure. I think I gave people the
answer they wanted. I think the speaker feels he should,
too, like in Hollywood films where everything is clear,
where people live happily ever after. But here in a
subtle way, Frost is admitting that he doesn't have all
the answers.

Perhaps this kind of compromise is necessary in life.
Indeed, the speaker of "Stopping by Woods on a Snowy
Evening" seems equally conflicted. He stops to watch
"woods fill up with snow" even though from the response
of his horse this is not business as usual. Perhaps the
driver is a hard-working country doctor or a salesman
used to stopping only at houses. But he is doing more
than sightseeing: He is seriously questioning his life.
When he says it is "the darkest evening of the year," he
is referring to his mood. Everyone says the holidays are
the most joyful season of the year, but when my children
were two and three and wild with energy and my husband
was working overtime at the garage, I was not celebra-
tory. My old friends were home for Christmas vacation
and full of stories of trips to Florida and plans for

graduate school and jobs in New York and Atlanta. I was morose, and I think Frost's speaker is, too. He needs a long rest. He might even be suicidal. Everything around him is peaceful, serene, restful. The lines "the only other sound's the sweep / Of easy wind and downy flake" are more than pleasant alliteration; they are what his mind longs for: stillness, pause. To me the line "the woods are lovely, dark and deep" is a symbolic way of saying death might be quite appealing. I know that tension between retreat and moving on, between sleep and work, between the longing for rest and the necessity to do your duty.

After reading this poem several times and studying its rhyme scheme, I found that the rhyme moves us forward but then takes us back. The last word in the third line ("here," "lake," "sweep") in each stanza becomes the major repeated rhyme of the next. When we read each stanza aloud, we can hear an echo of the previous one, almost as if Frost is duplicating the choice between movement and retreat the speaker is contemplating. But he does go on; he does accept the harsh reality that a working life offers little real rest. If we are content or not, we must endure. That is what I felt for years: that "I have promises to keep." And I probably repeated words like this too, droning them like a mantra I truly had to believe in.

Does the speaker of "Mending Wall" truly believe that "good fences make good neighbors"? At the very beginning he does seem to suggest that there is almost a cosmic presence that doesn't love a wall. And later he wants to encourage his neighbor to question his conformist way of thinking. The speaker claims he would be careful about building a wall, but I notice that he doesn't say he plans to take this one down, just that he might not want another. The wall here seems symbolic of emotional restraint or a psychological barrier. Might it also sug-

gest privacy or secrets of the heart? Could he be suggesting that emotional honesty (for example, "we tell
each other everything") is like living without walls?
This is too complex to say, and like the other two speak-
ers, I think this one isn't so sure. True, he seems to
employ a negative connotation, calling his neighbor a
"savage armed," who "moves in darkness." But why then
does the speaker make repairs? Why does he invite his
neighbor to join him in mending the wall? He seems to
disagree with the neighbor's conformity but then he himself conforms with him. Why?

Because he wants it both ways; he wants to travel
both roads; he wants to retreat from the world and
embrace it. He wants to be close with his neighbor (or
perhaps his family and friends), but he also wants to
keep them at a safe distance. Since this has definitely
been a part of my personality for years, I have no
trouble understanding such contradictory thinking.
Even now, as I look forward to seeing my family during
the holidays, I know that after I have been there awhile,
I will be eager to return home to the serenity behind my
own wall.

Robert Frost is willing to suggest easy answers to
those who long for certainty. If you need to believe that
a choice you made years ago was the right one, then you
can get comfort from "The Road Not Taken." If you want to
plow ahead without doubting what you are doing, then
"Stopping by Woods" will confirm your certainty. If you
think honesty is always the best policy, then you will
think the speaker of "Mending Wall" wise. But if like me,
you face life with a certain tentativeness, if the past
is still a puzzle, if the future is an enigma, then
Frost's poetry will suggest that uncertainty is our lot
and that those who would have it otherwise are the real
"old-stone savage[s]," moving in the "darkness" of
illusions.

5

Writing about Plays

Most plays incorporate elements also found in short fiction, such as plot, characterization, dialogue, setting, and theme. But unlike short fiction and other literary genres, plays are typically enacted live, in front of an audience. Theater professionals distinguish between the written *script* of a play and its actual *performances*. When you write about a play, you may wind up saying little or nothing about performances of it. When you first read and analyze a play, however, try to imagine ways of staging it. You might even research past productions of the play, noting how scenery, costumes, and lighting—as well as particular actors—were used.

Because a play is usually meant to be staged, its readers are rarely its only interpreters. Theater audiences also ponder its meanings. So, too, do cast members; no doubt you have heard of actors "interpreting" their parts. When a play is put on, even members of the backstage team are involved in interpreting it. The technical designers' choices of sets, costumes, and lighting reflect their ideas about the play, while the director works with cast and crew to implement a particular vision of it. No matter what the author of the script intended, theater is a collaborative art: All of the key figures involved in a play's production are active interpreters of the play in that they influence the audience's understanding and experience of it. Therefore, you can develop good ideas when you read a play if you imagine yourself directing a production of it. More specifically, think what you would say to the actors as you guided them through their parts. As you engage in this thought experiment, you will see that you have options, for even directors keen on staying faithful to the script know it can be staged in any number of ways. Perhaps your course will give you and other students the chance to perform a scene together; if so, you will be deciding what interpretation of the scene to set forth.

To help you understand how to write about plays, we will refer often to the two one-act plays that follow. Both works explore relations between women. The first play, *The Stronger,* had its stage debut in 1889. Its author, the Swedish playwright August Strindberg (1849–1912), is widely acknowledged as a founder of modern drama. Throughout his career, Strindberg experimented with theatrical styles. For this particular play about an encounter between two actresses, he unconventionally chose to have one character speak and the other remain silent. The second play, Susan Glaspell's *Trifles*, premiered in 1916 with the author and her husband, the novelist George Cram Cook, in the cast. Glaspell (1876–1948) is best known for her association with the Provincetown Players, which was considered avant-garde in its day. Glaspell and Cook had founded the company a year earlier while vacationing in Provincetown, Massachusetts. Since its debut, the play has continued to be performed and read, in part because it is a compelling detective story as well as an analysis of female relations.

AUGUST STRINDBERG
The Stronger
Translated by Elizabeth Sprigge

CHARACTERS

MRS. X, *actress, married*
MISS Y, *actress, unmarried*
A WAITRESS

SCENE: *A corner of a ladies' café [in Stockholm in the eighteen eighties].° Two small wrought-iron tables, a red plush settee, and a few chairs.*

Miss Y is sitting with a half-empty bottle of beer on the table before her, reading an illustrated weekly which from time to time she exchanges for another.

Mrs. X enters, wearing a winter hat and coat and carrying a decorative Japanese basket.

MRS. X: Why, Millie, my dear, how are you? Sitting here all alone on Christmas Eve like some poor bachelor.

Miss Y looks up from her magazine, nods, and continues to read.

MRS. X: You know it makes me feel really sad to see you. Alone. Alone in a café and on Christmas Eve of all times. It makes me feel as sad as when once in Paris I saw a wedding party at a restaurant. The bride was reading a comic paper and the bridegroom playing billiards with the witnesses. Ah me, I said to myself, with such a beginning how will it go, and how will it end? He was playing billiards on his wedding day! And she, you were going to say, was reading a comic paper on hers. But that's not quite the same.

A waitress brings a cup of chocolate to Mrs. X and goes out.

MRS. X: Do you know, Amelia, I really believe now you would have done better to stick to him. Don't forget I was the first who told you to forgive him. Do you remember? Then you would be married now and have a home. Think how happy you were that Christmas when you stayed with your fiancé's

Addition to scene bracketed. First mention of Miss Y and Mrs. X reversed. [Translator's note]

people in the country. How warmly you spoke of domestic happiness! You really quite longed to be out of the theatre. Yes, Amelia dear, home is best — next best to the stage, and as for children — but you couldn't know anything about that.

Miss Y's expression is disdainful. Mrs. X sips a few spoonfuls of chocolate, then opens her basket and displays some Christmas presents.

MRS. X: Now you must see what I have bought for my little chicks. *(Takes out a doll.)* Look at this. That's for Lisa. Do you see how she can roll her eyes and turn her head. Isn't she lovely? And here's a toy pistol for Maja.° *(She loads the pistol and shoots it at Miss Y who appears frightened.)*

MRS. X: Were you scared? Did you think I was going to shoot you? Really, I didn't think you'd believe that of me. Now if *you* were to shoot *me* it wouldn't be so surprising, for after all I did get in your way, and I know you never forget it — although I was entirely innocent. You still think I intrigued to get you out of the Grand Theatre, but I didn't. I didn't, however much you think I did. Well, it's no good talking, you will believe it was me . . . *(Takes out a pair of embroidered slippers.)* And these are for my old man, with tulips on them that I embroidered myself. As a matter of fact I hate tulips, but he has to have tulips on everything.

Miss Y looks up, irony and curiosity in her face.

MRS. X *(putting one hand in each slipper)*:   Look what small feet Bob has, hasn't he? And you ought to see the charming way he walks — you've never seen him in slippers, have you?

Miss Y laughs.

MRS. X: Look, I'll show you. *(She makes the slippers walk across the table, and Miss Y laughs again.)*

MRS. X: But when he gets angry, look, he stamps his foot like this. "Those damn girls who can never learn how to make coffee! Blast! That silly idiot hasn't trimmed the lamp properly!" Then there's a draught under the door and his feet get cold. "Hell, it's freezing, and the damn fools can't even keep the stove going!" *(She rubs the sole of one slipper against the instep of the other. Miss Y roars with laughter.)*

MRS. X: And then he comes home and has to hunt for his slippers, which Mary has pushed under the bureau . . . Well, perhaps it's not right to make fun of one's husband like this. He's sweet anyhow, and a good, dear husband. You ought to have had a husband like him, Amelia. What are you laughing at? What is it? Eh? And, you see, I know he is faithful to me. Yes, I know it. He told me himself — what *are* you giggling at? — that while I was on tour in Norway that horrible Frederica came and tried to seduce him. Can you imagine anything more abominable? *(Pause.)* I'd have scratched her eyes out if she had come around while I was at home. *(Pause.)* I'm glad Bob told me about it himself, so I didn't just hear it from gossip. *(Pause.)* And, as a matter of fact,

---

Maja: Pronounced Maya.

Frederica wasn't the only one. I can't think why, but all the women in the Company° seem to be crazy about my husband. They must think his position gives him some say in who is engaged at the Theatre. Perhaps you have run after him yourself? I don't trust you very far, but I know he has never been attracted by you, and you always seemed to have some sort of grudge against him, or so I felt. *(Pause. They look at one another guardedly.)*

MRS. X: Do come and spend Christmas Eve with us tonight, Amelia — just to show that you're not offended with us, or anyhow not with me. I don't know why, but it seems specially unpleasant not to be friends with you. Perhaps it's because I did get in your way that time . . . *(slowly)* or — I don't know — really, I don't know at all why it is.

Pause. Miss Y gazes curiously at Mrs. X.

MRS. X *(thoughtfully)*:   It was so strange when we were getting to know one another. Do you know, when we first met, I was frightened of you, so frightened I didn't dare let you out of my sight. I arranged all my goings and comings to be near you. I dared not be your enemy, so I became your friend. But when you came to our home, I always had an uneasy feeling, because I saw my husband didn't like you, and that irritated me — like when a dress doesn't fit. I did all I could to make him be nice to you, but it was no good — until you went and got engaged. Then you became such tremendous friends that at first it looked as if you only dared show your real feelings then — when you were safe. And then, let me see, how was it after that? I wasn't jealous — that's queer. And I remember at the christening, when you were the godmother, I told him to kiss you. He did, and you were so upset . . . As a matter of fact I didn't notice that then . . . I didn't think about it afterwards either . . . I've never thought about it — until *now!* *(Rises abruptly.)* Why don't you say something? You haven't said a word all this time. You've just let me go on talking. You have sat there with your eyes drawing all these thoughts out of me — they were there in me like silk in a cocoon — thoughts . . . Mistaken thoughts? Let me think. Why did you break off your engagement? Why did you never come to our house after that? Why don't you want to come to us tonight?

Miss Y makes a motion, as if about to speak.

MRS. X: No. You don't need to say anything, for now I see it all. That was why — and why — and why. Yes. Yes, that's why it was. Yes, yes, all the pieces fit together now. That's it. I won't sit at the same table as you. *(Moves her things to the other table.)* That's why I have to embroider tulips, which I loathe, on his slippers — because you liked tulips. *(Throws the slippers on the floor.)* That's why we have to spend the summer on the lake — because you couldn't bear the seaside. That's why my son had to be called Eskil — because it was your father's name. That's why I had to wear your colours, read your books, eat the dishes you liked, drink your drinks — your chocolate, for instance. That's why — oh my God, it's terrible to think of, terrible! Everything, everything came to me from

---

in the Company: Translator's addition.

you — even your passions. Your soul bored into mine like a worm into an apple, and ate and ate and burrowed and burrowed, till nothing was left but the skin and a little black mould. I wanted to fly from you, but I couldn't. You were there like a snake, your black eyes fascinating me. When I spread my wings, they only dragged me down. I lay in the water with my feet tied together, and the harder I worked my arms, the deeper I sank — down, down, till I reached the bottom, where you lay in waiting like a giant crab to catch me in your claws — and now here I am. Oh how I hate you! I hate you, I hate you! And you just go on sitting there, silent, calm, indifferent, not caring whether the moon is new or full, if it's Christmas or New Year, if other people are happy or unhappy. You don't know how to hate or to love. You just sit there without moving — like a cat° at a mouse-hole. You can't drag your prey out, you can't chase it, but you can out-stay it. Here you sit in your corner — you know they call it the rat-trap after you — reading the papers to see if anyone's ruined or wretched or been thrown out of the Company. Here you sit sizing up your victims and weighing your chances — like a pilot his shipwrecks for the salvage. *(Pause.)* Poor Amelia! Do you know, I couldn't be more sorry for you. I know you are miserable, miserable like some wounded creature, and vicious because you are wounded. I can't be angry with you. I should like to be, but after all you are the small one — and as for your affair with Bob, that doesn't worry me in the least. Why should it matter to me? And if you, or somebody else taught me to drink chocolate, what's the difference? *(Drinks a spoonful. Smugly.)* Chocolate is very wholesome anyhow. And if I learnt from you how to dress, *tant mieux!*° — that only gave me a stronger hold over my husband, and you have lost what I gained. Yes, to judge from various signs, I think you have now lost him. Of course, you meant me to walk out, as you once did, and which you're now regretting. But I won't do that, you may be sure. One shouldn't be narrow-minded, you know. And why should nobody else want what I have? *(Pause.)* Perhaps, my dear, taking everything into consideration, at this moment it is I who am the stronger. You never got anything from me, you just gave away — from yourself. And now, like the thief in the night, when you woke up I had what you had lost. Why was it then that everything you touched became worthless and sterile? You couldn't keep a man's love — for all your tulips and your passions — but I could. You couldn't learn the art of living from your books — but I learnt it. You bore no little Eskil, although that was your father's name. *(Pause.)* And why is it you are silent — everywhere, always silent? Yes, I used to think this was strength, but perhaps it was because you hadn't anything to say, because you couldn't think of anything. *(Rises and picks up the slippers.)* Now I am going home, taking the tulips with me — *your* tulips. You couldn't learn from others, you couldn't bend, and so you broke like a dry stick. I did not. Thank you, Amelia, for all your good lessons. Thank you for teaching my husband how to love. Now I am going home — to love him.

Exit. [1907]

---

cat: In Swedish, "stork."   ***tant mieux:*** French for "so much the better."

SUSAN GLASPELL
Trifles

CHARACTERS

GEORGE HENDERSON, *county attorney*
HENRY PETERS, *sheriff*
LEWIS HALE, *a neighboring farmer*
MRS. PETERS
MRS. HALE

SCENE: *The kitchen in the now abandoned farmhouse of John Wright, a gloomy kitchen, and left without having been put in order — the walls covered with a faded wall paper. Down right is a door leading to the parlor. On the right wall above this door is a built-in kitchen cupboard with shelves in the upper portion and drawers below. In the rear wall at right, up two steps is a door opening onto stairs leading to the second floor. In the rear wall at left is a door to the shed and from there to the outside. Between these two doors is an old-fashioned black iron stove. Running along the left wall from the shed door is an old iron sink and sink shelf, in which is set a hand pump. Downstage of the sink is an uncurtained window. Near the window is an old wooden rocker. Centerstage is an unpainted wooden kitchen table with straight chairs on either side. There is a small chair down right. Unwashed pans under the sink, a loaf of bread outside the breadbox, a dish towel on the table — other signs of incompleted work. At the rear the shed door opens and the Sheriff comes in followed by the County Attorney and Hale. The Sheriff and Hale are men in middle life, the County Attorney is a young man; all are much bundled up and go at once to the stove. They are followed by the two women — the Sheriff's wife, Mrs. Peters, first; she is a slight wiry woman, a thin nervous face. Mrs. Hale is larger and would ordinarily be called more comfortable looking, but she is disturbed now and looks fearfully about as she enters. The women have come in slowly, and stand close together near the door.*

COUNTY ATTORNEY (*at stove rubbing his hands*):   This feels good. Come up to the fire, ladies.

MRS. PETERS (*after taking a step forward*):   I'm not — cold.

SHERIFF (*unbuttoning his overcoat and stepping away from the stove to right of table as if to mark the beginning of official business*):   Now, Mr. Hale, before we move things about, you explain to Mr. Henderson just what you saw when you came here yesterday morning.

COUNTY ATTORNEY (*crossing down to left of the table*):   By the way, has anything been moved? Are things just as you left them yesterday?

SHERIFF (*looking about*):   It's just about the same. When it dropped below zero last night I thought I'd better send Frank out this morning to make a fire for us — (*sits right of center table*) no use getting pneumonia with a big case on, but I told him not to touch anything except the stove — and you know Frank.

COUNTY ATTORNEY: Somebody should have been left here yesterday.

SHERIFF: Oh—yesterday. When I had to send Frank to Morris Center for that man who went crazy—I want you to know I had my hands full yesterday. I knew you could get back from Omaha by today and as long as I went over everything here myself——

COUNTY ATTORNEY: Well, Mr. Hale, tell just what happened when you came here yesterday morning.

HALE *(crossing down to above table)*:   Harry and I had started to town with a load of potatoes. We came along the road from my place and as I got here I said, "I'm going to see if I can't get John Wright to go in with me on a party telephone." I spoke to Wright about it once before and he put me off, saying folks talked too much anyway, and all he asked was peace and quiet—I guess you know about how much he talked himself; but I thought maybe if I went to the house and talked about it before his wife, though I said to Harry that I didn't know as what his wife wanted made much difference to John——

COUNTY ATTORNEY: Let's talk about that later, Mr. Hale. I do want to talk about that, but tell now just what happened when you got to the house.

HALE: I didn't hear or see anything; I knocked at the door, and still it was all quiet inside. I knew they must be up, it was past eight o'clock. So I knocked again, and I thought I heard somebody say, "Come in." I wasn't sure, I'm not sure yet, but I opened the door—this door *(indicating the door by which the two women are still standing)* and there in that rocker—*(pointing to it)* sat Mrs. Wright. *(They all look at the rocker down left.)*

COUNTY ATTORNEY: What—was she doing?

HALE: She was rockin' back and forth. She had her apron in her hand and was kind of—pleating it.

COUNTY ATTORNEY: And how did she—look?

HALE: Well, she looked queer.

COUNTY ATTORNEY: How do you mean—queer?

HALE: Well, as if she didn't know what she was going to do next. And kind of done up.

COUNTY ATTORNEY *(takes out notebook and pencil and sits left of center table)*: How did she seem to feel about your coming?

HALE: Why, I don't think she minded—one way or other. She didn't pay much attention. I said, "How do, Mrs. Wright, it's cold, ain't it?" And she said, "Is it?"—and went on kind of pleating at her apron. Well, I was surprised; she didn't ask me to come up to the stove, or to set down, but just sat there, not even looking at me, so I said, "I want to see John." And then she—laughed. I guess you would call it a laugh. I thought of Harry and the team outside, so I said a little sharp: "Can't I see John?" "No," she says, kind o' dull like. "Ain't he home?" says I. "Yes," says she, "he's home." "Then why can't I see him?" I asked her, out of patience. "'Cause he's dead," says she. *"Dead?"* says I. She just nodded her head, not getting a bit excited, but rockin' back and forth. "Why—where is he?" says I, not knowing what to say. She just pointed upstairs—like that. *(Himself pointing to the room above.)* I started for the stairs, with the idea of going up there. I walked from there to here—then I says, "Why, what did he die of?" "He died of a rope round his neck," says she, and just went on pleatin' at her apron. Well, I went out and called Harry. I thought I might — need help. We went upstairs and there he was lyin' ——

COUNTY ATTORNEY: I think I'd rather have you go into that upstairs, where you can point it all out. Just go on now with the rest of the story.

HALE: Well, my first thought was to get that rope off. It looked . . . (*stops; his face twitches*) . . . but Harry, he went up to him, and he said, "No, he's dead all right, and we'd better not touch anything." So we went back downstairs. She was still sitting that same way. "Has anybody been notified?" I asked. "No," says she, unconcerned. "Who did this, Mrs. Wright?" said Harry. He said it businesslike — and she stopped pleatin' of her apron. "I don't know," she says. "You don't *know?*" says Harry. "No," says she. "Weren't you sleepin' in the bed with him?" says Harry. "Yes," says she, "but I was on the inside." "Somebody slipped a rope round his neck and strangled him and you didn't wake up?" says Harry. "I didn't wake up," she said after him. We must 'a' looked as if we didn't see how that could be, for after a minute she said, "I sleep sound." Harry was going to ask her more questions but I said maybe we ought to let her tell her story first to the coroner, or the sheriff, so Harry went fast as he could to Rivers' place, where there's a telephone.

COUNTY ATTORNEY: And what did Mrs. Wright do when she knew that you had gone for the coroner?

HALE: She moved from the rocker to that chair over there (*pointing to a small chair in the down right corner*) and just sat there with her hands held together and looking down. I got a feeling that I ought to make some conversation, so I said I had come in to see if John wanted to put in a telephone, and at that she started to laugh, and then she stopped and looked at me — scared. (*The County Attorney, who has had his notebook out, makes a note.*) I dunno, maybe it wasn't scared. I wouldn't like to say it was. Soon Harry got back, and then Dr. Lloyd came and you, Mr. Peters, and so I guess that's all I know that you don't.

COUNTY ATTORNEY (*rising and looking around*): I guess we'll go upstairs first — and then out to the barn and around there. (*To the Sheriff.*) You're convinced that there was nothing important here — nothing that would point to any motive?

SHERIFF: Nothing here but kitchen things. (*The County Attorney, after again looking around the kitchen, opens the door of a cupboard closet in right wall. He brings a small chair from right — gets on it and looks on a shelf. Pulls his hand away, sticky.*)

COUNTY ATTORNEY: Here's a nice mess. (*The women draw nearer up center.*)

MRS. PETERS (*to the other woman*): Oh, her fruit; it did freeze. (*To the Lawyer.*) She worried about that when it turned so cold. She said the fire'd go out and her jars would break.

SHERIFF (*rises*): Well, can you beat the woman! Held for murder and worryin' about her preserves.

COUNTY ATTORNEY (*getting down from chair*): I guess before we're through she may have something more serious than preserves to worry about. (*Crosses down right center.*)

HALE: Well, women are used to worrying over trifles. *(The two women move a little closer together.)*

COUNTY ATTORNEY *(with the gallantry of a young politician):*   And yet, for all their worries, what would we do without the ladies? *(The women do not unbend. He goes below the center table to the sink, takes a dipperful of water from the pail, and pouring it into a basin, washes his hands. While he is doing this the Sheriff and Hale cross to cupboard, which they inspect. The County Attorney starts to wipe his hands on the roller towel, turns it for a cleaner place.)* Dirty towels! *(Kicks his foot against the pans under the sink.)* Not much of a housekeeper, would you say, ladies?

MRS. HALE *(stiffly):*   There's a great deal of work to be done on a farm.

COUNTY ATTORNEY: To be sure. And yet *(with a little bow to her)* I know there are some Dickson County farmhouses which do not have such roller towels. *(He gives it a pull to expose its full-length again.)*

MRS. HALE: Those towels get dirty awful quick. Men's hands aren't always as clean as they might be.

COUNTY ATTORNEY: Ah, loyal to your sex, I see. But you and Mrs. Wright were neighbors. I suppose you were friends, too.

MRS. HALE *(shaking her head):*   I've not seen much of her of late years. I've not been in this house — it's more than a year.

COUNTY ATTORNEY *(crossing to women up center):*   And why was that? You didn't like her?

MRS. HALE: I liked her all well enough. Farmers' wives have their hands full, Mr. Henderson. And then ——

COUNTY ATTORNEY: Yes —— ?

MRS. HALE *(looking about):*   It never seemed a very cheerful place.

COUNTY ATTORNEY: No — it's not cheerful. I shouldn't say she had the home-making instinct.

MRS. HALE: Well, I don't know as Wright had, either.

COUNTY ATTORNEY: You mean that they didn't get on very well?

MRS. HALE: No, I don't mean anything. But I don't think a place'd be any cheer-fuller for John Wright's being in it.

COUNTY ATTORNEY: I'd like to talk more of that a little later. I want to get the lay of things upstairs now. *(He goes past the women to up right where steps lead to a stair door.)*

SHERIFF: I suppose anything Mrs. Peters does'll be all right. She was to take in some clothes for her, you know, and a few little things. We left in such a hurry yesterday.

COUNTY ATTORNEY: Yes, but I would like to see what you take, Mrs. Peters, and keep an eye out for anything that might be of use to us.

MRS. PETERS: Yes, Mr. Henderson. *(The men leave by up right door to stairs. The women listen to the men's steps on the stairs, then look about the kitchen.)*

MRS. HALE *(crossing left to sink):*   I'd hate to have men coming into my kitchen, snooping around and criticizing. *(She arranges the pans under sink which the lawyer had shoved out of place.)*

MRS. PETERS: Of course it's no more than their duty. *(Crosses to cupboard up right.)*

MRS. HALE: Duty's all right, but I guess that deputy sheriff that came out to make the fire might have got a little of this on. *(Gives the roller towel a pull.)* Wish I'd thought of that sooner. Seems mean to talk about her for not having things slicked up when she had to come away in such a hurry. *(Crosses right to Mrs. Peters at cupboard.)*

MRS. PETERS *(who has been looking through cupboard, lifts one end of towel that covers a pan):* She had bread set. *(Stands still.)*

MRS. HALE *(eyes fixed on a loaf of bread beside the breadbox, which is on a low shelf of the cupboard):* She was going to put this in there. *(Picks up loaf, abruptly drops it. In a manner of returning to familiar things.)* It's a shame about her fruit. I wonder if it's all gone. *(Gets up on the chair and looks.)* I think there's some here that's all right, Mrs. Peters. Yes — here; *(holding it toward the window)* this is cherries, too. *(Looking again.)* I declare I believe that's the only one. *(Gets down, jar in her hand. Goes to the sink and wipes it off on the outside.)* She'll feel awful bad after all her hard work in the hot weather. I remember the afternoon I put up my cherries last summer. *(She puts the jar on the big kitchen table, center of the room. With a sigh, is about to sit down in the rocking chair. Before she is seated realizes what chair it is; with a slow look at it, steps back. The chair which she has touched rocks back and forth. Mrs. Peters moves to center table and they both watch the chair rock for a moment or two.)*

MRS. PETERS *(shaking off the mood which the empty rocking chair has evoked. Now in a businesslike manner she speaks):* Well I must get those things from the front room closet. *(She goes to the door at the right but, after looking into the other room, steps back.)* You coming with me, Mrs. Hale? You could help me carry them. *(They go in the other room; reappear, Mrs. Peters carrying a dress, petticoat, and skirt, Mrs. Hale following with a pair of shoes.)* My, it's cold in there. *(She puts the clothes on the big table and hurries to the stove.)*

MRS. HALE *(right of center table examining the skirt):* Wright was close. I think maybe that's why she kept so much to herself. She didn't even belong to the Ladies' Aid. I suppose she felt she couldn't do her part, and then you don't enjoy things when you feel shabby. I heard she used to wear pretty clothes and be lively, when she was Minnie Foster, one of the town girls singing in the choir. But that — oh, that was thirty years ago. This all you want to take in?

MRS. PETERS: She said she wanted an apron. Funny thing to want, for there isn't much to get you dirty in jail, goodness knows. But I suppose just to make her feel more natural. *(Crosses to cupboard.)* She said they was in the top drawer in this cupboard. Yes, here. And then her little shawl that always hung behind the door. *(Opens stair door and looks.)* Yes, here it is. *(Quickly shuts door leading upstairs.)*

MRS. HALE *(abruptly moving toward her):* Mrs. Peters?

MRS. PETERS: Yes, Mrs. Hale? *(At up right door.)*

MRS. HALE: Do you think she did it?

MRS. PETERS (*in a frightened voice*): Oh, I don't know.

MRS. HALE: Well, I don't think she did. Asking for an apron and her little shawl. Worrying about her fruit.

MRS. PETERS (*starts to speak, glances up, where footsteps are heard in the room above. In a low voice*): Mr. Peters says it looks bad for her. Mr. Henderson is awful sarcastic in a speech and he'll make fun of her sayin' she didn't wake up.

MRS. HALE: Well, I guess John Wright didn't wake when they was slipping that rope under his neck.

MRS. PETERS (*crossing slowly to table and placing shawl and apron on table with other clothing*): No, it's strange. It must have been done awful crafty and still. They say it was such a — funny way to kill a man, rigging it all up like that.

MRS. HALE (*crossing to left of Mrs. Peters at table*): That's just what Mr. Hale said. There was a gun in the house. He says that's what he can't understand.

MRS. PETERS: Mr. Henderson said coming out that what was needed for the case was a motive; something to show anger, or — sudden feeling.

MRS. HALE (*who is standing by the table*): Well, I don't see any signs of anger around here. (*She puts her hand on the dish towel, which lies on the table, stands looking down at table, one-half of which is clean, the other half messy.*) It's wiped to here. (*Makes a move as if to finish work, then turns and looks at loaf of bread outside the breadbox. Drops towel. In that voice of coming back to familiar things.*) Wonder how they are finding things upstairs. (*Crossing below table to down right.*) I hope she had it a little more red-up up there. You know, it seems kind of *sneaking*. Locking her up in town and then coming out here and trying to get her own house to turn against her!

MRS. PETERS: But, Mrs. Hale, the law is the law.

MRS. HALE: I s'pose 'tis. (*Unbuttoning her coat.*) Better loosen up your things, Mrs. Peters. You won't feel them when you go out. (*Mrs. Peters takes off her fur tippet, goes to hang it on chair back left of table, stands looking at the work basket on floor near down left window.*)

MRS. PETERS: She was piecing a quilt. (*She brings the large sewing basket to the center table and they look at the bright pieces, Mrs. Hale above the table and Mrs. Peters left of it.*)

MRS. HALE: It's a log cabin pattern. Pretty, isn't it? I wonder if she was goin' to quilt it or just knot it? (*Footsteps have been heard coming down the stairs. The Sheriff enters followed by Hale and the County Attorney.*)

SHERIFF: They wonder if she was going to quilt it or just knot it! (*The men laugh, the women look abashed.*)

COUNTY ATTORNEY (*rubbing his hands over the stove*): Frank's fire didn't do much up there, did it? Well, let's go out to the barn and get that cleared up. (*The men go outside by up left door.*)

MRS. HALE (*resentfully*): I don't know as there's anything so strange, our takin' up our time with little things while we're waiting for them to get the evidence. (*She sits in chair right of table smoothing out a block with decision.*) I don't see as it's anything to laugh about.

MRS. PETERS (*apologetically*): Of course they've got awful important things on their minds. (*Pulls up a chair and joins Mrs. Hale at the left of the table.*)

MRS. HALE (*examining another block*): Mrs. Peters, look at this one. Here, this is the one she was working on, and look at the sewing! All the rest of it has been so nice and even. And look at this! It's all over the place! Why, it looks as if she didn't know what she was about! (*After she has said this they look at each other, then start to glance back at the door. After an instant Mrs. Hale has pulled at a knot and ripped the sewing.*)

MRS. PETERS: Oh, what are you doing, Mrs. Hale?

MRS. HALE (*mildly*): Just pulling out a stitch or two that's not sewed very good. (*Threading a needle.*) Bad sewing always made me fidgety.

MRS. PETERS (*with a glance at door, nervously*): I don't think we ought to touch things.

MRS. HALE: I'll just finish up this end. (*Suddenly stopping and leaning forward.*) Mrs. Peters?

MRS. PETERS: Yes, Mrs. Hale?

MRS. HALE: What do you suppose she was so nervous about?

MRS. PETERS: Oh—I don't know. I don't know as she was nervous. I sometimes sew awful queer when I'm just tired. (*Mrs. Hale starts to say something, looks at Mrs. Peters, then goes on sewing.*) Well, I must get these things wrapped up. They may be through sooner than we think. (*Putting apron and other things together.*) I wonder where I can find a piece of paper, and string. (*Rises.*)

MRS. HALE: In that cupboard, maybe.

MRS. PETERS (*crosses right looking in cupboard*): Why, here's a bird-cage. (*Holds it up.*) Did she have a bird, Mrs. Hale?

MRS. HALE: Why, I don't know whether she did or not—I've not been here for so long. There was a man around last year selling canaries cheap, but I don't know as she took one; maybe she did. She used to sing real pretty herself.

MRS. PETERS (*glancing around*): Seems funny to think of a bird here. But she must have had one, or why would she have a cage? I wonder what happened to it?

MRS. HALE: I s'pose maybe the cat got it.

MRS. PETERS: No, she didn't have a cat. She's got that feeling some people have about cats—being afraid of them. My cat got in her room and she was real upset and asked me to take it out.

MRS. HALE: My sister Bessie was like that. Queer, ain't it?

MRS. PETERS (*examining the cage*): Why, look at this door. It's broke. One hinge is pulled apart. (*Takes a step down to Mrs. Hale's right.*)

MRS. HALE (*looking too*): Looks as if someone must have been rough with it.

MRS. PETERS: Why, yes. (*She brings the cage forward and puts it on the table.*)

MRS. HALE (*glancing toward up left door*): I wish if they're going to find any evidence they'd be about it. I don't like this place.

MRS. PETERS: But I'm awful glad you came with me, Mrs. Hale. It would be lonesome for me sitting here alone.

MRS. HALE:　It would, wouldn't it? (*Dropping her sewing.*) But I tell you what I do wish, Mrs. Peters. I wish I had come over sometimes when *she* was here. I — (*looking around the room*) — wish I had.

MRS. PETERS:　But of course you were awful busy, Mrs. Hale — your house and your children.

MRS. HALE (*rises and crosses left*):　I could've come. I stayed away because it weren't cheerful — and that's why I ought to have come. I — (*looking out left window*) — I've never liked this place. Maybe because it's down in a hollow and you don't see the road. I dunno what it is, but it's a lonesome place and always was. I wish I had come over to see Minnie Foster sometimes. I can see now — (*Shakes her head.*)

MRS. PETERS (*left of table and above it*):　Well, you mustn't reproach yourself, Mrs. Hale. Somehow we just don't see how it is with other folks until — something turns up.

MRS. HALE:　Not having children makes less work — but it makes a quiet house, and Wright out to work all day, and no company when he did come in. (*Turning from window.*) Did you know John Wright, Mrs. Peters?

MRS. PETERS:　Not to know him; I've seen him in town. They say he was a good man.

MRS. HALE:　Yes — good; he didn't drink, and kept his word as well as most, I guess, and paid his debts. But he was a hard man, Mrs. Peters. Just to pass the time of day with him — (*Shivers.*) Like a raw wind that gets to the bone. (*Pauses, her eye falling on the cage.*) I should think she would 'a' wanted a bird. But what do you suppose went with it?

MRS. PETERS:　I don't know, unless it got sick and died. (*She reaches over and swings the broken door, swings it again, both women watch it.*)

MRS. HALE:　You weren't raised round here, were you? (*Mrs. Peters shakes her head.*) You didn't know — her?

MRS. PETERS:　Not till they brought her yesterday.

MRS. HALE:　She — come to think of it, she was kind of like a bird herself — real sweet and pretty, but kind of timid and — fluttery. How — she — did — change. (*Silence: then as if struck by a happy thought and relieved to get back to everyday things. Crosses right above Mrs. Peters to cupboard, replaces small chair used to stand on to its original place down right.*) Tell you what, Mrs. Peters, why don't you take the quilt in with you? It might take up her mind.

MRS. PETERS:　Why, I think that's a real nice idea, Mrs. Hale. There couldn't possibly be any objection to it could there? Now, just what would I take? I wonder if her patches are in here — and her things. (*They look in the sewing basket.*)

MRS. HALE (*crosses to right of table*):　Here's some red. I expect this has got sewing things in it. (*Brings out a fancy box.*) What a pretty box. Looks like something somebody would give you. Maybe her scissors are in here. (*Opens box. Suddenly puts her hand to her nose.*) Why —— (*Mrs. Peters bends nearer, then turns her face away.*) There's something wrapped up in this piece of silk.

MRS. PETERS:　Why, this isn't her scissors.

MRS. HALE *(lifting the silk)*: Oh, Mrs. Peters — it's —— *(Mrs. Peters bends closer.)*

MRS. PETERS: It's the bird.

MRS. HALE: But, Mrs. Peters — look at it! Its neck! Look at its neck! It's all — other side *to.*

MRS. PETERS: Somebody — wrung — its — neck. *(Their eyes meet. A look of growing comprehension, of horror. Steps are heard outside. Mrs. Hale slips box under quilt pieces, and sinks into her chair. Enter Sheriff and County Attorney. Mrs. Peters steps down left and stands looking out of window.)*

COUNTY ATTORNEY *(as one turning from serious things to little pleasantries)*: Well, ladies, have you decided whether she was going to quilt it or knot it? *(Crosses to center above table.)*

MRS. PETERS: We think she was going to — knot it. *(Sheriff crosses to right of stove, lifts stove lid, and glances at fire, then stands warming hands at stove.)*

COUNTY ATTORNEY: Well, that's interesting, I'm sure. *(Seeing the bird-cage.)* Has the bird flown?

MRS. HALE *(putting more quilt pieces over the box)*: We think the — cat got it.

COUNTY ATTORNEY *(preoccupied)*: Is there a cat? *(Mrs. Hale glances in a quick covert way at Mrs. Peters.)*

MRS. PETERS *(turning from window takes a step in)*: Well, not *now.* They're superstitious, you know. They leave.

COUNTY ATTORNEY *(to Sheriff Peters, continuing an interrupted conversation)*: No sign at all of anyone having come from the outside. Their own rope. Now let's go up again and go over it piece by piece. *(They start upstairs.)* It would have to have been someone who knew just the —— *(Mrs. Peters sits down left of table. The two women sit there not looking at one another, but as if peering into something and at the same time holding back. When they talk now it is in the manner of feeling their way over strange ground, as if afraid of what they are saying, but as if they cannot help saying it.)*

Mrs. Hale (hesitatively and in hushed voice): She liked the bird. She was going to bury it in that pretty box.

MRS. PETERS *(in a whisper)*: When I was a girl — my kitten — there was a boy took a hatchet, and before my eyes — and before I could get there —— *(Covers her face an instant.)* If they hadn't held me back I would have — *(catches herself, looks upstairs where steps are heard, falters weakly)* — hurt him.

MRS. HALE *(with a slow look around her)*: I wonder how it would seem never to have had any children around. *(Pause.)* No, Wright wouldn't like the bird — a thing that sang. She used to sing. He killed that, too.

MRS. PETERS *(moving uneasily)*: We don't know who killed the bird.

MRS. HALE: I knew John Wright.

MRS. PETERS: It was an awful thing was done in this house that night, Mrs. Hale. Killing a man while he slept, slipping a rope around his neck that choked the life out of him.

MRS. HALE: His neck. Choked the life out of him. *(Her hand goes out and rests on the bird-cage.)*

MRS. PETERS *(with rising voice)*: We don't know who killed him. We don't *know.*

MRS. HALE (*her own feeling not interrupted*):   If there'd been years and years of nothing, then a bird to sing to you, it would be awful — still, after the bird was still.

MRS. PETERS (*something within her speaking*):   I know what stillness is. When we homesteaded in Dakota, and my first baby died — after he was two years old, and me with no other then ——

MRS. HALE (*moving*):   How soon do you suppose they'll be through looking for the evidence?

MRS. PETERS: I know what stillness is. (*Pulling herself back.*) The law has got to punish crime, Mrs. Hale.

MRS. HALE (*not as if answering that*):   I wish you'd seen Minnie Foster when she wore a white dress with blue ribbons and stood up there in the choir and sang. (*A look around the room.*) Oh, I *wish* I'd come over here once in a while! That was a crime! That was a crime! Who's going to punish that?

MRS. PETERS (*looking upstairs*):   We mustn't — take on.

MRS. HALE: I might have known she needed help! I know how things can be — for women. I tell you, it's queer, Mrs. Peters. We live close together and we live far apart. We all go through the same things — it's all just a different kind of the same thing. (*Brushes her eyes, noticing the jar of fruit, reaches out for it.*) If I was you I wouldn't tell her her fruit was gone. Tell her it *ain't.* Tell her it's all right. Take this in to prove it to her. She — she may never know whether it was broke or not.

MRS. PETERS (*takes the jar, looks about for something to wrap it in; takes petticoat from the clothes brought from the other room, very nervously begins winding this around the jar. In a false voice*):   My, it's a good thing the men couldn't hear us. Wouldn't they just laugh! Getting all stirred up over a little thing like a — dead canary. As if that could have anything to do with — with — wouldn't they *laugh!* (*The men are heard coming downstairs.*)

MRS. HALE (*under her breath*):   Maybe they would — maybe they wouldn't.

COUNTY ATTORNEY: No, Peters, it's all perfectly clear except a reason for doing it. But you know juries when it comes to women. If there was some definite thing. (*Crosses slowly to above table. Sheriff crosses down right. Mrs. Hale and Mrs. Peters remain seated at either side of table.*) Something to show — something to make a story about — a thing that would connect up with this strange way of doing it —— (*The women's eyes meet for an instant. Enter Hale from outer door.*)

HALE (*remaining by door*):   Well, I've got the team around. Pretty cold out there.

COUNTY ATTORNEY: I'm going to stay awhile by myself. (*To the Sheriff.*) You can send Frank out for me, can't you? I want to go over everything. I'm not satisfied that we can't do better.

SHERIFF: Do you want to see what Mrs. Peters is going to take in? (*The Lawyer picks up the apron, laughs.*)

COUNTY ATTORNEY: Oh, I guess they're not very dangerous things the ladies have picked out. (*Moves a few things about, disturbing the quilt pieces which cover the box. Steps back.*) No, Mrs. Peters doesn't need supervising. For that matter a sheriff's wife is married to the law. Ever think of it that way, Mrs. Peters?

MRS. PETERS: Not—just that way.

SHERIFF *(chuckling)*:   Married to the law. *(Moves to down right door to the other room.)* I just want you to come in here a minute, George. We ought to take a look at these windows.

COUNTY ATTORNEY *(scoffingly)*:   Oh, windows!

SHERIFF: We'll be right out, Mr. Hale. *(Hale goes outside. The Sheriff follows the County Attorney into the room. Then Mrs. Hale rises, hands tight together, looking intensely at Mrs. Peters, whose eyes make a slow turn, finally meeting Mrs. Hale's. A moment Mrs. Hale holds her, then her own eyes point the way to where the box is concealed. Suddenly Mrs. Peters throws back quilt pieces and tries to put the box in the bag she is carrying. It is too big. She opens box, starts to take bird out, cannot touch it, goes to pieces, stands there helpless. Sound of a knob turning in the other room. Mrs. Hale snatches the box and puts it in the pocket of her big coat. Enter County Attorney and Sheriff, who remains down right.)*

COUNTY ATTORNEY *(crosses to up left door facetiously)*:   Well, Henry, at least we found out that she was not going to quilt it. She was going to—what is it you call it, ladies?

MRS. HALE *(standing center below table facing front, her hand against her pocket)*:   We call it—knot it, Mr. Henderson.

Curtain.   [1916]

A WRITING EXERCISE

Once you have read the two plays, write your reaction to them off the top of your head, spending at least ten minutes on each. Note any personal experiences affecting your response to each play. Note as well the questions you have about each, for one or more of these questions can serve as the basis for a paper of your own.

A Student's Personal Response to the Plays

Trish Carlisle was enrolled in a class that read and discussed both Strindberg's *The Stronger* and Glaspell's *Trifles*. Members of her class even performed these plays. Here is some freewriting that Trisha did about each of them:

> Near the end of Strindberg's play, Mrs. X says that
> "at this moment it is I who am the stronger." But is she?
> I guess that depends on what Strindberg meant by "the
> stronger" when he gave his play that title. As I was
> reading, I started to think that the stronger woman is

actually the silent one, Miss Y, because she seems to
have more self-control than Mrs. X does. I mean, Miss Y
doesn't apparently feel that she has to make long, loud
speeches in defense of her way of life. I can even
believe that with her silence she is manipulating Mrs. X
into getting fairly hysterical. Also, I guess we're to
think that Amelia has managed to lure away Mrs. X's husband, at least for a while. Furthermore, we don't have to
believe Mrs. X when at the end she claims that she has
triumphed over Miss Y. Maybe people who have really succeeded in life don't need to proclaim that they have, as
Mrs. X does.

Nevertheless, I can see why some students in this
class feel that Mrs. X is in fact the stronger. If she
has her husband back and wants her husband back, and if
Miss Y is really without companionship at the end and has
even lost her job at the theater, then probably Mrs. X is
entitled to crow. Was Strindberg being deliberately
unclear? Did he want his audience to make up their own
minds about who is stronger? Maybe neither of these women
is strong, because each of them seems dependent on a man,
and Mrs. X's husband may not even be such a great person
in the first place. If I were Mrs. X, maybe I wouldn't
even take him back. I guess someone could say that it's
Mrs. X's husband who is the stronger, since he has managed to make the two women fight over him while he enjoys
his creature comforts. Anyway, Strindberg makes us guess
what he is really like. Because he's offstage, he's just
as silent as Miss Y is, although his wife imitates his
voice at one point.

In a way, I feel that this play is too short. I want
it to go on longer so that I can be sure how to analyze
the two women and the man. But I realize that one of the
reasons the play is dramatic is that it's brief. I might
not be interested in it if it didn't leave me hanging.
And it's also theatrical because Miss Y is silent even as
Mrs. X lashes out at her. I wonder what the play would be

like if we could hear Miss Y's thoughts in a sort of
voice-over, like we find in some movies. It's interesting
to me that the play is <u>about</u> actresses. I wonder if these
characters are still "performing" with each other even if
they're not acting in a theater at the moment.

   <u>Trifles</u> is a clearer play to me because obviously I'm
supposed to agree with the two women that Minnie Wright
was justified in killing her husband. Glaspell steers all
our sympathies toward the two women onstage and Minnie.
I'm hazy about the offstage husband in Strindberg's play,
but Glaspell makes clear how we're to feel about the offstage Minnie. Meanwhile, the men in her play come across
as insensitive dummies. They're not really brutal or
mean, but they don't seem to understand or appreciate
women. Their wives seem a heck of a lot smarter about
women's daily lives than they are. Glaspell did keep me
guessing about how John Wright died. I figured early on
that his wife played a big role in his death, but I
didn't know exactly how she contributed to it. I liked
how slowly her motives were revealed; the use of the dead
bird as a prop must be very theatrical on a real stage.
At the end, I despised the men for thinking that their
wives were still just concerned with trivial things. A
lot of men I know would probably say that men today
aren't nearly as condescending as Glaspell's men are in
this play. But I think men today really are inclined to
consider women's interests as a bunch of trifles.

   I'm undecided, though, about whether women who kill
their husbands should go free if those husbands are
cruel. It's interesting to me that Minnie's husband evidently didn't beat her. Glaspell implies that Minnie is
more a victim of psychological abuse rather than physical
abuse. I realize that a woman out in the country couldn't
go to a counselor, but I think that she had more options
than Glaspell suggests. Why didn't Minnie just leave her
husband if he was so mean to her? Mrs. Hale seems to feel
guilty about not doing more to help Minnie, but can't we

```
expect Minnie to have tried to help herself? I guess I
wish that Minnie and her husband had been onstage so that
I could see better what they're really like. As things
stand, I feel that Glaspell is pushing me to accept Mrs.
Peters's and Mrs. Hale's interpretation and evaluation of
the marriage. I can imagine a second act to this play,
where we get to see Minnie thinking in her jail cell and
maybe even talking with some other prisoners about her
marriage. Of course, then I'd have to decide whether to
accept Minnie's own account of her marriage and her
explanation of why she killed her husband. In Glaspell's
play, there's some reference to the possibility that
Minnie has gone insane. If I saw Minnie and heard her
speak, I'd have to decide whether she's crazy and whether
her degree of sanity should even matter to me as I con-
sider whether she should go free.
```

Trish's freewriting will eventually help her develop ideas for one of her major class assignments, a paper in which she has to analyze either Strindberg's play or Glaspell's. Compare your responses to the plays with hers. Did the same issues come up for you? How do you feel about the two plays' women characters? What, if anything, do you wish the playwrights had made clearer? What would you advise Trish to think about as she moved from freewriting to drafting a paper?

The Elements of Drama

You will strengthen your ability to write about plays like Strindberg's and Glaspell's if you grow familiar with typical elements of drama. These elements include plot and structure, characterization, stage directions and setting, language, and theme.

Plot and Structure

Most plays, like most short stories, have a **plot**. When you read them, you find yourself following a **narrative**, a sequence of interrelated events. Even plays as short as *The Stronger* and *Trifles* feature plots, though in their cases the onstage action occurs in just one place and takes just a little while. As with short fiction, the reader of a play is often anxious to know how the events will turn out. The reader may especially feel this way when the play contains a mystery that characters are trying to solve. In Strindberg's play, for example, Mrs. X is apparently bent on discovering what relation her husband has had with her friend, while the two women onstage in Glaspell's play attempt to figure out the circumstances of John Wright's death.

In summarizing these two plays, you might choose to depict each plot as a detective story. Then again, you might prefer to emphasize the characters' emotional conflicts as you describe how these plays proceed. In fact, there are various ways you can describe Strindberg's and Glaspell's plots; just bear in mind that your accounts should be grounded in actual details of the texts. However you summarize a play's **structure** will reflect your sense of which characters are central to it. How prominent in Glaspell's plot is Minnie Wright, would you say? Is she as important as the two women onstage? More important than them? Less important? Your summary will also reflect your sense of which characters have power. Do you think the two women in Strindberg's drama equally influence that play's events? In addition, your summary ought to acknowledge the human motives that drive the play's action. Why, evidently, did Minnie Wright kill her husband?

Summarizing the plot of a play can mean arranging its events chronologically. Yet bear in mind that some of the play's important events may have occurred in the characters' pasts. In many plays, characters learn things about the past that they did not know and must now try to accept. For example, several of the important events in *Trifles* take place before the play begins. By the time the curtain rises, John Wright has already tormented his wife, and she has already killed him. Now, onstage, Mrs. Hale and Mrs. Peters proceed to investigate how John Wright died. A summary of Glaspell's play could begin with the sad state of the Wrights' marriage, then move to the murder, and then chronicle the subsequent investigation. But you can also summarize the play by starting with the investigation, which is what the audience first sees. Only later would you bring up the past events that Mrs. Hale and Mrs. Peter learn about through their detective work.

A WRITING EXERCISE

List in chronological order the events referred to and shown in *The Stronger*. Start with the earliest event that Mrs. X mentions; end with the event that concludes the play. Next, choose from this list an event that apparently occurred before the characters appear onstage. Then, write at least a paragraph analyzing the moment when the audience is made aware of this event. Most likely the audience learns of the event from Mrs. X. Why do you think Strindberg has her announce it at this particular moment?

In discussing the structure of short stories, we noted that many of them follow Alice Adams's formula ABDCE (**action, background, development, climax,** and **ending**). This scheme, however, does not fit many plays. In a sense, the average play is entirely action, for its performers are constantly engaged in physical movement of various sorts. Furthermore, as we have been suggesting, information about background can surface quite often as the play's characters talk. Yet the terms *development, climax,* and *ending* do seem appropriate for many plays. Certainly the plot of *The Stronger* develops, as Mrs. X becomes increasingly hostile to Miss Y. Certainly the play can be said to reach a climax, a moment of great significance and intensity, when Mrs. X moves to another table and declares her hatred for Miss Y. The term *ending* can also apply to this play, although readers may disagree about exactly when its climax turns into its ending. Certainly Mrs. X is in a different state of mind at the play's last moment; at that point, she stops haranguing Miss Y and leaves, declaring that she will save her own marriage.

Like short stories, plays often use repetition as an organizational device. The characters in a play may repeat certain words; for example, trace the multiple appearances of the word *knot* in *Trifles*. Also, a play may show repeated actions, as when the men in Glaspell's drama repeatedly interrupt the two women's conversation. In addition, a play may suggest that the onstage situation echoes previous events; when the men onstage in *Trifles* utter obnoxious comments about women, these remarks make Mrs. Hale and Mrs. Peters more aware of the abuse that Minnie Wright's husband inflicted on her.

The Stronger and *Trifles* are both short one-act plays. But many other plays are longer and divided conspicuously into subsections. Ancient Greek drama alternates scenes where major characters perform actions with sections in which a chorus comments on the actions. All of Shakespeare's plays, and most modern ones, are divided into acts, which are often further divided into scenes. Detecting various stages in the action is easier when the play is fairly lengthy, but you can also break Strindberg's and Glaspell's one-act plays down into stages.

A WRITING EXERCISE

Outline either *The Stronger* or *Trifles*, breaking down its action into at least three stages. Write at least a couple of sentences describing each stage you have identified.

Characters

Many short stories have a narrator who reveals the characters' inner thoughts. Most plays, however, have no narrator. To figure out what the characters think, you must study what they say and how they move. Some characters say a great deal, leaving you with several clues to their psyche. Shakespeare's play *Hamlet*, for example, contains thousands of lines. Moreover, when Hamlet is alone onstage making long speeches to the audience, he seems to be baring his very soul. Yet despite such moments, Hamlet's mental state remains far from clear; scholars continue to debate his sanity. Thus, as a reader of *Hamlet* and other plays, you have much room for interpretation. Often you will have to decide whether to accept the judgments that characters express about one another. For example, how fair and accurate does Strindberg's Mrs. X seem to you as she berates Miss Y?

As with short stories, a good step toward analyzing a play's characters is to consider what each desires. The drama or comedy of many plays arises when the desires of one character conflict with those of another. Strindberg's Mrs. X feels that Miss Y has been a threat to her marriage, and while we cannot be sure of Miss Y's thoughts, evidently she is determined not to answer Mrs. X's charges. At the end of the play, the women's conflict seems to endure, even though Mrs. X proclaims victory. Many other plays end with characters managing to resolve conflict because one or more of them experiences a change of heart. Whatever play you are studying, consider whether any of its characters change. For example, is anyone's thinking transformed in *Trifles*? If so, whose?

The main character of a play is referred to as its **protagonist**, and a character who notably opposes this person is referred to as the **antagonist**. As you might guess without even reading Shakespeare's play, Hamlet is the protagonist of *Hamlet*; his uncle Claudius serves as his antagonist. Applying these terms may be tricky or impossible in some instances. The two women in *The Stronger* oppose each other, but each can be called the protagonist and each can be called the antagonist. *Trifles* also seems a challenging case. How, if at all, would you apply the two terms to Glaspell's characters?

In discussing the elements of short fiction, we referred to point of view, the perspective from which a story is told. Since very few plays are narrated, the term *point of view* fits this genre less well. While it is possible to claim that much of Shakespeare's *Hamlet* reflects the title character's point of view, he is offstage for stretches, and the audience may focus on other characters even when he appears. Also, think about the possible significance of characters who are not physically present. A character may be important even if he or she never appears onstage. In *The Stronger*, the two women's conflict is partly about Mrs. X's unseen husband. In *Trifles*, everyone onstage aims to discover what happened between two unseen people, Minnie and John Wright.

In most plays, characters' lives are influenced by their social standing, which in turn is influenced by particular traits of theirs. These may include their gender, social class, race, ethnic background, nationality, sexual orientation, and the kind of work they do. Obviously *Trifles* deals with gender relationships. Mrs. Peters and Mrs. Hale come to feel an affinity with Minnie Wright because they sense she has been an oppressed wife; meanwhile, their husbands scoff at women's obsession with "trifles."

A WRITING EXERCISE

Susan Glaspell's play *Trifles* depicts Mrs. Peters and Mrs. Hale covering up evidence to protect Minnie Wright. They seem to act out of loyalty to their gender. Do you feel that there are indeed times when you should be someone's ally because that person is of the same gender as you? What would you say to someone who is generally comfortable with alliances between women but less comfortable with alliances between men, since throughout history women have been oppressed by bands of men? Freewrite for fifteen minutes in response to these questions.

Stage Directions and Setting

When analyzing a script, pay attention to the **stage directions** it gives, and try to imagine additional ways that the actors might move around. Through a slight physical movement, performers can indicate important developments in their characters' thoughts. A good example is Glaspell's stage directions when Mr. Hale declares that "women are used to worrying over trifles." By having Mrs. Hale and Mrs. Peters "move a little closer together," Glaspell suggests that these two women *grow* closer because of Mr. Hale's scorn. As we have noted, Mrs. Hale and Mrs. Peters do seem to develop a kinship based on their common gender, and in turn they both seem increasingly sensitive to Minnie's plight.

You can get a better sense of how a play might be staged if you research its actual production history. Granted, finding out about its previous stagings may be difficult. But at the very least, you can discover some of the theatrical conventions that must have shaped presentations of the play, even one that is centuries old. Take the case of Sophocles' *Antigone* and Shakespeare's *Hamlet*. While classical scholars would like to learn more about early performances of *Antigone*, they already know that it and other ancient Greek plays were staged in open-air arenas. They know, too, that, *Antigone*'s Chorus turned in unison at particular moments, and that the whole cast wore large masks. Although the premiere of *Hamlet* was not videotaped, Shakespeare scholars are sure that, like other productions in Renaissance England, it made spare use of scenery and featured an all-male cast.

Most of the modern plays we include in this book were first staged in a style alien to Sophocles and Shakespeare, a style most often called **realism**. Realism marked, for example, the first production of Lorraine Hansberry's *A Raisin in the Sun*. When the curtain rose on that play's opening night in 1959, the audience saw a vivid re-creation of a shabby Chicago apartment. Indeed, when a production seems quite true to life, audiences may think it has no style at all. Nevertheless, even realism uses a set of identifiable conventions. That first production of Hansberry's play relied on what theater professionals call the *illusion of the fourth wall*. Although the actors pretended the "apartment" was completely enclosed, the set had just three walls, and the audience looked in. Similarly, an audience watching a production of *Trifles* is encouraged to think that it is peering into Minnie Wright's kitchen.

Some plays can be staged in any number of styles and still work well. Shakespeare wrote *Hamlet* back in Renaissance England, but quite a few successful productions of it have been set in later times, such as late-nineteenth-century England. Even modern plays that seem to call for realistic productions can be staged in a variety of ways. Note Strindberg's description of the setting for *The Stronger*: "A corner of a ladies' café [in Stockholm in the eighteen eighties]. Two small wrought-iron tables, a red plush settee, and a few chairs." Many productions of this play have remained within the conventions of realism, striving to make the audience believe that it is seeing a late-nineteenth-century Stockholm café. But a production of *The Stronger* may present the audience with only a few pieces of furniture that barely evoke the café. Furthermore, the production might have Mrs. X's husband physically hover in the background, as if he were a ghost haunting both women's minds. You may feel that such a production would horribly distort Strindberg's drama; a boldly experimental staging of a play can indeed become a virtual rewriting of it. Nevertheless, remember that productions of a play may be more diverse in style than the script would indicate.

A WRITING EXERCISE

A particular theater's architecture may affect a production team's decisions. Realism's illusion of the "fourth wall" works best on a proscenium stage, which is the kind probably most familiar to you. A **proscenium stage** is a boxlike space where the actors perform in front of the entire audience. In a proscenium production of *Trifles*, Minnie Wright's kitchen can be depicted in great detail. The performing spaces at some theaters, however, are "in the round": that is, the audience completely encircles the stage. What would have to be done with Minnie's kitchen then? List some items in the kitchen that an "in the round" staging could accommodate.

In referring to possible ways of staging a play, we inevitably refer as well to its setting. A play may not be all that precise in describing its setting; Strindberg provides set designers with few guidelines for creating his Stockholm café. More significant, perhaps, than the place of the action is its *timing*: Mrs. X finds Miss Y sitting alone on Christmas Eve. Yet a play may stress to its audience that its characters are located in particular places, at particular moments in their personal histories, or at a particular moment in *world* history. For example, *Trifles* repeatedly calls attention to the fact that it is set in a kitchen, traditionally a female domain. Furthermore, the audience is reminded that Minnie Wright's kitchen is in an isolated rural area, where a spouse's abuse and a neighbor's indifference can have devastating impact on a woman. Furthermore, as Mrs. Peters and Mrs. Hale explore Minnie's kitchen, they increasingly see its physical decline as a symptom of the Wrights' failing marriage.

You can learn much about a play's characters by studying how they accommodate themselves—or fail to accommodate themselves—to their settings. When Strindberg's Mrs. X can no longer bear sitting next to Miss Y, her shift to another table dramatically signifies her feelings. In *Trifles*, Mrs. Peters and Mrs. Hale are clearly interlopers in Minnie Wright's kitchen; they analyze its condition like detectives, or even like anthropologists. Increasingly they realize that they should have been more familiar with this kitchen—in other words, they should have been better neighbors for Minnie. Of course, much of the drama in Strindberg's and Glaspell's plays occurs because there is a single setting, which in both plays makes at least one character feel confined. Other plays employ a wider variety of settings to dramatize their characters' lives.

Imagery

When plays use images to convey meaning, sometimes they do so through **dialogue**. At the beginning of *The Stronger*, for instance, Mrs. X recalls "a wedding party at a restaurant," where "the bride was reading a comic paper and the bridegroom playing billiards with the witnesses." The play proceeds to become very much about divisions between husband and wife; moreover, the two women engage in a tense "game" that seems analogous to billiards. But just as often, a play's meaningful images are physically presented in the staging: through gestures, costumes, lighting, and props. For instance, perhaps the key image in *Trifles* is the dead bird wrapped in silk, which the audience is encouraged to associate with Minnie Wright. While Glaspell presents dialogue about the bird, the physical presence of the bird and cage props may make the audience more inclined to see the bird as a **symbol**, the term traditionally used for an image that represents some concept or concepts.

A WRITING EXERCISE

Imagine that you have been asked to stage a production of *The Stronger.* List the key props and gestures you would use to stress the meanings you find in the play. Then exchange lists with a classmate, and write a brief interpretation of each item on that classmate's list. Then, get your own list back and see whether the interpretations written there are what you wanted to convey.

Keep in mind that you may interpret an image differently than the characters within the play do. When Strindberg's Mrs. X refers to billiards, she may not think at all that she will be playing an analogous game with Miss Y. You, however, may make this connection, especially as the play proceeds.

Language

You can learn much about a play's meaning and impact from studying the **language** in its script. Start with the play's title. At the climax of Strindberg's play, for example, Mrs. X even refers to herself as "the stronger"; in Glaspell's play, the men and women express conflicting views about women's apparent concern with "trifles." Obviously both playwrights are encouraging audiences to think about their titles' implications. Yet not always will the meaning of a play's title be immediately clear. In her freewriting, Trish wonders how to define *stronger* and which of Strindberg's characters fits the term. Even if you think the title of a play is easily explainable, pause to see whether that title actually leads to an issue of definition.

In most plays, language is a matter of dialogue. The audience tries to figure out the play by focusing on how the characters address one another. At the beginning of Glaspell's play, the dialogue between Mrs. Peters and Mrs. Hale reveals that they do not completely agree about how to view Minnie Wright's situation:

MRS. PETERS: But, Mrs. Hale, the law is the law.
MRS. HALE: I s'pose 'tis. (*Unbuttoning her coat.*) Better loosen up your
things, Mrs. Peters. You won't feel them when you go out.

Mrs. Hale's response seems half-hearted. Unlike Mrs. Peters, the wife of the sheriff, she seems more disposed to believe that Minnie's situation may justify sparing Minnie the force of the law. To bring up issues of definition again, you might say that Mrs. Hale subtly questions just what "the law" should be, whereas Mrs. Peters says only that "the law is the law." Furthermore, when Mrs. Hale advises Mrs. Peters to "loosen up your things," perhaps the playwright is suggesting that Mrs. Peters should also "loosen up" her moral code.

Remember that the pauses or silences within a play may be just as important as its dialogue. In fact, a director may add moments of silence that the script does not explicitly demand. In many plays, however, the author does specify moments when one or more characters significantly fail to speak. *The Stronger* is a prominent example: Miss Y is notably silent throughout the play, and as a reader you probably find yourself wondering why she is. Ironically, the play's absence of true dialogue serves to remind us that plays usually *depend* on dialogue.

A WRITING EXERCISE

Choose a moment in *The Stronger* when Miss Y notably fails to speak — perhaps one in which she makes a sound but does not utter words. Then, write a brief monologue for her in which you express what she may be thinking at that moment. Next, write a paragraph or two in which you identify what Strindberg conceivably gains by *not* having Miss Y speak at that moment.

Theme

We have already discussed **theme** on pages 17–19, and here we will build on some points from our earlier discussion. A theme is the main claim — an assertion, proposition, or statement — that a work seems to make. As with other literary genres, try to state a play's theme as a midlevel generalization. If expressed in very broad terms, it will seem to fit many other works besides the one you have read; if narrowly tied to the play's characters and their particular situation, it will seem irrelevant to most other people's lives. With *The Stronger*, an example of a very broad theme would be "Women should not fight over a man." At the opposite extreme, a too-narrow theme would be "Women should behave well toward each other on Christmas Eve, even if one of them has slept with the other's husband." If you are formulating Strindberg's theme, you might start with the broad generalization we have cited and then try to narrow it down to a midlevel one. You might even think of ways that Strindberg's play *complicates* that broad generalization. What might, in fact, be a good midlevel generalization in Strindberg's case?

As we have noted, the titles of *The Stronger* and *Trifles* seem significant. Indeed, a play's theme may be related to its title. Nevertheless, be wary of couching the theme in terms drawn solely from the title. The play's theme may not be reducible to these words alone. Remember that the titles of Strindberg's and Glaspell's plays can give rise to issues of definition in the first place.

You can state a play's theme as an **observation** or as a **recommendation**. With Strindberg's play, an observation-type theme would be "Marriage and career may disrupt relations between women." A recommendation-type theme would be either the broad or narrow generalization that we cited earlier. Neither way of stating the theme is automatically preferable, but remain aware of the different tones and effects they may carry. Consider, too, the possibility of stating the theme as a problem, as in this example: "We may be inclined to defend our marriages when they seem threatened, but in our defense we may cling to illusions that can easily shatter." Furthermore, consider the possibility of referring to *a* theme of the play rather than *the* theme, thereby acknowledging the possibility that the play is making several important claims.

A WRITING EXERCISE

Write three different versions of the theme of *Trifles*: a version that is excessively broad, one that is a midlevel generalization, and one that is too narrow.
Then, exchange sheets with several of your classmates. (Your instructor may
have all the sheets circulated quickly through the entire class.) As a group,
select the best midlevel generalization. Be prepared to say why it is the best.

When you write about a play, certainly you will refer to the text of it, its
script. But probably the play was meant to be staged, and most likely it has been.
Thus, you might refer to actual productions of it and to ways it can be performed.
Remember, though, that different productions of the play may stress different
meanings and create different effects. In your paper, you might discuss how
much room for interpretation the script allows those who would stage it. For any
paper you write about the play, look beyond the characters' dialogue and study
whatever stage directions the script gives.

Undoubtedly your paper will have to offer some plot summary, even if your
audience has already read the play. After all, certain details of the plot will be
important support for your points. But, as with papers about short fiction, keep
the amount of plot summary small, mentioning only events in the play that are
crucial to your overall argument. Your reader should feel that you are analyzing
the play rather than just recounting it.

To understand more what analysis of a play involves, let's return to Trish
Carlisle, the student whose freewriting you read earlier. Trish was assigned to
write a 600-word paper about Strindberg's *The Stronger* or Glaspell's *Trifles*. She
was asked to imagine herself writing to a particular audience: performers rehears-
ing a production of the play she chose. More specifically, she was to identify and
address some question that these performers might have, an issue that might be
bothering them as they prepared to put on the play. Trish knew that, besides presenting an issue, her paper would have to make a main claim and support it with
evidence. Moreover, the paper might have to spell out some of the warrants or
assumptions behind her evidence.

Trish found both Strindberg's play and Glaspell's interesting, so she was not
immediately sure which one to choose. Because finding an issue was such an
important part of the assignment, she decided to review her freewriting about
each play, noting questions she had raised there about them. Trish saw that the
chief issue posed for her by *The Stronger* was, "Which character is the stronger?"
She also saw that, for her, *Trifles* was a more clear-cut play, although it did leave
her with the question, "Should women who kill their husbands go free if their
husbands are cruel?" Eventually Trish decided to focus on Strindberg's play and
the issue of how to apply its title. Much as she liked *Trifles*, she thought the issue
she associated with it went far beyond the play itself, whereas the issue she associated with *The Stronger* would enable her to discuss many of that play's specific
details. Also, she thought that performers of Strindberg's play would be anxious to
clarify its title, whereas performers of *Trifles* need not be sure how to judge the
Minnie Wrights of this world.

Nevertheless, Trish recognized that the issue "Which character is the stronger?" still left her with various decisions to make. For one thing, she had to decide what kind of an issue she would call it. Trish saw that it could be considered an issue of fact, an issue of evaluation, or an issue of definition. Although it could fit into all of these categories, Trish knew that the category she chose would influence the direction of her paper. Eventually she decided to treat "Which character is the stronger?" as primarily an issue of definition, because she figured that, no matter what, she would be devoting much of her paper to defining *stronger* as a term.

Of course, there are many different senses in which someone may be "stronger" than someone else. Your best friend may be a stronger tennis player than you, in the sense that he or she always beats you at that game. But you may be a stronger student than your friend, in the sense that you get better grades in school. In the case of Strindberg's play, Trish came to see that a paper focused on which character is *morally* stronger would differ from one focused on who is *emotionally* stronger, and these papers would differ in turn from one focused on which character is *politically* stronger, more able to impose his or her will. These reflections led Trish to revise her issue somewhat. She decided to address the question, "Which particular sense of the word 'stronger' is most relevant to Strindberg's play?" In part, Trish came up with this reformulation of her issue because she realized that the two women feuding in the play are actresses, and that they behave as actresses even when they are not professionally performing. Trish's answer to her revised question was that the play encourages the audience to consider which woman is the stronger *actress*—which woman is more able, that is, to convey her preferred version of reality.

When you write about a play, you may have to be selective, for your paper may not be able to accommodate all the ideas and issues that occur to you. Trish was not sure which woman in Strindberg's play is the stronger actress. She felt that a case can be made for Mrs. X or Miss Y; indeed, she suspected that Strindberg was letting his audience decide. But she decided that her paper was not obligated to resolve this matter; she could simply mention the various possible positions in her final paragraph. In the body of her paper, Trish felt she would contribute much if she focused on addressing her main issue with her main claim. Again, her main issue was, "Which particular sense of the word 'stronger' is most relevant to Strindberg's play?" Her main claim was that, "The play is chiefly concerned with which woman is the stronger actress, 'stronger' here meaning 'more able to convey one's version of reality.'"

Although a paper about a play need not explicitly mention the elements of plays we have identified, thinking about these elements can provide you with a good springboard for analysis. Trish saw that her paper would be very much concerned with the title of Strindberg's play, especially as that title applied to the characters. Also, she would have to refer to stage directions and imagery, because Miss Y's silence leaves the reader having to look at her physical movements and the play's props for clues to her thinking. The play does not really include dialogue, a term that implies people talking with each other. Nevertheless, Trish saw that there are utterances in the script she could refer to, especially as she made points about the play's lone speaker, Mrs. X. Indeed, a persuasive paper about a play is one that quotes from characters' lines and perhaps from the stage directions, too. Yet the paper needs to quote selectively, for a paper chock full of quotations may obscure instead of enhance the writer's argument.

Sample Student Paper: Final Draft

Here is Trish's final draft of her paper about *The Stronger*. It emerged out of several drafts, and after Trish had consulted classmates and her instructor. As you read this version of her paper, note its strengths, but also think of any suggestions that might help Trish make the paper even better.

Trish Carlisle

Professor Zelinsky

English 102

28 April ----

Which Is the Stronger Actress

in August Strindberg's Play?

You have asked me to help you solve difficulties you may be experiencing with August Strindberg's script for The Stronger as you prepare to play the roles of Mrs. X and Miss Y. These female characters seem harder to judge than the three women who are the focus of Susan Glaspell's play Trifles, the play you are performing next month. Obviously Glaspell is pushing us to think well of Mrs. Hale, Mrs. Peters, and Minnie Wright. The two women in Strindberg's play are another matter; in particular, you have probably been wondering which of these two women Strindberg thinks of as "the stronger." If you knew which character he had in mind with that term, you might play the roles accordingly. As things stand, however, Strindberg's use of the term in his title is pretty ambiguous. It is not even clear, at least not immediately, which particular sense of the word stronger is most relevant to the play. I suggest that the play is chiefly concerned with which character is the stronger actress. In making this claim, I am defining stronger as "more able to convey one's version of reality."

You may feel that Strindberg is clarifying his use of the word stronger when he has Mrs. X bring up the word in the long speech that ends the play. In that final speech, she declares to Miss Y that "it is I who am the stronger" and that Miss Y's silence is not the "strength" that Mrs. X previously thought it was. At this point in the play, Mrs. X is evidently defining stronger as "more able to keep things, especially a man." She feels that she is the stronger because she is going home to her husband, while Miss Y is forced to be alone on Christmas Eve. Yet there is little reason to believe that Mrs. X is using the word stronger in the sense that the playwright has chiefly in mind. Furthermore, there is little reason to believe that Mrs. X is an accurate judge of the two women's situations. Perhaps she is telling herself that she is stronger because she simply needs to believe that she is. Similarly, perhaps she is telling herself that she now has control over her husband when in actuality he may still be emotionally attached to Miss Y. In addition, because Miss Y does not speak and because Mrs. X sweeps out without giving her any further opportunity to do so, we don't know if Miss Y agrees with Mrs. X's last speech.

Since Mrs. X's final use of the word stronger is so questionable, we are justified in thinking of other ways that the term might be applied. In thinking about this play, I have entertained the idea that the stronger character is actually Mrs. X's husband Bob, for he has two women fighting over him and also apparently has the creature comforts that servants provide. But now I tend to think that the term applies to one or both of the two women. Unfortunately, we are not given many facts about them, for it is a brief one-act play and one of the major characters does not even speak. But as we try to figure out how Strindberg is defining the term stronger, we should notice one fact that we are indeed given: Each of these women is an actress. Both of them have worked at Stockholm's Grand Theater, although apparently Mrs. X got Miss Y fired from the company. Furthermore, Mrs. X engages in a bit of theatrical illusion when she scares

Miss Y by firing the toy pistol at her. Soon after, Mrs. X
plays the role of her own husband when she puts her hands
in the slippers she has bought for him and imitates not
only his walk but also the way he scolds his servants.
Miss Y even laughs at this "performance," as if she is
being an appreciative audience for it. In addition, if
Mrs. X is right about there being an adulterous affair
between her husband and Miss Y, then those two people
have basically been performing an act for Mrs. X. It is
possible, too, that Mrs. X has not been quite so naive;
perhaps she has deliberately come to the café in order to
confront Miss Y about the affair and to proclaim ultimate
victory over her. In that case, Mrs. X is performing as
someone more innocent than she really is. On the other
hand, Miss Y might be using her silence as an actress
would, manipulating her audience's feelings by behaving
in a theatrical way.

Because we do know that these women are professional
actresses, and because Strindberg gives us several hints
that they are performing right there in the café, we
should feel encouraged to think that he is raising the
question of which is the stronger actress. Of course, we
would still have to decide how he is defining the term
stronger. But if he does have in mind the women's careers
and behavior as actresses, then he seems to be defining
stronger as "more able to convey one's version of reality." Obviously Mrs. X is putting forth her own version
of reality in her final speech, although we do not know
how close her version comes to the actual truth. Again,
we cannot be sure of Miss Y's thoughts because she does
not express them in words; nevertheless, she can be said
to work at influencing Mrs. X's version of reality by
making strategic use of silence.

I realize that the claim I am making does not solve
every problem you might have with the play as you prepare
to perform it. Frankly, I am not sure who is the stronger
actress. I suspect that Strindberg is being deliberately

ambiguous; he wants the performers to act in a way that will let each member of the audience arrive at his or her own opinion. Still, if you accept my claim, each of you will think of yourself as playing the part of an actress who is trying to shape the other woman's sense of reality.

6

Writing about Essays

Many readers do not think of nonfiction as a literary genre. They believe dealing with information and facts, science and technology, history and biography, memories and arguments is too ordinary, too far from traditional literary works such as sonnets, short stories, and plays. But what counts as literature is often more a matter of tradition and perspective than content, language, or merit. Many contemporary critics have noticed that definitions of literature are quite subjective, even arbitrary. We are told that literature must move us emotionally; it must contain imaginative, extraordinary language; it must deal with profound, timeless, and universal themes. If all of these claims are true of poems, stories, and plays, they might also be true of essays, autobiographies, memoirs, and historical writing.

Essays demand as much of a reader's attention as fiction, drama, and poetry. They also demand a reader's active participation. And, as with more conventional literature, the intellectual, emotional, and aesthetic rewards of attentively reading essays are significant.

Writing about essays in college is best done as a process, one that begins with a first response and ends with editing and proofreading. Author Henry David Thoreau once noted that books should be read with the same care and deliberation with which they were written. This is as true for essays as it is for complex modern poetry. One's understanding is enhanced by careful reading and a composing process that calls for a cycle of reading, writing, and reflecting. Few people, even professionals, can read a text and write cogently about it the first time. Writing well about essays takes as much energy and discipline as writing about other genres. And the results are always worth it.

To begin practicing the process, read the following essays carefully, underlining interesting passages and jotting down brief comments in the margins. The three essays deal with revisiting an important place in one's past. It is something we have all done and, whether we have written about it or not, it would be unusual if the experience did not make us reflect about the effects the passage of time has on us all. The first essay, "Once More to the Lake," is a classic reprinted in scores of college anthologies. E. B. White's (1899–1985) reminiscence about his boyhood vacation in Maine is beautifully vivid and finally a bit unsettling. Joan Didion's

(b. 1934) brief essay is almost as popular, perhaps because most of us can remember the rush of conflicting feelings one has on going home after being away for a while. The last essay, written by Andrea Lee (b. 1953), appeared in a recent issue of *The New Yorker* and reflects our culture's contemporary focus on coming to terms with the inequalities of our racial past, especially in schooling.

E. B. WHITE
Once More to the Lake

One summer, along about 1904, my father rented a camp on a lake in Maine and took us all there for the month of August. We all got ringworm from some kittens and had to rub Pond's Extract on our arms and legs night and morning, and my father rolled over in a canoe with all his clothes on; but outside of that the vacation was a success and from then on none of us ever thought there was any place in the world like that lake in Maine. We returned summer after summer—always on August 1st for one month. I have since become a salt-water man, but sometimes in summer there are days when the restlessness of the tides and the fearful cold of the sea water and the incessant wind which blows across the afternoon and into the evening make me wish for the placidity of a lake in the woods. A few weeks ago this feeling got so strong I bought myself a couple of bass hooks and a spinner and returned to the lake where we used to go, for a week's fishing and to revisit old haunts.

I took along my son, who had never had any fresh water up his nose and who had seen lily pads only from train windows. On the journey over to the lake I began to wonder what it would be like. I wondered how time would have marred this unique, this holy spot—the coves and streams, the hills that the sun set behind, the camps and the paths behind the camps. I was sure that the tarred road would have found it out and I wondered in what other ways it would be desolated. It is strange how much you can remember about places like that once you allow your mind to return into the grooves which lead back. You remember one thing, and that suddenly reminds you of another thing. I guess I remembered clearest of all the early mornings, when the lake was cool and motionless, remembered how the bedroom smelled of the lumber it was made of and the wet woods whose scent entered through the screen. The partitions in the camp were thin and did not extend clear to the top of the rooms, and as I was always the first up I would dress softly so as not to wake the others, and sneak out into the sweet outdoors and start out in the canoe, keeping close along the shore in the long shadows of the pines. I remembered being very careful never to rub my paddle against the gunwale for fear of disturbing the stillness of the cathedral.

The lake had never been what you would call a wild lake. There were cottages sprinkled around the shores, and it was in farming country although the shores of the lake were quite heavily wooded. Some of the cottages were owned by nearby farmers, and you would live at the shore and eat your meals at the farmhouse. That's what our family did. But although it wasn't wild, it was a fairly large and undisturbed lake and there were places in it which, to a child at least, seemed infinitely remote and primeval.

I was right about the tar: it led to within half a mile of the shore. But when I got back there, with my boy, and we settled into a camp near a farmhouse and into the kind of summertime I had known, I could tell that it was going to be pretty much the same as it had been before—I knew it, lying in bed the first morning, smelling the bedroom, and hearing the boy sneak quietly out and go off along the shore in a boat. I began to sustain the illusion that he was I, and therefore, by simple transposition, that I was my father. This sensation persisted, kept cropping up all the time we were there. It was not an entirely new feeling, but in this setting it grew much stronger. I seemed to be living a dual existence. I would be in the middle of some simple act, I would be picking up a bait box or laying down a table fork, or I would be saying something, and suddenly it would be not I but my father who was saying the words or making the gesture. It gave me a creepy sensation.

We went fishing the first morning. I felt the same damp moss covering the   5
worms in the bait can, and saw the dragonfly alight on the tip of my rod as it hovered a few inches from the surface of the water. It was the arrival of this fly that convinced me beyond any doubt that everything was as it always had been, that the years were a mirage and there had been no years. The small waves were the same, chucking the rowboat under the chin as we fished at anchor, and the boat was the same boat, the same color green and the ribs broken in the same places, and under the floor-boards the same freshwater leavings and débris—the dead helgramite, the wisps of moss, the rusty discarded fishhook, the dried blood from yesterday's catch. We stared silently at the tips of our rods, at the dragonflies that came and went. I lowered the tip of mine into the water, tentatively, pensively dislodging the fly, which darted two feet away, poised, darted two feet back, and came to rest again a little farther up the rod. There had been no years between the ducking of this dragonfly and the other one—the one that was part of memory. I looked at the boy, who was silently watching his fly, and it was my hands that held his rod, my eyes watching. I felt dizzy and didn't know which rod I was at the end of.

We caught two bass, hauling them in briskly as though they were mackerel, pulling them over the side of the boat in a businesslike manner without any landing net, and stunning them with a blow on the back of the head. When we got back for a swim before lunch, the lake was exactly where we had left it, the same number of inches from the dock, and there was only the merest suggestion of a breeze. This seemed an utterly enchanted sea, this lake you could leave to its own devices for a few hours and come back to, and find that it had not stirred, this constant and trustworthy body of water. In the shallows, the dark, water-soaked sticks and twigs, smooth and old, were undulating in clusters on the bottom against the clean ribbed sand, and the track of the mussel was plain. A school of minnows swam by, each minnow with its small individual shadow, doubling the attendance, so clear and sharp in the sunlight. Some of the other campers were in swimming, along the shore, one of them with a cake of soap, and the water felt thin and clear and unsubstantial. Over the years there had been this person with the cake of soap, this cultist, and here he was. There had been no years.

Up to the farmhouse to dinner through the teeming, dusty field, the road under our sneakers was only a two-track road. The middle track was missing, the one with the marks of the hooves and the splotches of dried, flaky manure. There had always been three tracks to choose from in choosing which track to walk in; now the choice was narrowed down to two. For a moment I missed terribly the middle alternative. But the way led past the tennis court, and something about the way it lay there in the sun reassured me; the tape had loosened along the backline, the alleys were green with plantains and other weeds, and the net (installed in June and removed in September) sagged in the dry noon, and the whole place steamed with midday heat and hunger and emptiness. There was a choice of pie for dessert, and one was blueberry and one was apple, and the waitresses were the same country girls, there having been no passage of time, only the illusion of it as in a dropped curtain — the waitresses were still fifteen; their hair had been washed, that was the only difference — they had been to the movies and seen the pretty girls with the clean hair.

Summertime, oh summertime, pattern of life indelible, the fade-proof lake, the woods unshatterable, the pasture with the sweetfern and the juniper forever and ever, summer without end; this was the background, and the life along the shore was the design, the cottages with their innocent and tranquil design, their tiny docks with the flagpole and the American flag floating against the white clouds in the blue sky, the little paths over the roots of the trees leading from camp to camp and the paths leading back to the outhouses and the can of lime for sprinkling, and at the souvenir counters at the store the miniature birch-bark canoes and the post cards that showed things looking a little better than they looked. This was the American family at play, escaping the city heat, wondering whether the newcomers in the camp at the head of the cove were "common" or "nice," wondering whether it was true that the people who drove up for Sunday dinner at the farmhouse were turned away because there wasn't enough chicken.

It seemed to me, as I kept remembering all this, that those times and those summers had been infinitely precious and worth saving. There had been jollity and peace and goodness. The arriving (at the beginning of August) had been so big a business in itself, at the railway station the farm wagon drawn up, the first smell of the pineladen air, the first glimpse of the smiling farmer, and the great importance of the trunks and your father's enormous authority in such matters, and the feel of the wagon under you for the long ten-mile haul, and at the top of the last long hill catching the first view of the lake after eleven months of not seeing this cherished body of water. The shouts and cries of the other campers when they saw you, and the trunks to be unpacked, to give up their rich burden. (Arriving was less exciting nowadays, when you sneaked up in your car and parked it under a tree near the camp and took out the bags and in five minutes it was all over, no fuss, no loud wonderful fuss about trunks.)

Peace and goodness and jollity. The only thing that was wrong now, really, was 10 the sound of the place, an unfamiliar nervous sound of the outboard motors. This was the note that jarred, the one thing that would sometimes break the illusion and set the years moving. In those other summertimes all motors were inboard; and when they were at a little distance, the noise they made was a sedative, an ingredient of summer sleep. They were one-cylinder and two-cylinder engines, and some were make-and-break and some were jump-spark, but they all made a sleepy sound across the lake. The one-lungers throbbed and fluttered, and the twin-cylinder ones purred and purred, and that was a quiet sound too. But now the campers all had outboards. In the daytime, in the hot mornings, these motors made a petulant, irritable sound; at night, in the still evening when the afterglow lit the water, they whined about one's ears like mosquitoes. My boy loved our rented outboard, and his great desire was to achieve singlehanded mastery over it, and authority, and he soon learned the trick of choking it a little (but not too much), and the adjustment of the needle valve. Watching him I would remember the things you could do with the old one-cylinder engine with the heavy flywheel, how you could have it eating out of your hand if you got really close to it spiritually. Motor boats in those days didn't have clutches, and you would make a landing by shutting off the motor at the proper time and coasting in with a dead rudder. But there was a way of reversing them, if you learned the trick, by cutting the switch and putting it on again exactly on the final dying revolution of the flywheel, so that it would kick back against compression and begin reversing. Approaching a dock in a strong following breeze, it was difficult to slow up sufficiently by the ordinary coasting method, and if a boy felt he had complete mastery over his motor, he was tempted to keep it running beyond its time and then reverse it a few feet from the dock. It took a cool nerve, because if you threw the switch a twentieth of a second too soon you could catch the flywheel when it still had speed enough to go up past center, and the boat would leap ahead, charging bull-fashion at the dock.

We had a good week at the camp. The bass were biting well and the sun shone endlessly, day after day. We would be tired at night and lie down in the accumulated heat of the little bedrooms after the long hot day and the breeze would stir almost imperceptibly outside and the smell of the swamp drift in through the rusty screens. Sleep would come easily and in the morning the red squirrel would be on the roof, tapping out his gay routine. I kept remembering everything, lying in bed in the mornings—the small steamboat that had a long rounded stern like the lip of a Ubangi,° how quietly she ran on the moonlight sails, when the older boys played their mandolins and the girls sang and we ate doughnuts dipped in sugar, and how sweet the music was on the water in the shining night, and what it had felt like to think about girls then. After breakfast we would go up to the store and the things were in the same place—the minnows in a bottle, the plugs and spinners disarranged and pawed over by the youngsters from the boys' camp, the fig newtons and the Beeman's gum. Outside, the road was tarred and cars stood in front of the store. Inside, all was just as it had always been, except there was more Coca-Cola and not so much Moxie and root beer and birch beer and sarsaparilla. We would walk out with a bottle of pop apiece and sometimes the pop would backfire up our noses and hurt. We explored the streams, quietly, where the turtles slid off the sunny logs and dug their way into

Ubangi: A member of an African tribe whose customary dress includes disk-shaped mouth ornaments that stretch the wearer's lips.

the soft bottom; and we lay on the town wharf and fed worms to the tame bass. Everywhere we went I had trouble making out which was I, the one walking at my side, the one walking in my pants.

One afternoon while we were there at that lake a thunderstorm came up. It was like the revival of an old melodrama that I had seen long ago with childish awe. The second-act climax of the drama of the electrical disturbance over a lake in America had not changed in any important respect. This was the big scene, still the big scene. The whole thing was so familiar, the first feeling of oppression and heat and a general air around camp of not wanting to go very far away. In midafternoon (it was all the same) a curious darkening of the sky, and a lull in everything that had made life tick; and then the way the boats suddenly swung the other way at their moorings with the coming of a breeze out of the new quarter, and the premonitory rumble. Then the kettle drum, then the snare, then the bass drum and cymbals, then crackling light against the dark, and the gods grinning and licking their chops in the hills. Afterward the calm, the rain steadily rustling in the calm lake, the return of light and hope and spirits, and the campers running out in joy and relief to go swimming in the rain, their bright cries perpetuating the deathless joke about how they were getting simply drenched, and the children screaming with delight at the new sensation of bathing in the rain, and the joke about getting drenched linking the generations in a strong indestructible chain. And the comedian who waded in carrying an umbrella.

When the others went swimming my son said he was going in too. He pulled his dripping trunks from the line where they had hung all through the shower, and wrung them out. Languidly, and with no thought of going in, I watched him, his hard little body, skinny and bare, saw him wince slightly as he pulled up around his vitals the small, soggy, icy garment. As he buckled the swollen belt suddenly my groin felt the chill of death.   [1941]

JOAN DIDION
On Going Home

I am home for my daughter's first birthday. By "home" I do not mean the house in Los Angeles where my husband and I and the baby live, but the place where my family is, in the Central Valley of California. It is a vital although troublesome distinction. My husband likes my family but is uneasy in their house, because once there I fall into their ways, which are difficult, oblique, deliberately inarticulate, not my husband's ways. We live in dusty houses ("D-U-S-T," he once wrote with his finger on surfaces all over the house, but no one noticed it) filled with mementos quite without value to him (what could the Canton dessert plates mean to him? how could he have known about the assay scales, why should he care if he did know?), and we appear to talk exclusively about people we know who have been committed to mental hospitals, about people we know who have been booked on drunk-driving charges, and about property, particularly about property, land, price per acre and C-2 zoning and assessments and freeway access. My brother does not understand my husband's inability to perceive the advantage in the rather common real-estate transaction known as "sale-leaseback," and my husband in turn does not understand why so many of the people he hears about in my father's house have recently been committed to mental hospitals or booked on drunk-driving charges. Nor does he understand that when we talk about sale-leasebacks and right-of-way condemnations we are talking in code about the things we like best, the yellow fields and the cotton-woods and the rivers rising and falling and the mountain roads closing when the heavy snow comes in. We miss each other's points, have another drink and regard the fire. My brother refers to my husband, in his presence, as "Joan's husband." Marriage is the classic betrayal.

Or perhaps it is not any more. Sometimes I think that those of us who are now in our thirties were born into the last generation to carry the burden of "home," to find in family life the source of all tension and drama. I had by all objective accounts a "normal" and a "happy" family situation, and yet I was almost thirty years old before I could talk to my family on the telephone without crying after I had hung up. We did not fight. Nothing was wrong. And yet some nameless anxiety colored the emotional charges between me and the place that I came from. The question of whether or not you could go home again was a very real part of the sentimental and largely literary baggage with which we left home in the fifties; I suspect that it is irrelevant to the children born of the frag-mentation after World War II. A few weeks ago in a San Francisco bar I saw a pretty young girl on crystal take off her clothes and dance for the cash prize in an "amateur-topless" contest. There was no particular sense of moment about this, none of the effect of romantic degradation, of "dark journey," for which my gen-eration strived so assiduously. What sense could that girl possibly make of, say, *Long Day's Journey into Night*? Who is beside the point?

That I am trapped in this particular irrelevancy is never more apparent to me than when I am home. Paralyzed by the neurotic lassitude engendered by meet-ing one's past at every turn, around every corner, inside every cupboard, I go aim-lessly from room to room. I decide to meet it head-on and clean out a drawer, and I spread the contents on the bed. A bathing suit I wore the summer I was seven-teen. A letter of rejection from *The Nation*, an aerial photograph of the site for a shopping center my father did not build in 1954. Three teacups hand-painted with cabbage roses and signed "E.M.," my grandmother's initials. There is no final solution for letters of rejection from *The Nation* and teacups hand-painted in 1900. Nor is there any answer to snapshots of one's grandfather as a young man on skis, surveying around Donner Pass in the year 1910. I smooth out the snap-shot and look into his face, and do and do not see my own. I close the drawer, and have another cup of coffee with my mother. We get along very well, veterans of a guerrilla war we never understood.

Days pass. I see no one. I come to dread my husband's evening call, not only because he is full of news of what by now seems to me our remote life in Los Angeles, people he has seen, letters which require attention, but because he asks what I have been doing, suggests uneasily that I get out, drive to San Francisco or

Berkeley. Instead I drive across the river to a family graveyard. It has been vandal-ized since my last visit and the monuments are broken, overturned in the dry grass. Because I once saw a rattlesnake in the grass I stay in the car and listen to a country-and-Western station. Later I drive with my father to a ranch he has in the foothills. The man who runs his cattle on it asks us to the roundup, a week from Sunday, and although I know that I will be in Los Angeles I say, in the oblique way my family talks, that I will come. Once home I mention the broken monu-ments in the graveyard. My mother shrugs.

I go to visit my great-aunts. A few of them think now that I am my cousin, or their daughter who died young. We recall an anecdote about a relative last seen in 1948, and they ask if I still like living in New York City. I have lived in Los Angeles for three years, but I say that I do. The baby is offered a horehound drop, and I am slipped a dollar bill "to buy a treat." Questions trail off, answers are abandoned, the baby plays with the dust motes in a shaft of afternoon sun.

It is time for the baby's birthday party: a white cake, strawberry-marshmallow ice cream, a bottle of champagne saved from another party. In the evening, after she has gone to sleep, I kneel beside the crib and touch her face, where it is pressed against the slats, with mine. She is an open and trusting child, unpre-pared for and unaccustomed to the ambushes of family life, and perhaps it is just as well that I can offer her little of that life. I would like to give her more. I would like to promise her that she will grow up with a sense of her cousins and of rivers and of her great-grandmother's teacups, would like to pledge her a picnic on a river with fried chicken and her hair uncombed, would like to give her *home* for her birthday, but we live differently now and I can promise her nothing like that. I give her a xylophone and a sundress from Madeira, and promise to tell her a funny story.   [1967]

ANDREA LEE
Back to School

A couple of weeks ago, I paid a visit to the girls' preparatory school outside Philadelphia where, about thirty years ago, I enrolled as one of the first two black students. It wasn't my first return trip, but it was one that had a peculiarly defini-tive feeling: this time, I was going back to look at classes with my daughter, who is eleven — exactly the age I was when I first put on a blue-and-white uniform and walked in the front entrance of an institution where black people had always used the back door. My daughter, who was born in Europe, and who views the civil-rights struggle of the sixties as an antique heroic cycle not much removed in drama and time frame from the *Iliad*, sees her mother's experience as a singularly tame example of integration. There were, after all no jeering mobs, no night rid-ers, no police dogs or fire hoses — just a girl going to school and learning with quiet thoroughness the meaning of isolation.

The air inside the schoolhouse smelled exactly as it used to on rainy April days — that mysterious school essence of damp wood and ancient chalk dust and pent-up young flesh. For an instant, I relived precisely what it felt like to walk those halls with girls who never included me in a social event, with teachers and administrators who regarded me with bemused incomprehension — halls where the only other black faces I saw were those of maids and cooks, and where I never received the slightest hint that books had been written and discoveries made by people whose skin wasn't white. I remembered the defensive bravado that I once used as a cover for a constant and despairing sense of worthlessness, born and reinforced at school.

As I delivered my daughter to the sixth-grade classroom where she would spend the day, I saw that in the intervening time not only had the school sprouted a few glossy modern additions — an art wing, science and computer facilities, and a new lower school — but the faculty and the student body had also been transformed. Black and Asian girls mingled in the crowd of students rushing back and forth between classrooms and playing fields, giddy with excitement over the impending Easter and Passover weekend. A black teacher with braids strode out of the room where long ago I'd conjugated Latin verbs. Posters celebrating African-American artists and scientists hung on the walls, and the school's curriculum included dozens of works by black, Native American, and Hispanic writers. The director of the middle school was, miracle of miracles, a young black woman — a woman who combined an old-fashioned headmistress's unflappable good sense with a preternatural sensitivity to the psychology of culture and identity. She explained to me that she herself had once been a student at a mostly white East Coast prep school. When I asked who on her staff in particular, was responsible for the self-esteem of minority students, she said firmly, "Every person who works here."

That day, I finally forgave my old school. I'd held a touchy rancor toward it through much of my adult life, like someone heaping blame on a negligent parent, and had taken the institution rather churlishly to task during a Commencement address I gave there some years ago. The changes I saw now disarmed and delighted me. Watching my daughter run by with a group of girls, I realized with envy how different her experience would be from mine if she were enrolled there. "Just think, I used to dream of burning the place down," I remarked to her, as we drove away, along the school's winding drive. She looked at me impatiently. "Can't you just forget all that?" she asked. The sound of her voice — half childish and half adolescent — made it clear to me that I wouldn't do any such thing. Wounds that have healed bring a responsibility to avoid repeating the past. The important thing is to pardon, even with joy, when the time comes — but never, I thought, driving on in silence, to forget.   [1996]

A WRITING EXERCISE

Skim the essays, and jot down notes and comments in the margins. Consider your immediate reactions; don't ignore personal associations. Your experiences, age, gender, race, and so forth are as relevant as noting the voice, style, structure, and ideas in the text. "Meaning," as one critic put it, "exists in the margin of overlap between the writer's experience and the reader's." After skimming the three pieces and considering your comments, freewrite for fifteen minutes.

A Student's Personal Response to the Essays

Stevie Goronski, a college sophomore from Queens, New York, wrote the following response to the three essays:

I was surprised by the ending of "Once More to the Lake." I thought the father was enjoying the drama of the summer storm and the memories that he was having about when he was a boy at the lake in Maine with his father in 1904. When he mentioned the "chill of death," I thought that I probably missed his point. Almost forty years after his first visit he has returned with his son who I imagined was a preteen. I guess his own father is dead. He seems to enjoy being back at the camp, remembering the old sights and smells around the lake. I had somewhat of a hard time relating to this, since I never have been to a lake in the woods. I've been to the lake in Central Park which has trees and is nice, but I don't think it's anything like Maine. In fact, I've only been on vacation twice. Both times my father and mother, my twin sisters, and I went to the beach at Atlantic City for a long weekend. I remembered this when he says his son never had "fresh water up his nose." Since I never swam in Central Park, and since city pools certainly aren't fresh, then neither have I.

I was a little puzzled when they go fishing and he says "I felt dizzy and didn't know which rod I was at the end of." This must have something to do with remembering when he and his father were sitting there fishing forty years ago. Then he says there had been no years, as if everything was the same then as it is now. He must really want it to be that way. I guess there wasn't much development at this lake; it must be a lot more isolated than the lakes I've heard about. Later he does say that it is noisier now because of outboard motors. But he still seems to love it at the lake, especially when he says "summertime, oh, summertime," like in a song or a poem, but then a lot of the writing here reminds me of a poem. I noticed he says that

the people at the lake were "the American family" which is
a bit of an exaggeration since most of the people in my
neighborhood in Queens go to the beach just for the day and
can't afford vacations, especially not for a week or a
month in Maine, which probably costs a small fortune.

Toward the end he brings up the idea again that he is
confused if he is his son or himself. Since this seems
unlikely I guess it's just a way to say that everything
is the same as it was forty years ago when he and his
father were doing exactly what he is doing now with his
son. This seems to be an essay about memories that were
important and how we want to relive them or hold on to
them even though almost a lifetime has passed.

I can relate better to "On Going Home" since I have my
own apartment near campus which is about fifty miles from
my home in Queens. I haven't been away from home as long
as Didion seems to have been, but I don't live there anymore and probably never will again. Yet I still call it
home; and I say I'm going to my apartment. Like me, when
Didion goes home she has a lot of mixed feelings. This
happens to me especially if I bring my boyfriend home
with me; he grew up in a suburb of Charlotte and is
amazed at how differently my family lives in Queens. In
fact, Didion leaves her husband at their house because he
usually can't relate to their different ways. She says
that marriage is a classic betrayal which means that when
you get married, you have a new family and can't relate
like you once did to your birth family. But then she
talks about what I would call sociology and claims that
for her generation the family was everything, but not
anymore. I think there are a lot of Italian families (and
I'm half Italian) who see each other every week and are
always involved in each other's business. I know Irish
and Asian families where this is also true. But maybe
this is only true for ethnic families and Didion's sounds
more like an upper-middle-class family that has been in
America for generations.

She also talks about tension with her mother and uncomfortable conversations with her old aunts. My take on these events is that you get used to talking to people you live with but when you leave, that comfortable connection never comes back. Perhaps she goes home expecting the fond experiences of childhood but what she finds is awkwardness and paralysis. She does seem to get over these negative feelings in the last paragraph, however. At the party for her baby, she wonders if it really would be so great for her daughter to have the family life she had. I think this is a good point because the past is over anyhow, and wishing for the good old days is just a fantasy that leads to disappointment. My favorite line is "we live different now." I think it's fine to think of what Bruce Springsteen calls our "glory days," but the thing that is the most important is the present.

In "Back to School" the narrator also looks back to a former time through the eyes of her daughter, who is about E. B. White's son's age. She also remembers the sights and smells of her past, although I was puzzled by what "pent-up young flesh" might mean. She seemed to live in a segregated society, except for a few token minorities. I suspect the only reason she was allowed to go to this fancy school was because she was smart. Maybe it made the school look good. But even so, her self-esteem must have been damaged by the general atmosphere of white privilege. At the school, things have changed, unlike at the lake in Maine. Now there are lots of minorities, and their cultures are also being studied in English and history. In fact, the principal is a black woman. All of these changes make the narrator forgive the indignities she suffered in the past. She must be a fairly famous person because she gave the commencement address at some point. Her daughter can't relate to these past experiences and seems like she just wants to get on with her life, which is very healthy. Because the girl is young, the mother can't completely heed the daughter's

advice to get over it. The mother decides to forgive but
not forget, which seems reasonable to me since we should
remember history for the lessons it might teach us.

In all three essays, people are confronted with their
past. E. B. White seems to be a bit dazed by the experience of going back to a beloved place. He seems to imagine that everything stays the same. I think it does but
only in his memories. When he comes to his senses after
the storm, he realizes that he is a middle-aged man who
will eventually die. Didion is also dazed by the past,
but she is able to see that change is inevitable and, for
better or worse, this fact needs to be accepted. Lee's
memories of a white-only world were so negative that she
doesn't want to forget out of a sense of social responsibility, like remembering the Holocaust. Lee could have
been the one and only black camp counselor at White's
lake and she wants to remember that kind of exclusion.
But she does forgive the school and society, which makes
sense to me because bitterness hurts you more than those
you're angry with. Visiting our past is risky and you
have to be mature enough to see what really happened,
what is gone, and how to move on. If not, you could try
to hold on to the past and that could be damaging.

A WRITING EXERCISE

An exceptional paper can grow out of probing, thoughtful, early responses
like this one. Stevie seems to have several promising ideas that are worth pur-
suing. Which of Stevie's ideas seem interesting to you? Did she overlook any
ideas that you noticed? Make note of what you admired in her response, and
what you think she may have overlooked.

The Elements of Essays

First impressions are valuable, but writing intelligently about essays should
not be completely spontaneous. We can be personal and insightful, but persuad-
ing others about the validity of our reading takes a more focused and textually
informed presentation. The following discussion of the basic elements of the
essay is meant to increase your ability to analyze and write about essays. The elements include voice, style, structure, and idea.

Voice

When we read the first few sentences of an essay, we usually hear the narrator's voice: We hear a person speaking to us, and we begin to notice if he or she sounds friendly or hostile, stuffy or casual, self-assured or tentative. The voice might be austere and technical or personal and flamboyant. The voice may be intimate or remote. It may be sincere, hectoring, hysterical, meditative, or ironic. The possibilities are endless.

We usually get a sense of the writer's voice from the **tone** the writer takes. In the first paragraph of "Once More to the Lake," E. B. White's voice is casual and folksy; it is filled with admiration for the lake and for the fun his family enjoyed there. As soon as he mentions fresh water up his son's nose, we suspect that White's tone is going to combine informality and seriousness. Indeed, we can see in the second paragraph that the narrator is filled with complex emotions on returning to his beloved childhood lake. He wonders if time has marred "this holy spot." Deeply nostalgic, White is probably worried that he might sound sentimental. The phrase about the "stillness of the cathedral" indeed sounds reverential, perhaps too reverential. He doesn't linger in reverence, however, quickly returning to more specific, less figurative details about the lake.

Just as White's voice approaches confusion and dreaminess — "I felt dizzy and didn't know which rod I was at the end of" — he suddenly grounds himself in the concrete reality of bass fishing. Just when his emotions seem to bubble to the surface with his rapturous "summertime, oh, summertime . . . summer without end," White returns to the specifics of arrival and a detailed paragraph about boats.

A WRITING EXERCISE

Make a list of details you can remember from the first several paragraphs of E. B. White's "Once More to the Lake." How do you react to a writer who notices and presents such concrete details? Now look at the last two paragraphs and try to describe White's voice, including his stance toward the drama of the storm. Did the last sentence surprise you? Look back through the essay to see how White might have set up the final sentence.

After assigning Joan Didion's "On Going Home," Stevie's instructor asked the class to freewrite on the voice they heard. Stevie wrote the following response:

```
Didion seems anxious to me, maybe a bit confused
about how she should behave on returning home. She claims
"marriage is the classic betrayal" and then says "perhaps
it is not." She is honest though, telling us how para-
lyzed she is at home and how strange she becomes around
her family. The last paragraph shows us that she finally
relaxes and faces things as they are.
```

Although Stevie's response is her subjective view of what she hears, Didion also seems to us to be tentative, hedging with her statements. Didion's attitude toward her home is certainly ambivalent, a mixture of nostalgia, resentment, and wariness. She is unwilling to delude herself; denial and repression will not do. Inappropriate optimism and sentimental nostalgia are to be avoided at all costs: better to see things as they are. The persona that emerges seems to face reality squarely and bravely. The past is over, and she will endure: no picnics on the river perhaps, but certainly music, and stories, and love. We find Didion's voice ultimately to be unsentimental, realistic, and yet hopeful.

A WRITING EXERCISE

Describe the voice you hear when you read Andrea Lee's "Back to School." Be specific about the tone, her attitude toward the school, toward her daughter, and toward the past.

Stevie hears some irony in Andrea Lee's first paragraph, and then notes in the second paragraph some of the same sensory alertness White felt when he returned to the lake. But, unlike White, Lee is negative about her previous experiences. Some sarcasm surfaces when she uses the phrase "miracle of miracles," but like Didion she seems willing to surrender bad feelings from the past, since there have been so many positive changes. Her voice also conveys honesty and a certain self-reflectiveness especially when she realizes that "envy" is influencing her. Like Didion, Lee speaks in an ambivalently optimistic voice when she notes that she is willing to forgive but not forget.

Style

We all have stylish friends. They look good. Their shoes and pants and shirts seem to complement each other perfectly. It's not that they are color-coordinated — that would be too obvious for them — it's something more subtle. They seem to make just the right choices. When they go to a party, to the movies, or to school, they have a personal style that is their own.

Writers also have **style**. They make specific choices in words, in syntax and sentence length, in diction, in metaphors, even in sentence beginnings and endings. Writers use parallelism, balance, formal diction, poetic language, even sentence fragments to create their own styles. Read again the opening paragraphs of each of the three essays with an eye to comparing the styles of White, Didion, and Lee.

This is what Stevie wrote about the differing styles:

```
    I noticed that White's sentences are much longer than
mine. But Didion also has lengthy sentences and so does
Lee. Didion seems to write in a plainer style, especially
the first sentence (I guess each paragraph begins this
way). White uses the phrase "long about 1904" which
```

```
sounds informal, even countryish, but he also uses fancy
words like "placidity" and phrases like "the restlessness
of the tides and the fearful cold of the sea water and
the incessant wind." He seems both literary and conversa-
tional. Didion's style is clear and forceful and concrete
with lots of details. Lee's style is less literary and
more matter-of-fact, almost like a newspaper story.
```

Stevie's comments are perceptive. Indeed, White is famous for his skilled blending of the high and the low and for sensual details, focusing our attention on the sights, smells, and sounds of the lake, the woods, and the cabin. Look especially at paragraph 7 for visual details and paragraphs 10, 11, and 12 for sound and sense details. How does such rich stylistic detail affect you?

White's sentences can be elegant, filled with the rhythms of repeated words and phrases. Notice the use of *same* in the fourth sentence in paragraph 5. White repeats *jollity* and *good* in paragraphs 9 and 10 and alternates simple, compound, and complex sentences. Consider the various ways he begins sentences, sometimes using the usual subject/verb/object pattern, other times inverting this order. Find other examples of these stylistic variations. Notice also the sentence pattern called a **cumulative sentence** that begins with a brief direct statement and then adds parallel words, phrases, or clauses. The opening sentence of paragraph 6 is a good example. Notice that *hauling, pulling,* and *stunning* all end with *ing*.

A WRITING EXERCISE

Find other cumulative sentences in White's essay. Notice that you can actually invert the order by beginning with the phrases. Read some of White's cumulative sentences out loud, then invert them. Which order do you prefer? Why? Why do you think White uses cumulative sentences? Try to write several cumulative sentences yourself by simply describing the room you are in or the people surrounding you.

Didion also varies the length of her sentences and inverts normal word order. But mostly she writes in an unadorned, crisp, lean style with brief and direct assertions.

Stevie noted that Lee's style was journalistic. The piece did appear in *The New Yorker*, a weekly magazine, but her essay seems more polished than a simple news account. When you read the second paragraph aloud, notice the sensual details, the inverted sentence patterns, the repetition and rhythm of the elegant second sentence. Lee is also fond of the dash. Notice the ways in which she uses it. Is there a comparison with White's cumulative phrases? In the last paragraph she begins like Didion with a direct assertion, and then she ends with an interesting sentence. See how many ways you can rearrange the parts of this sentence. Which variation do you like best?

A WRITING EXERCISE

We've pointed out several different kinds of sentences, suggesting that variety of sentence structure is an essential element of style. Find an especially striking paragraph in one of the three essays, and characterize the tone (for example, ironic, pained, matter of fact, dreamy). Then, try to change the tone by rewriting it. Focus on changing sentence structure — simplifying compound sentences, complicating simple sentences, and so forth — rather than substantially changing diction.

Structure

The way essayists put their work together is not very mysterious. The best writers create a **structure** to fit their needs. Most do not have a prearranged structure in mind or feel the need to obey the composition rules many students think they have to follow: topic sentence first and three examples following. Writers of essays aren't so inclined to follow formulas. Essayists begin and end as they see fit; they give explicit topic sentences or create narratives that imply themes; they begin with an assertion and support it, or vice versa. Essayists are inventors of structures that fit the occasion and their own way of seeing the world. The thought of the essay significantly influences its structure. Like the relationship between mind and body, form and thought are inseparable.

A WRITING EXERCISE

Briefly respond to the following writing suggestions and then compare your answer to Stevie's. How would you map the structure of Didion's essay? Is there an introduction, a body, and a conclusion? Pick any two paragraphs and describe the relationship between them.

Here is Stevie's analysis of Didion's structure:

```
    The way Joan Didion put her six paragraphs together
seems traditional, with an introduction, a body, and
a conclusion. We first learn that Didion is going home
and about the difficulty her husband has relating to
her family in the opening paragraph. Then she talks about
the tension that used to exist in families but doesn't
much anymore. Then she realizes that she is still a kind
of victim of this old way of thinking. Then she tells us
about how she is spending her time, visiting aunts and
such. In the last paragraph, she talks about the birthday
party, realizes the past is gone and what she plans to
give her daughter. I like the transition between the
```

```
first two paragraphs. The last sentence of the first
paragraph leads nicely into the next. Very smooth.
```

Didion likes to begin her essays concretely with lots of specific detail, allowing readers to draw conclusions; she does not begin with an abstraction that she must support, although her second paragraph is quite speculative. Mostly she grounds her ideas about the cultural change in families in her own experience. Her conclusion is concrete, as if she were too tentative or suspicious about the confident conclusions found in most academic essays.

White also divides his essays between speculation and narration, although the organizational frame for the thirteen paragraphs opens with White's planned trip to the Maine woods and then moves on by giving us many concrete details of the actual vacation. The simple introduction, body, and conclusion also works well. The lyrical description of the lake and the narrative of the father and son fishing, rowing, and swimming move the essay along nicely. Notice how effortlessly the narrator guides us from one paragraph to the next, acting like an attentive host who wants to be sure guests know where they're going next. It is bad manners to confuse guests or readers. The transition to the last paragraph, for example, is especially smooth. Here White simply uses "others" in the first sentence to connect the reader to the previous episode. And his last sentence nicely brings to a conclusion the connection between father and son that White has been playing with throughout the vacation.

Since Lee's essay is shorter, the structure of her piece is perhaps easier to see. But it is still quite efficient, giving us the usual who, what, when, where, why, and how in the first few sentences. Lee's walk through the school becomes the organizing center. She notices, she comments, she interacts. Her first-person point of view dominates and orchestrates the four paragraphs, ending with her thematic observation as she drives away.

Ideas

All writers have something on their minds when they write. That seems especially true when writers decide to put their **ideas** into a nonfictional form such as the essay. Of course, lots of ideas fill poems and short stories too, but they are usually expressed more indirectly. Although essays seem more idea-driven, this does not mean that as readers we have a responsibility to extract the precise idea or argument the writer had in mind. That may not even be possible since in the creative process of all writing, ideas get modified or changed. Sometimes a writer's original intention is significantly transformed; sometimes writers are not fully conscious of all their hidden intentions. Regardless, readers of essays are not simply miners unearthing hidden meanings; they are more like coproducers. And in creating that meaning, ideas are central. In responding to "Once More to the Lake," for example, Stevie was interested in several ideas, from the disparity between White's summer vacations and Stevie's more urban experience to White's concern for the past and his hope that things at the lake would not have changed. Stevie does not specifically mention what we considered an important idea—White's final realization of his inevitable death—perhaps because Stevie is a twenty-year-old student and the editors of this book are middle-aged professors. That is important to remember. Your perception of the ideas in an essay come partially from the author and partially from your own experiences, your opinions, your sense of what is important and what is not. It is a collaborative and creative process.

White does his part in providing food for thought. One way to think about "Once More to the Lake" is to focus on time. White wants to believe that little has changed at the lake as a way to avoid the fact that he has indeed changed, that he is no longer a boy but a middle-aged man, that death, while not around the corner, is no longer a remote possibility. The epiphany or sudden insight that White has in the last line deals with age and death, with White's mortality. Although it is reasonable to note that White also exhibits a love of nature, a nostalgia for the past, an affection for his son, and even a certain blindness about his privileged status, it seems to us that White's essay revolves around the idea that everything changes, that our eventual fate cannot be denied. It is this thought that animates the whole essay, that gives the piece its structure, its reason for being.

Indeed, it may be that Didion is playing with something like the same idea. Although she seems to have more mixed feelings about the past than White, she does seem attached to the tradition of the extended American family. She sees the good in that kind of rooted past, in small-town closeness and love of place, but she also understands that things change, that new family arrangements are replacing the old. The cliché "you can't go home again" is one way to characterize Didion's acceptance that the past is gone. She seems comfortable rather than pessimistic about her present life. Perhaps she is a realist, rejecting a false hope for a world that no longer exists (and perhaps never did). Although a "picnic on a river with fried chicken" sounds romantically nostalgic, she seems more committed to her nuclear family. If she cannot give her daughter the same kind of childhood she had, she can give her music, style, culture, and love.

Lee's "Back to School" also allows us to see a writer confronting her past and thinking her way through to a resolution. She certainly does not share White's sentimental view of the past since she was made to feel so different and alienated from mainstream culture. She also sees that her bad memories are in the past, that progress has been made. And so she forgives her old school. She comes to a separate peace with discrimination. She is delighted and disarmed by progress, but she cannot forget what was. She is healed but feels a responsibility to remember. This seems less like bitterness than a desire not to let the past repeat itself.

It is interesting to note that in all three essays the narrators confront and deal with the past through their children. The three children represent the future, a realization that each writer uses to establish a mature and healthy relationship with the past. All three writers move on, apparently wiser.

A WRITING EXERCISE

The essays by White, Didion, and Lee work against the notion that an essay should begin with a thesis statement that the rest of the essay supports.

Instead, all three writers capture us with their tone and gradually initiate us into their thought, into the direction their essays are headed. We propose two possible exercises. For the first, try to rewrite one of the essays as a traditional five-paragraph paper: thesis paragraph, supporting paragraphs, closing paragraphs. What, if anything, is gained? What is lost? For the second, if you have at hand a five-paragraph essay you have written recently, try rewriting it in the style of White, Didion, or Lee. Try to engage your reader with concrete details and fluent style, letting the thesis emerge as the essay builds.

Sample Student Paper: Final Draft

After writing journal entries and then a freewrite, Stevie planned her essay and then wrote a draft. On receiving responses from several students in a small-group workshop and from her instructor, she revised her essay, sharpening her focus and supporting her claims more explicitly. Here is Stevie's final version:

```
Stevie Goronski

Professor McLaughlin

English 102

21 April ----
                    The Return of the Past
    In her essay "On Going Home," Joan Didion notes that
when she returns home she wanders about her former home
"meeting [her] past at every turn . . . I decide to meet it
head-on." This is a courageous position to take, one that
requires self-awareness, confidence, and the ability to
deal realistically with life's disappointments. Didion
works hard to deal with the challenge of letting the past
go in order to face the present, to be ready for the
future. In his essay "Once More to the Lake," E. B. White
is not ready to face the reality that his youth is over
until the last sentence when he is shocked into a sudden
insight. Andrea Lee in "Back to School" also refuses to
let the past go, but this time for good reason. When
writers tell us stories about their past, part of their
motivation is to come to a separate peace with unre-
solved, troublesome memories. As Didion claimed in
another essay, "The White Album," "we tell ourselves
stories in order to live . . . we interpret what we see."
Didion, White, and Lee do just this; they shape the past
```

to understand it. We also read these tales for understanding. But in the process, we also come to know ourselves better. I read these three essays as a warning
that the past never completely disappears; we can bump
into it unexpectedly. We should realize that and develop
mature strategies to deal with reality.

In her essay "On Going Home," Didion tells us of her
return to her childhood home for her daughter's first
birthday. She does so with understandably mixed feelings.
Returning to one's old home is psychologically unnerving,
as Didion suggests when she goes "aimlessly from room to
room." She examines such mementos from her adolescence as
a bathing suit, a photo, a letter of rejection. More
importantly she resumes the emotionally tense relationship with her mother that she refers to as a "nameless
anxiety." Didion has been living away from home for many
years and has become a productive writer in the larger
world. But at home, things are the same; at home the
present gets gobbled up by the past; at home Didion, the
famous writer, is seventeen again. As Didion says, "I
fall into their ways." Her husband can't take this
strange time warp and so stays at their home. He is used
to an independent adult Didion and cannot relate to her
psychological regression. This return to the past is evident when she visits her great-aunts who are so trapped
in the past they slip her a dollar bill as a gift.

But in the last paragraph Didion regains her sense of
reality when she kneels beside her daughter's crib. When
she contemplates her child's future, she realizes that
her past with her family is over. She writes that "it is
just as well that I can offer her little of that life."
So Didion's return home only temporarily paralyzes her.
She is ambushed by her past ways but recovers nicely when
she realizes that the lifestyle of the large extended
family is no longer. Instead she promises her daughter
not the past but music, style, and stories: "a xylophone

and a sundress from Madeira, and promise to tell her a funny story."

Something like this also happens at the end of White's "Once More to the Lake." In this essay, White revisits a lake in the Maine woods where he and his father used to vacation some forty years ago. This time around, however, White is now a middle-aged man who has his own son. White visits this lake with great expectations and reverence, calling it a "holy spot" and "a cathedral." He obviously has fond memories of these long ago vacations, so much so that when White says that "we settled into . . . the kind of summertime I had known . . . it was going to be pretty much the same as it had been before," White actually starts to get the present and the past confused. The middle-aged White begins to imagine that he is his father and his son is himself as a boy ("he was I . . . I was my father"). This feeling continues throughout the essay. While they are both fishing, for example, White says:

> there had been no years . . . I looked at the boy, who was silently watching his fly, and it was my hands that held his rod, my eyes watching. I felt dizzy and didn't know which rod I was at the end of.

If Didion was a bit dazed by the past walking around her mother's home, White is in a hallucinatory trance. Over and over he says, "There had been no years." It is perhaps plausible that the lake would stay the same, but what about him? He has not stood still. But maybe that is just the point. White is in denial about growing old. Some men buy red sports cars in middle age; some dye their hair and date women half their age. White returns to a sacred spot from his youth and tries to convince himself everything is like it always was. But, as in Didion's essay, White does finally gain some self-awareness. After a thunderstorm at the lake during which the campers react with the same lighthearted behavior

they did years ago, White watches his son put on a pair
of cold, wet swim trunks. The last line is startling: "As
he buckled the swollen belt suddenly my groin felt the
chill of death." Reality finally sets in. White is not a
young boy cavorting in a summer storm; he is, instead,
some forty years closer to his death. That might be
regrettable, but it is reality and White is better off by
facing the truth: The past is irretrievable.

Lee's journey to her past in "Back to School" is to a
time thirty years ago when racial integration was still a
novelty. She returns to her former prep school with a
daughter who might be the same age as White's son. When
she attended school there, she was one of only two
African American pupils. She felt like an outsider, as if
the curriculum was culturally biased. But when she
returns to see if her own daughter might attend this
school, she finds a different place. Unlike White's lake
or Didion's home, her old school is now integrated and
multicultural with a young black woman in charge. She is
also carried back in time by the school's smells: "For an
instant, I relived precisely what it felt like to walk
those halls." However she is not dazzled by the past. She
sees clearly that the atmosphere is more tolerant, more
progressive. And so she decides to forgive the school its
previous insensitivity to her. Her daughter responds to
her mother's statement that she had wanted to burn this
place down by saying, "'Can't you just forget all that?'"
Like Didion and White, Lee comes to a sudden realization:
It is good to forgive but not to forget. This seems quite
mature. The past will not haunt us if it is put to rest
with understanding and tolerance. Lee is now more interested in avoiding the mistakes of the past.

In all three essays, adults are confronted by a past
that keeps popping up around every corner. Didion and Lee
seem to have achieved a measure of peace by seeing that
the past cannot, and should not, be relived. White is
probably on the verge of accepting this insight, once he

comes to terms with his own mortality. In many ways, we are our past; consequently, it helps to face it straight-forwardly, to see what it was, what it can never be again, and finally to get beyond its staleness into the fresh air of the future.

7

Writing a Research Paper

You may imagine that writing a research paper for your English class is a significantly different, and perhaps more difficult, assignment than others you have had. Because more steps are involved in their writing (for example, additional reading and analysis of sources), research papers tend to be long-range projects. They also tend to be more formal than other kinds of papers because they involve integrating and documenting source material.

Despite the common misconception (cause of much unnecessary anxiety) that writing a research paper requires a special set of knowledge and skills, it draws principally on the same kind of knowledge and skills needed to write other types of papers. A writer still needs to begin with an arguable **issue** and a **claim**, still needs to marshal **evidence** to defend that claim, and still needs to present that evidence persuasively to convince an audience that the claim has merit. Writing about literature begins with a **primary research source** — the story, poem, play, or essay on which the paper is focused. In addition to this primary source, however, research papers call on **secondary research sources** — historical, biographical, cultural, and critical documents that writers use to support their claims.

Identifying an Issue and a Tentative Claim

Your first task in writing a research paper is to identify an issue that you genuinely want to think and to learn more about. The more interested you are in your issue, the better your paper will be. You may choose, for example, to write about issues of theme, symbolism, pattern, or genre, or you may prefer to explore contextual issues of social policy, or of the author's biography, culture, or historical period. Any of the types of issues described on pages 17–24 are potentially suitable for research. The type of secondary research materials you use will depend largely on the issue you choose to pursue.

First, read your primary source carefully, taking notes as you do so. If you work with the texts in this book, you will want to read the biographical and contextual information about the author and any editorial commentary that we have provided. Then, ask questions of your own to figure out what really interests you about the literature. Do not look for simple issues or questions that can be easily answered with a few factual statements; instead, try to discover a topic that will challenge you to perform serious research and do some hard thinking.

Before you begin looking for secondary research sources for your paper, formulate a tentative claim, much like a scientist who begins research with a hypothesis to be tested and affirmed or refuted. Since this tentative claim is unlikely to find its way into your final paper, do not worry if it seems a little vague or obvious. You will have opportunities to refine it as your research proceeds. Having a tentative claim in mind — or, better still, on paper — will prevent you from becoming overwhelmed by the multitude of secondary sources available to you.

Rebecca Stanley, who wrote the research paper that begins on page 196, chose to write on Kate Chopin after reading the following story.

KATE CHOPIN
Désirée's Baby

Kate Chopin (1851–1904) is known for her evocations of the unique, multiethnic Creole and Cajun societies of late-nineteenth-century Louisiana; however, her characters transcend the limitation of regional genre writing, striking a particularly resonant note among feminist readers. Born Katherine O'Flaherty in St. Louis, Missouri, she married Oscar Chopin in 1870 and went to live with him in New Orleans and on his Mississippi River plantation. Her short stories were collected in Bayou Folk *(1894) and* A Night in Acadie *(1897).* Chopin's last novel, The Awakening, *scandalized readers at the time of its publication in 1899 because of its frank portrayal of female sexuality in the context of an extramarital affair. Long ignored by readers and critics, her work was revived in the 1960s and continues to provoke heated discussion: Do her female characters seek freedom in the only ways available to them, or are they willing participants in their own victimhood?*

"Désirée's Baby" was written in 1892 and published in Bayou Folk. *The story reflects Chopin's experience among the French Creoles in Louisiana.*

As the day was pleasant, Madame Valmondé drove over to L'Abri to see Désirée and the baby.

It made her laugh to think of Désirée with a baby. Why, it seemed but yesterday that Désirée was little more than a baby herself; when Monsieur in riding through the gateway of Valmondé had found her lying asleep in the shadow of the big stone pillar.

The little one awoke in his arms and began to cry for "Dada." That was as much as she could do or say. Some people thought she might have strayed there of her own accord, for she was of the toddling age. The prevailing belief was that she had been purposely left by a party of Texans, whose canvas-covered wagon, late in the day, had crossed the ferry that Coton Maïs kept, just below the plantation. In time Madame Valmondé abandoned every speculation but the one that Désirée had been sent to her by a beneficent Providence to be the child of her affection, seeing that she was without child of the flesh. For the girl grew to be beautiful and gentle, affectionate and sincere, — the idol of Valmondé.

It was no wonder, when she stood one day against the stone pillar in whose shadow she had lain asleep, eighteen years before, that Armand Aubigny riding by and seeing her there, had fallen in love with her. That was the way all the Aubignys fell in love, as if struck by a pistol shot. The wonder was that he had not loved her before; for he had known her since his father brought him home from Paris, a boy of eight, after his mother died there. The passion that awoke in him that day, when he saw her at the gate, swept along like an avalanche, or like a prairie fire, or like anything that drives headlong over all obstacles.

Monsieur Valmondé grew practical and wanted things well considered: that   5
is, the girl's obscure origin. Armand looked into her eyes and did not care. He was reminded that she was nameless. What did it matter about a name when he could give her one of the oldest and proudest in Louisiana? He ordered the *corbeille* from Paris, and contained himself with what patience he could until it arrived; then they were married.

Madame Valmondé had not seen Désirée and the baby for four weeks. When she reached L'Abri she shuddered at the first sight of it, as she always did. It was a sad looking place, which for many years had not known the gentle presence of a mistress, old Monsieur Aubigny having married and buried his wife in France, and she having loved her own land too well ever to leave it. The roof came down steep and black like a cowl, reaching out beyond the wide galleries that encircled the yellow stuccoed house. Big, solemn oaks grew close to it, and their thick-leaved, far-reaching branches shadowed it like a pall. Young Aubigny's rule was a strict one, too, and under it his negroes had forgotten how to be gay, as they had been during the old master's easy-going and indulgent lifetime.

The young mother was recovering slowly, and lay full length, in her soft white muslins and laces, upon a couch. The baby was beside her, upon her arm, where he had fallen asleep, at her breast. The yellow nurse woman sat beside a window fanning herself.

Madame Valmondé bent her portly figure over Désirée and kissed her, holding her an instant tenderly in her arms. Then she turned to the child.

"This is not the baby!" she exclaimed, in startled tones. French was the language spoken at Valmondé in those days.

"I knew you would be astonished," laughed Désirée, "at the way he has   10
grown. The little *cochon de lait!*° Look at his legs, mamma, and his hands and fingernails, — real fingernails. Zandrine had to cut them this morning. Isn't it true, Zandrine?"

The woman bowed her turbaned head majestically, "Mais si, Madame."

"And the way he cries," went on Désirée, "is deafening. Armand heard him the other day as far away as La Blanche's cabin."

Madame Valmondé had never removed her eyes from the child. She lifted it and walked with it over to the window that was lightest. She scanned the baby

---

cochon de lait: French for "suckling pig"; an endearment.

narrowly, then looked as searchingly at Zandrine, whose face was turned to gaze across the fields.

"Yes, the child has grown, has changed," said Madame Valmondé, slowly, as she replaced it beside its mother. "What does Armand say?"

Désirée's face became suffused with a glow that was happiness itself.   15

"Oh, Armand is the proudest father in the parish, I believe, chiefly because it is a boy, to bear his name; though he says not,—that he would have loved a girl as well. But I know it isn't true. I know he says that to please me. And mamma," she added, drawing Madame Valmondé's head down to her and speaking in a whisper, "he hasn't punished one of them—not one of them—since baby is born. Even Négrillon, who pretended to have burnt his leg that he might rest from work—he only laughed, and said Négrillon was a great scamp. Oh, mamma, I'm so happy; it frightens me."

What Désirée said was true. Marriage, and later the birth of his son had softened Armand Aubigny's imperious and exacting nature greatly. This was what made the gentle Désirée so happy, for she loved him desperately. When he frowned she trembled, but loved him. When he smiled, she asked no greater blessing of God. But Armand's dark, handsome face had not often been disfigured by frowns since the day he fell in love with her.

When the baby was about three months old, Désirée awoke one day to the conviction that there was something in the air menacing her peace. It was at first too subtle to grasp. It had only been a disquieting suggestion; an air of mystery among the blacks; unexpected visits from far-off neighbors who could hardly account for their coming. Then a strange, an awful change in her husband's manner, which she dared not ask him to explain. When he spoke to her, it was with averted eyes, from which the old love-light seemed to have gone out. He absented himself from home; and when there, avoided her presence and that of her child, without excuse. And the very spirit of Satan seemed suddenly to take hold of him in his dealings with the slaves. Désirée was miserable enough to die.

She sat in her room, one hot afternoon, in her *peignoir*, listlessly drawing through her fingers the strands of her long, silky brown hair that hung about her shoulders. The baby, half naked, lay asleep upon her own great mahogany bed, that was like a sumptuous throne, with its satin-lined half-canopy. One of La Blanche's little quadroon boys—half naked too—stood fanning the child slowly with a fan of peacock feathers. Désirée's eyes had been fixed absently and sadly upon the baby, while she was striving to penetrate the threatening mist that she felt closing about her. She looked from her child to the boy who stood beside him, and back again; over and over. "Ah!" It was a cry that she could not help; which she was not conscious of having uttered. The blood turned like ice in her veins, and a clammy moisture gathered upon her face.

She tried to speak to the little quadroon boy; but no sound would come, at   20 first. When he heard his name uttered, he looked up, and his mistress was pointing to the door. He laid aside the great, soft fan, and obediently stole away, over the polished floor, on his bare tiptoes.

She stayed motionless, with gaze riveted upon her child, and her face the picture of fright.

Presently her husband entered the room, and without noticing her, went to a table and began to search among some papers which covered it.

"Armand," she called to him, in a voice which must have stabbed him, if he was human. But he did not notice. "Armand," she said again. Then she rose and tottered towards him. "Armand," she panted once more, clutching his arm, "look at our child. What does it mean? tell me."

He coldly but gently loosened her fingers from about his arm and thrust the hand away from him. "Tell me what it means!" she cried despairingly.

"It means," he answered lightly, "that the child is not white; it means that you are not white." 25

A quick conception of all that this accusation meant for her nerved her with unwonted courage to deny it. "It is a lie; it is not true, I am white! Look at my hair, it is brown; and my eyes are gray, Armand, you know they are gray. And my skin is fair," seizing his wrist. "Look at my hand; whiter than yours, Armand," she laughed hysterically.

"As white as La Blanche's," he returned cruelly; and went away leaving her alone with their child.

When she could hold a pen in her hand, she sent a despairing letter to Madame Valmondé.

"My mother, they tell me I am not white. Armand has told me I am not white. For God's sake tell them it is not true. You must know it is not true. I shall die. I must die. I cannot be so unhappy, and live."

The answer that came was as brief: 30

"My own Désirée: Come home to Valmondé; back to your mother who loves you. Come with your child."

When the letter reached Désirée she went with it to her husband's study, and laid it open upon the desk before which he sat. She was like a stone image: silent, white, motionless after she placed it there.

In silence he ran his cold eyes over the written words. He said nothing. "Shall I go, Armand?" she asked in tones sharp with agonized suspense.

"Yes, go."

"Do you want me to go?" 35

"Yes, I want you to go."

He thought Almighty God had dealt cruelly and unjustly with him; and felt, somehow, that he was paying Him back in kind when he stabbed thus into his wife's soul. Moreover he no longer loved her, because of the unconscious injury she had brought upon his home and his name.

She turned away like one stunned by a blow, and walked slowly towards the door, hoping he would call her back.

"Good-by, Armand," she moaned.

He did not answer her. That was his last blow at fate. 40

Désirée went in search of her child. Zandrine was pacing the sombre gallery with it. She took the little one from the nurse's arms with no word of explanation, and descending the steps, walked away, under the live-oak branches.

It was an October afternoon; the sun was just sinking. Out in the still fields the negroes were picking cotton.

Désirée had not changed the thin white garment nor the slippers which she wore. Her hair was uncovered and the sun's rays brought a golden gleam from its brown meshes. She did not take the broad, beaten road which led to the far-off plantation of Valmondé. She walked across a deserted field, where the stubble bruised her tender feet, so delicately shod, and tore her thin gown to shreds.

She disappeared among the reeds and willows that grew thick along the banks of the deep, sluggish bayou; and she did not come back again.

Some weeks later there was a curious scene enacted at L'Abri. In the centre   45
of the smoothly swept back yard was a great bonfire. Armand Aubigny sat in the wide hallway that commanded a view of the spectacle; and it was he who dealt out to a half dozen negroes the material which kept this fire ablaze.

A graceful cradle of willow, with all its dainty furbishings, was laid upon the pyre, which had already been fed with the richness of a priceless *layette*. Then there were silk gowns, and velvet and satin ones added to these; laces, too, and embroideries; bonnets and gloves; for the *corbeille* had been of rare quality.

The last thing to go was a tiny bundle of letters; innocent little scribblings that Désirée had sent to him during the days of their espousal. There was the remnant of one back in the drawer from which he took them. But it was not Désirée's; it was part of an old letter from his mother to his father. He read it. She was thanking God for the blessing of her husband's love: —

"But, above all," she wrote, "night and day, I thank the good God for having so arranged our lives that our dear Armand will never know that his mother, who adores him, belongs to the race that is cursed with the brand of slavery."   [1892]

Having read the story, Rebecca Stanley found herself wondering about the racial issues raised by "Désirée's Baby." She was horrified by the racism depicted by Chopin but also fascinated by Chopin's unusual and apparently sensitive treatment of the topic. Still, she knew that she lacked a clear sense of direction for her paper and would have to do more reading and thinking. On her second reading, she began to notice how Chopin's vivid, descriptive language, especially her use of light and dark imagery, seemed to create a mood and comment on the theme of racism. She decided on a tentative claim: that there is a connection between the imagery in "Désirée's Baby" and Chopin's attitude towards race relations in her society. Clearly this claim would need refining, but it gave Rebecca a starting point as she headed to the library to begin her research.

Finding and Using Secondary Sources

Once you have your topic in mind and have sketched a tentative claim, begin looking for secondary research sources. Many different types of sources for literary research are available, and the types you will need will depend largely on the type of claim you choose to defend. If your issue is primarily one of interpretation — about the theme, patterns, or symbolism of the text, for instance — you will most likely need to consult literary criticism to see what has been said in the past about the literature you are discussing. If your issue concerns historical or cultural context, including issues of social policy, you may need to consult newspapers, magazines, and similar sorts of cultural documents. Some topics, like Rebecca's, might require several different types of sources.

Researching your project divides into two main activities. First, you will need to identify several secondary sources and construct a **working bibliography**—that is, a list of the materials you might use. Most researchers find it useful to record this working bibliography on a stack of note cards, with one entry per card containing all the pertinent information to help find the source and later to list it in the paper's bibliography, called the **Works Cited.** (Some researchers with laptop computers prefer to record their working bibliographies on a computer file.) Once you have compiled a working bibliography, you will be ready to move on to the second stage: tracking down the materials you have identified, reading and evaluating them, and writing notes from (and about) them as a preliminary step to writing your own paper.

As you make note of potentially useful sources, it is important that you include in your working bibliography all of the information—including names, titles, publication information, and page numbers—that will eventually be needed for your Works Cited list. An explanation of the Works Cited format for each type of source (from books and articles to CD-ROMs and Web sites) begins on page 188. Acquaint yourself with this format before you begin compiling your working bibliography; otherwise, you may forget to record crucial information that you will need when you prepare the final version of your paper.

FINDING SOURCES IN THE LIBRARY

A good place to commence your research is your college or university library's computerized **catalog**. Be aware that scholarly books are often quite specialized, and that you may want to start with one or two fairly general titles to orient you before venturing into more sharply focused scholarship. Because Rebecca was interested in race relations in the South during Chopin's time, she searched the catalog using the very general key words *race relations* and *United States*, which turned up references to a number of books. Among the most interesting titles was Stetson Kennedy's *Jim Crow Guide*, which provided her with a good deal of useful information for her paper.

Perhaps an even better place than the library catalog to begin research for your paper is the **MLA *International Bibliography***, published each year by the Modern Language Association. Most college and university libraries carry both the CD-ROM and print versions of this work, which lists scholarly books and articles on a wide range of topics in literary criticism and history. The CD-ROM version is a powerful and flexible tool that allows a researcher to enter a topic or the name of an author or work of literature and then to see on-screen a list of books and articles addressing that topic. These references can be copied by hand, printed out, or downloaded to a floppy disk for your working bibliography.

The print version of the *Bibliography* is also useful, though you must understand its organization to use it efficiently. The bibliographic references are subdivided first by the nationality of the literature, then by its date of publication, then by the author and title of the work. To find information from this source for her paper, Rebecca first located the most recent edition of the *MLA International Bibliogra-*

phy, then moved to the section devoted to American literature, then to literature of 1800–99, then finally to Kate Chopin and the specific story, "Désirée's Baby." If you find few or no references to your topic in an edition of the bibliography, try the editions for the previous few years. Chances are your topic will show up.

Sources of cultural information other than literary criticism and history can be found by using other excellent options widely available in college and university libraries. These include *infotrac*, a user-friendly electronic index of academic and general-interest periodicals including scholarly journals, magazines, and several prominent newspapers. Many researchers also like to use the *Readers' Guide to Periodical Literature* (available in both print and CD-ROM versions), the *Newspaper Abstracts*, and the many specialized indexes devoted to particular fields of study, from science, to history, to education. Let your topic lead you to the information sources that will be most valuable to you. Your reference librarians will be happy to tell you what is available in your particular library as well as how to use any of these books and databases.

EVALUATING SOURCES

Whatever method you use to locate your research materials, remember that not all sources are created equal. Be sure to allot some time for **evaluating** the materials you find. In general, the best and most reliable sources of information for academic papers are (1) books published by academic and university presses; (2) articles appearing in scholarly and professional journals; and (3) articles in prominent, reputable newspapers, such as the *New York Times* or the *Washington Post*. Many other types of sources—from CD-ROMs to popular magazines—may prove useful to you as well, but if you have any hesitation about the trustworthiness of a source, approach it with healthy skepticism. Also, the more recent your information, the better (unless, of course, you are doing historical research).

In general, basic questions you should ask of your sources include: (1) Is the information recent, and if not, is the validity of the information likely to have changed significantly over time? (2) How credible is the author? Is he or she a recognized expert on the subject? (3) Is the source published by an established, respectable press, or does it appear in a well-respected journal or periodical (the *Los Angeles Times* has more credibility than the *National Enquirer*, for example) or Web site (one supported by a university or library, for instance)? (4) Based on what you've learned about responsible argument, do the arguments in your source seem sound, fair, and thoughtful? Is the evidence convincing? Is the development of the argument logical?

You increase your own credibility with your audience by using the most credible research materials available to you, so do not just settle for whatever comes to hand if you have the opportunity to find a stronger source.

FINDING SOURCES WITH A COMPUTER

These days, reliable information is widely and conveniently available on CD-ROMs, many of which may be found in college and university libraries. These include texts of literary works (often with commentaries on these works), bibliographies and indexes to help you locate more traditional sources of information, and even the texts of historical and cultural documents. (For example, a CD-ROM about Robert Frost includes not only the texts of his poems but also critical commentaries, relevant source materials, biographical and autobiographical passages, and recordings of Frost reading his own poetry.) In addition, standard reference works such as encyclopedias and dictionaries are often available on CD-ROM, where they can be efficiently searched for background information or factual corroboration (names, dates, spelling) for your paper. Keep in mind that you may need to rely on your librarian to tell you about your library's holdings, because many CD-ROMs are not yet indexed in the same way as traditional books and magazines.

A wealth of information is available on the Internet as well, and, as with the information in the library, your goal is to find useful information efficiently, evaluate it carefully, and make effective use of it in your paper. Unfortunately, and unlike a library's sources, the information on the Internet is not indexed and organized to make it easily accessible to researchers. You will need to do a certain amount of "surfing" if you are to find appropriate materials for your project. Probably the most useful place to start your Internet research is with the text-and-graphics portion known as the World Wide Web. A number of **search engines** (programs for finding information) are designed to help you track down documents on the Web, and if you are an old hand on the Internet, you can probably depend on search engines that have served you well in the past. One of the most useful search engines for serious research, called *Yahoo!*, allows you continually to narrow a topic until you arrive at the information desired.

For example, to find information on Kate Chopin, Rebecca launched the Web browser on her computer and went to *Yahoo!* From the menu of categories, she chose the following path, clicking on each entry successively: Arts/Humanities/Literature/Authors/Literary Fiction/Chopin, Kate. *Yahoo!* then provided her with several Web sites she could choose to visit, one of which contained the complete text of Chopin's novel *The Awakening* and several of her short stories. Other sites on the list provided a wealth of biographical and critical information about Chopin and her work as well as contextual information about southern literature, Chopin's contemporaries, and her culture. (Similar information exists on-line for many of the other authors whose works appear in this book.)

Special care is needed to evaluate on-line sources, since anyone can put information on the Net. It will be up to you to determine if you are reading a piece of professional criticism or a middle-school term paper. When using on-line sources for serious research, look especially for work that has been signed by the author and is hosted by a respectable site, such as a university or a library.

Taking Notes: Summarizing, Paraphrasing, Quoting, and Avoiding Plagiarism

Once you have identified a number of sources for your paper and tracked down the books, periodicals, or other materials, it is time to begin reading, analyzing, and taking notes. At this point, it is especially important to keep yourself well organized and to write down *everything* that may be of use to you later. No matter how good your memory, do not count on remembering a few days (or even hours) later which notes or quotations come from which sources. Scrupulously write down page numbers and double-check facts and spellings.

Many researchers find it easier to stay organized if they take notes on large note cards, with each card containing just one key point from one source. The notes you take from sources will fall into one of three basic categories: summaries, paraphrases, and quotations. (A fourth category is notes of your own ideas, prompted by your research. Write these down as well, keeping them separate and clearly labeled, as you would any other notes.)

Student researchers often rely too heavily on **quotations**, copying verbatim large sections from their research sources. Do not make this mistake. Instead, start your note taking with a **summary** of the source in question—just one or two sentences indicating in your own words the author's main point. Such summaries guarantee that you understand the gist of an author's argument and (since they are your own words) can readily be incorporated in your paper. You might think of a summary as a restatement of the author's principal claim, perhaps with a brief indication of the types of supporting evidence he or she marshals. You can also write summaries of supporting points—subsections of an author's argument—if they seem applicable to your paper. A summary should not, however, include quotations, exhaustive detail about subpoints, or a list of all the evidence in a given source. A summary is meant to provide a succinct overview—to demonstrate that you have grasped a point and can convey it to your readers.

Chances are you will want to take more specific notes as well, ones that **paraphrase** the most germane passages in a particular source. Unlike a summary, a paraphrase does not condense an argument or leave out supporting evidence; instead it puts the information into new words. A paraphrase is generally no shorter than the material being paraphrased, but it still has two advantages over a quotation. First, as with a summary, an accurate paraphrase proves that you understand the material you've read. Second, again as with a summary, a paraphrase is easier to integrate into your paper than a quotation, since it is already written in your own words and style. When you include a paraphrase in your notes, indicate on the note the page numbers in the original source.

The rule of thumb about summarizing or paraphrasing is that you must always clearly indicate which ideas are yours and which are those of others. It is **plagiarism**—a serious violation of academic standards—to accept credit for another's ideas, even if you put them in your own words. Ideas in your paper that are not attributed to a source will be assumed to be your own, so to avoid plagiarism it is important to leave no doubt in your reader's mind about when you are summarizing or paraphrasing. Always cite the source.

An exception to the rule is **common knowledge**—factual information that the average reader can be expected to know or is readily available in many easily accessible sources—which need not be referenced. For example, it is common knowledge that Kate Chopin was an American writer. It is also considered common knowledge that her original name was Katherine O'Flaherty, and that she was born in St. Louis in 1851 and died there in 1904, even though most people would have to look that information up in an encyclopedia or biographical dictionary to verify it.

Sometimes, of course, you will want to copy quotations directly from a source. Do so sparingly, copying quotations only when the author's own words are especially succinct and pertinent. When you write down a quotation, enclose it in quotation marks and record the *exact* wording, right down to the punctuation. As with a paraphrase, make note of the original page numbers for the quotation, as you will need to indicate this in your final paper.

Each time you take a note, be it summary, paraphrase, or quotation, take a moment to consider why you wrote it down. Why is this particular note from this source important? Consider writing a brief commentary about the note's importance, maybe just a sentence or a few words, perhaps on the back of the note card (if you are using note cards). When the time comes to draft your paper, such commentaries will help you remember why you bothered to take the note, and may restart your train of thought if it gets stuck.

And do not forget: If something you read in a source sparks an original idea, write it down and label it clearly as your own. Keep these notes with your notes from the primary and secondary sources. Without your own ideas, your paper will be little more than a report, a record of what others have said. Your ideas will provide the framework for an argument that is your own.

Writing the Paper: Integrating Sources

With your research completed (at least for the moment), it is time to get down to drafting the paper. At this point, many students find themselves overwhelmed with information and wonder if they are really in any better shape to begin writing than they were before starting their research. But having read and thought about a number of authors' ideas and arguments, you are almost certainly more prepared to construct an argument of your own. You can, of course, use any method that has worked for you in the past to devise a first draft of your paper. If you are having trouble getting started, though, you might look to Chapters 2 through 6 of this book, which discuss general strategies for exploring, planning, and drafting papers as well as more specific ideas for working with individual literary genres.

Start by revisiting your tentative claim. Refine it to take into account what you have learned during your research. Rebecca Stanley began with the claim that there was a connection between Chopin's imagery and the attitudes she expressed towards race relations in her society. Having done some research, Rebecca was now ready to claim that the patterns of imagery Chopin uses indicate not only the racial heritage of the main characters in the story but also how guilty or innocent they are of racism. While this is still not quite the thesis of Rebecca's final paper, it reflects the major focus of her research.

With your revised-and-refined claim at hand, examine your assembled notes and try to subdivide them into groups of related ideas, each of which can form a single section of your paper, or even a single piece of supporting evidence for your claim. You can then arrange the groups of notes according to a logical developmental pattern—for example, from cause to effect, or from weakest to strongest evidence—which may provide a structure for the body of your essay. As you write, avoid using your own comments as a kind of glue to hold together other people's ideas. Instead, you are constructing an argument of your own, using secondary sources as bricks to build your own structure of claims and evidence.

Anytime you summarize, paraphrase, or quote another author, it should be clear how this author's ideas or words relate to your own argument. Keep in mind that, in your final paper, it is quite unlikely that every note you took deserves a place. Be prepared to discard any notes that do not, in some fashion, support your claim and strengthen your argument. Remember also that direct quotations should be used sparingly for greatest effect; papers that rely too heavily on them make for choppy reading. By contrast, summaries and paraphrases are in your own words and should be a clean and easy fit with your prose style.

Notice how Rebecca uses both summary and paraphrase in her essay (p. 196). For example, she summarizes two Supreme Court decisions on page 5 of her paper and paraphrases information from *The Jim Crow Guide* on pages 4 and 5. In both cases, her references clearly indicate that the information originated from a particular source. Notice also how smoothly she integrates these summaries and paraphrases into her own discussion of interracial relationships and shows how they connect to the Chopin story and to her claim. The following section on documenting sources (pp. 188–95) demonstrates the proper format for acknowledging authors whose work you summarize or paraphrase.

When you quote directly from either primary or secondary sources, you will need to follow special conventions of format and style. When quoting up to four lines of prose or three lines of poetry, integrate the quotation directly into your paragraph, enclosing the quoted material in double quotation marks and checking to make sure that the quotation accurately reflects the original. Longer quotations are set off from the text by starting a new line and indenting one inch on the left margin only; these are called **block quotations.** For these, quotation marks are omitted since the indention is enough to indicate that the material is a quotation. Examples of the correct format for both long and short quotations appear in Rebecca's paper.

When a short quotation is from a poem, line breaks in the poem are indicated by slash marks, with single spaces on either side. The example below demonstrates this using a short quotation from William Shakespeare's sonnet, "Let me not to the marriage of true minds." The number in parentheses is a page reference, and the format for these is explained in the next section, "Documenting Sources."

```
Shakespeare tells us that "Love is not love / Which
alters when it alteration finds, / Or bends with the
remover to remove" (716).
```

While it is essential to quote accurately, sometimes you may need to alter a quotation slightly, either by deleting text for brevity, or by adding or changing text to incorporate it grammatically. If you delete words from a quotation, indicate the deletion by inserting an ellipsis (three periods with spaces between them) as demonstrated below with another quotation from the Shakespeare sonnet.

```
Love, Shakespeare tells us, is "not Time's fool . . . But
bears it out even to the edge of doom" (716).
```

If you need to change or add words for clarity or grammatical correctness, indicate the changes with square brackets. If, for instance, you wanted to clarify the meaning of "It" in Shakespeare's line "It is the star to every wandering bark," you could do so like this:

```
Shakespeare claims that "[Love] is the star to every wan-
dering bark" (716).
```

In addition to these format considerations, remember a few general rules of thumb as you deploy primary and secondary sources in your paper. First, without stinting on necessary information, keep quotations as short as possible—your argument will flow more smoothly if you do. Quotations long enough to be blocked should be relatively rare. Second, never assume that a quotation is self-sufficient or its meaning self-evident. Every time you put a quotation in your paper, take the time to introduce it clearly and comment on it, to demonstrate why you chose to include it in the first place. Finally, quote fairly and accurately and stick to a consistent format (such as the MLA style explained below) when giving credit to your sources.

Documenting Sources: MLA Format

Documentation is the means by which you give credit to the authors of all primary and secondary sources cited within a research paper. It serves two principal purposes: (1) it allows your readers to find out more about the origin of the ideas you present; and (2) it protects you from charges of plagiarism. Every academic discipline follows slightly different conventions for documentation, but the method most commonly used for writing about literature is the format devised by the Modern Language Association (MLA). This documentation method encompasses **in-text citations**, which briefly identify within the body of your paper the source of a particular quotation, summary, or paraphrase, and a bibliography, called **Works Cited**, which gives more complete publication information.

While mastering the precise requirements of MLA punctuation and format can be time-consuming and even frustrating, getting it right adds immeasurably to the professionalism of a finished paper. More detailed information, including special circumstances and documentation styles for types of sources not covered here, will be found in the *MLA Handbook for Writers of Research Papers*, Fifth Edition, by Joseph Gibaldi (New York: Modern Language Association, 1999). Of course, if your instructor requests that you follow a different documentation method, you should follow his or her instructions instead.

MLA IN-TEXT CITATION

Each time you include information from any outside source — whether in the form of a summary, a paraphrase, or a quotation — you must provide your reader with a brief reference indicating the author and page number of the original. This reference directs the reader to the Works Cited list, where more complete information is available.

There are two basic methods for in-text citation. The first, and usually preferable, method is to include the author's name in the text of your essay and note the page number in parentheses at the end of the citation. The following paraphrase and quotation from James Joyce's "Araby" show the format to be followed for this method. Note that the page number (without the abbreviation "pg." or additional punctuation) is enclosed within the parentheses, and that the final punctuation for the sentence occurs after the parenthetical reference, effectively making the reference part of the preceding sentence. For a direct quotation, the closing quotation marks come before the page reference, but the final period is still saved until after the reference.

```
Joyce's narrator recounts how he thought of Mangan's sis-
ter constantly, even at the most inappropriate times
(729).

Joyce's narrator claims that he thought of Mangan's sis-
ter "even in places the most hostile to romance" (729).
```

The method is similar for long quotations (those set off from the main text of your essay). The only difference, as you can see on page 3 of Rebecca's essay, is that the final punctuation comes before the parenthetical page reference.

In those cases where citing the author's name in your text would be awkward or difficult, you may include both the author's last name and the page reference in the parenthetical citation. The example below draws a quotation from a commentary on love by the psychologist Nathaniel Branden. As demonstrated, the last name of the author (or authors) and the page number (or numbers) are the only thing included in such a reference. No additional punctuation or information is needed.

```
According to one psychologist, the relationships of imma-
ture persons "tend to be dependent and manipulative, not
the encounter of two autonomous selves who feel free to
express themselves honestly" (Branden 838).
```

Knowing the last name of the author is enough to allow your reader to find out more about the reference in the Works Cited, and having the page number makes it easy to find the original of the quotation, summary, or paraphrase should your reader choose to. The only time more information is needed is if you cite more than one work by the same author. In this case, you will need to specify from which of the author's works a particular citation comes. For instance, if you include more than one of Kate Chopin's works in your Works Cited list, you should make clear, either in your lead-in to a citation or in the parenthetical reference, which story is the basis of a paraphrase or source of a quotation. Electronic sources, such as CD-ROMs and Internet sources, are generally not divided into numbered pages. If you cite from such a source, the parenthetical reference need only include the author's last name (or, if the work is anonymous, an identifying title).

MLA WORKS CITED

The second feature of the MLA format is the Works Cited list, or bibliography. This list should begin on a new page of your paper and should be double spaced throughout and use hanging indention, which means that all lines except the first are indented one half inch. The list is alphabetized by author's last name (or by the title in the case of anonymous works) and includes every primary and secondary source referred to in your paper. The format for the most common types of entries is given below. If any of the information called for is unavailable for a particular source, simply skip that element and keep the rest of the entry as close as possible to the given format. An anonymous work, for instance, skips the author's name and is alphabetized under the title. In addition to the explanations below, you can see examples of MLA bibliographic format in Rebecca's Works Cited.

Books

Entries in your Works Cited for books should contain as much of the following information as is available to you. Follow the order and format exactly as given, with a period after each numbered element below (between author and title, and so on). Not all of these elements will be needed for most books. Copy the information directly from the title and publication pages of the book, not from a library catalog or other reference, because these sources often leave some information out.

1. The name(s) of the author(s) (or editor, if no author is listed, or organization in the case of a corporate author), last name first.
2. The full title, underlined or in italics. If the book has a subtitle, put a colon between title and subtitle.
3. The name(s) of the editor(s), if the book has both an author and an editor, following the abbreviation "Ed."
4. The name(s) of the translator or compiler, following the abbreviation "Trans.," or "Comp.," as appropriate.
5. The edition, if other than the first.

6. The volume(s) used, if the book is part of a multivolume set.
7. The name of any series to which the book belongs.
8. The city of publication (followed by a colon), name of the publisher (comma), and year.

The examples below cover the most common types of books you will encounter.

A book by a single author or editor.   Simply follow the elements and format as listed above. The first example below is for a book by a single author; note also the abbreviation UP, for "University Press." The second example is a book by a single editor. The third is for a book with both author (Conrad) and an editor (Murfin); note also that it is a second edition and a book in a series, so these facts are listed as well.

```
Cima, Gay Gibson. Performing Women: Female Char-
     acters, Male Playwrights, and the Modern Stage.
     Ithaca, NY: Cornell UP, 1993.
Tucker, Robert C., ed. The Marx-Engels Reader. New
     York: Norton, 1972.
Conrad, Joseph. Heart of Darkness. Ed. Ross C Murfin.
     2nd ed. Case Studies in Contemporary Criticism.
     Boston: Bedford/St. Martin's, 1996.
```

A book with multiple authors or editors.   If a book has two or three authors or editors , list all names, but note that only the first name is given last name first and the rest are in normal order. In cases where a book has four or more authors or editors, give only the first name listed on the title page, followed by a comma and the phrase *et al.* (Latin for "and others").

```
Leeming, David, and Jake Page. God: Myths of the Male
     Divine. New York: Oxford UP, 1996.
Arrow, Kenneth Joseph, et al., eds. Education in a
     Research University. Stanford: Stanford UP, 1996.
```

A book with a corporate author.   When a book has a group, government agency, or other organization listed as its author, treat that organization in your Works Cited just as you would a single author.

```
National Conference on Undergraduate Research. Pro-
     ceedings of the National Conference on Under-
     graduate Research. Asheville: U of North Carolina,
     1995.
```

Short Works from Collections and Anthologies

Many scholarly books are collections of articles on a single topic by several different authors. When you cite an article from such a collection, include the information given below. The format is the same for works of literature that appear in an anthology, such as this one.

1. The name of the author(s) of the article or literary work.
2. The title of the short work, enclosed in quotation marks.
3. Name(s) of the editor(s) of the collection or anthology.
4. All relevant publication information, in the same order and format as it would appear in a book citation.
5. The inclusive page numbers for the shorter work.

A single work from a collection or anthology. If you are citing only one article or literary work from any given collection or anthology, simply follow the format outlined above and demonstrated in the following examples.

```
Kirk, Russell. "Eliot's Christian Imagination." The
    Placing of T. S. Eliot. Ed. Jewel Spears Brooker.
    Columbia: U of Missouri P, 1991. 136-44.
Silko, Leslie Marmon. "Yellow Woman." Making
    Literature Matter: An Anthology for Readers and
    Writers. Ed. John Schilb and John Clifford.
    Boston: Bedford/St. Martin's, 2000. 720-27.
```

Multiple works from the same collection or anthology. If you are citing more than one short work from a single collection or anthology, it is often more efficient to set up a **cross-reference.** This means first writing a single general entry that provides full publication information for the collection or anthology as a whole. The entries for the shorter works then contain only the author and title of the shorter work, the names of the editors of the book, and the page numbers of the shorter work. The example below shows an entry for a short story cross-referenced with a general entry for the entire book; note that the entries remain in alphabetical order in your Works Cited, regardless of whether the general or specialized entry comes first.

```
Faulkner, William. "A Rose for Emily." Schilb and
    Clifford 849-56.
Schilb, John, and John Clifford, eds. Making Liter-
    ature Matter: An Anthology for Readers and
    Writers. Boston: Bedford/St. Martin's, 2000.
```

Works in Periodicals

The following information should be included, in the given order and format, when you cite articles and other short works from journals, magazines, or newspapers.

1. The name(s) of the author(s) of the short work.
2. The title of the short work, in quotation marks.

3. The title of the periodical, underlined or italicized.
4. All relevant publication information as explained in the examples below.
5. The inclusive page numbers for the shorter work.

A work in a scholarly journal. Publication information for work from scholarly and professional journals should include the volume number (and also the issue number, if the journal paginates each issue separately), the year of publication in parentheses and followed by a colon, and the page numbers of the shorter work.

```
Charles, Casey. "Gender Trouble in Twelfth Night."

    Theatre Journal 49 (1997): 121-41.
```

An article in a magazine. Publication information for articles in general-circulation magazines includes the month(s) of publication for a monthly (or bimonthly), and the date (day, month, then year) for a weekly or biweekly, followed by a colon and the page numbers of the article.

```
Cowley, Malcolm. "It Took a Village." Utne Reader

    Nov.-Dec. 1997: 48-49.

Levy, Steven. "On the Net, Anything Goes." Newsweek 7

    July 1997: 28-30.
```

An article in a newspaper. When citing an article from a newspaper include the date (day, month, year) and the edition if one is listed on the masthead, followed by a colon and the page numbers (including the section number or letter, if applicable).

```
Cobb, Nathan. "How to Dig Up a Family Tree." The

    Boston Globe 9 Mar. 1998: C7.
```

CD-ROMs

CD-ROMs come in two basic types, those published in a single edition — including major reference works like dictionaries and encyclopedias — and those published serially on a regular basis. In a Works Cited list, the first type is treated like a book and the second like a periodical. Details of citation appear in the following examples.

Single-edition CD-ROMs. An entry for a single-edition CD-ROM is formatted like one for a book, but with the word *CD-ROM* preceding publication information. Most CD-ROMs are divided into smaller subsections, and these should be treated like short works from anthologies.

```
"Realism." The Oxford English Dictionary. 2nd ed.

    CD-ROM. Oxford: Oxford UP, 1992.
```

Serial CD-ROMs. Treat information published on periodically released CD-ROMs just as you would articles in print periodical, but also include the title of the CD-ROM, underlined or italicized, the word *CD-ROM*, the name of the vendor distributing the CD-ROM, and the date of electronic publication. Many such CD-ROMs contain reprints and abstracts of print works, and in these cases, the publisher and date for the print version should be listed as well, preceding the information for the electronic version.

```
Brodie, James Michael and Barbara K. Curry. Sweet
    Words So Brave: The Story of African American
    Literature. Madison, WI: Knowledge Unlimited,
    1996. ERIC CD-ROM. SilverPlatter. 1997.
```

The Internet

Internet sources fall into several categories — World Wide Web documents and postings to newsgroups, listservs, and so on. Documentation for these sources should include as much of the following information as is available, in the order and format specified.

1. The name of the author(s), last name first (as for a print publication).
2. The title of the section of the work accessed (the subject line for e-mails and postings) in quotation marks.
3. The title of the full document or site, underlined or in italics.
4. Date the material was published or updated.
5. The protocol used for access (World Wide Web, FTP, USENET newsgroup, listserv, and so on).
6. The electronic address or path followed for access, in angle brackets.
7. The date you access a site, or the date specified on an e-mail or posting, in parentheses.

The examples below show entries for a Web site and a newsgroup citation, two of the most common sorts of Internet sources.

```
Brandes, Jay. "Maya Angelou: A Bibliography of
    Literary Criticism." 20 Aug. 1997. <http://
    www.geocities.com/ResearchTriangle/1221/
    Angelou.htm> (10 Feb. 1998).
Broun, Mike. "Jane Austen Video Package Launched."
    1 Mar. 1998. <rec.arts.prose> (11 Mar. 1998).
```

Personal Communication

In some cases you may get information directly from another person, either by conducting an interview or by receiving correspondence. In this case, include in your Works Cited the name of the person who gave you the information, the type of communication you had with that person, and the date of the communication.

```
McCorkle, Patrick. Personal [or Telephone] interview.
    12 Mar. 1998.
```

```
Aburrow, Clare. Letter [or E-mail] to the author. 15
    Apr. 1998.
```

Multiple Works by the Same Author

If you cite more than one work (in any medium) by a single author, the individual works are alphabetized by title. The author's full name is given only for the first citation in the Works Cited, after which it is replaced by three hyphens. The rest of the citation follows whatever format is appropriate for the medium of the source. The two entries below are for a work in an anthology and a book, both by the same author.

```
Faulkner, William. "A Rose for Emily." Making Litera-
    ture Matter: An Anthology for Readers and Writers.
    Ed. John Schilb and John Clifford. Boston:
    Bedford/St. Martin's, 2000. 849-56.
---. The Sound and the Fury. New York: Modern Li-
    brary, 1956.
```

Occasionally, you may have an idea or find a piece of information that seems important to your paper but that you just cannot work in smoothly without interrupting the flow of ideas. Such information can be included in the form of **endnotes**. A small superscript number in your text signals a note, and the notes themselves appear on a separate page at the end of your paper, before the Works Cited. Rebecca Stanley's paper includes an endnote, but for many research papers none will be needed.

Sample Student Research Paper

Of course, not all research follows exactly the pattern we have described; it varies from researcher to researcher and project to project. In working on your own research paper, you may find yourself taking more or less time on certain steps, doing the steps in a slightly different order, or looping back to further refine your claim or do more research. But if you take the time to think your project through, do the research right, and write and revise carefully, you should end up with a paper you can be proud of. Take a look at the paper Rebecca finally wrote, and note the annotations, which point out key features of her text and of the MLA format.

Stanley 1

Rebecca Stanley

Professor Gardner

English 102

15 March ----

Racial Disharmony and "Désirée's Baby"

The sensuous quality of Kate Chopin's works, as
well as the Creole and Cajun dialect that flavor
her diction, establish her as one of the nineteenth
century's foremost writers. Both her style and
themes have led to her being considered a precursor
to the "Southern Renaissance" of the 1920s (Evans).
In recent years, critics have especially focused on
the ground-breaking explorations of female autonomy
in her short novel The Awakening and in stories
like "The Story of an Hour." Another trait that
sets Chopin's writing ahead of her contemporaries'
is her advocacy of racial harmony, which is not
characteristic of early southern literature. The
racial issue is explored in "Désirée's Baby," in
which Chopin uses black and white imagery and an
ironic twist at the end to teach her audience a
profound truth about humanity. Rather than make
assumptions based upon appearance, individuals
should look beyond the exterior and notice the common humanity that binds all people together. Many
people in Chopin's audience had never learned this
lesson, and sadly enough, neither have many modern-
day Americans.

"Désirée's Baby" tells the tragic story of a
young woman's suffering in the face of her society's condemnation of mixed marriages. The reader
is introduced to the main character, Désirée, early
in her life, when she is a vulnerable infant, lack-
ing any familial ties. Désirée has been abandoned
at the Valmondé gates, and a kindhearted Madame
Valmondé takes pity and adopts the child as her

*Separate title page
unnecessary. First page
gives student name,
teacher's name, course,
and due date in upper
left corner. Centered
below is paper's title.
Student's last name
and page number
appear in upper right
corner.*

*Information cited from
World Wide Web
source; no page
number in
parenthetical
reference.*

*Rebecca immediately
introduces issue of race
and makes two related
claims — one about
Chopin's imagery and
one about American
society.*

own. Any doubts lurking in Madame Valmondé's mind
regarding the baby's obscure origin are assuaged as
the child blossoms into a "beautiful and gentle,
affectionate and sincere" young adult--"the idol of
Valmondé" (Chopin 776). This description is
Chopin's first association of Désirée with goodness, suggesting that the baby has been sent to
Madame Valmondé "by a beneficent Providence" (776).
Throughout the story, Chopin continually describes
Désirée as innately good, and she supports this
with imagery of light and undefiled whiteness.

Quotation cited with author's name and page number.

A character foil emerges when Armand Aubigny
enters the scene on horseback. A dark and handsome
knight of sorts, Armand's shadow falls across
Désirée's whiteness as she stands at the gate
of Valmondé. Eighteen years have passed since
Désirée's initial arrival at the gate, and she has
blossomed into an exquisite young woman. Their
encounter ignites a fiery passion in Armand's soul,
which "[sweeps] along like an avalanche, or like a
prairie fire, or like anything that drives headlong
over all obstacles" (776). The young girl's name-
lessness does not concern Armand, for his Aubigny
heritage--one of the oldest and proudest in
Louisiana (776)--will compensate for her lack
thereof. He hastily dismisses all differences,
marrying Désirée as soon as the <u>corbeille</u> arrives
from Paris.

Square brackets indicate alteration to quoted text. With the author's name already known, only the page number appears in parenthetical citation.

Désirée makes the symbolic transition from
undefiled light to darkness when she takes up resi-
dence in the Aubigny household, which, like the man
of the house, is immediately characterized by its
dark and somber presence:

The roof came down steep and black like a cowl,
    reaching out beyond the wide galleries that
    encircled the yellow stuccoed house. Big,

Format for block quotation, indented one inch on left margin only. Ellipses indicate deletion from quotation. Note format for page reference.

solemn oaks grew close to it, and their thick-
leaved, far-reaching branches shadowed it like
a pall. Young Aubigny's rule was a strict
one . . . and under it his negroes had forgotten
how to be gay. (776)

Désirée's presence brings sunshine to Armand's previously lonely world, and a new addition to the
Aubigny family further multiplies his joy as the
couple become the proud parents of a baby boy soon
after they are married. Chopin uses light imagery
in the description of Désirée's countenance, which
is "suffused with a glow that [is] happiness itself" (777), when she confides in Madame
Valmondé that Armand has undergone a total character change since the baby's arrival. Désirée
observes that the child's birth has indeed "softened Armand Aubigny's imperious and exacting nature
greatly" (777), marveling at the fact that none of
the blacks have been punished by him since the
baby's arrival. It is obvious that Désirée and
the baby bring an uncharacteristic happiness to
Armand, whose dark, handsome face, "[has] not
often been disfigured by frowns since the day he
fell in love" (777).

    As Désirée reclines upon a couch, glowing in
her soft white muslins and laces, she is a vision
of perfect happiness and purity. Unfortunately,
this idyllic existence is short-lived. Something is
wrong with the child, something which will ultimately break many hearts and split the family asun-
der. Désirée slowly realizes that her child does
not appear to be of entirely white heritage. "Look
at our child," she pleads with Armand. "What does
it mean? tell me" (778). She clutches her husband's
arm in desperation yet he, with his heart of
stone, pushes her hand away in disgust. Finally,

he replies that the child is not white because the
mother is not white. Eventually, bitter that
Désirée and the child are part black, he coldheart-
edly forces them both to leave.

Although Armand is guilty for harsh treatment
of someone whom he suspects is of mixed heritage,
the racism he demonstrates is common in the place
and time in which he lives. In New Orleans, where
"Désirée's Baby" takes place, personal relationships between the races were clearly forbidden by
society's rules of etiquette as well as by state
law. Southern society abided by certain unspoken
rules that governed every type of interracial
encounter. Even the shaking of hands between members of different races, under any set of circumstances, was taboo (Kennedy 212). Racist groups,
most notably the Ku Klux Klan, were constantly on
the prowl for those who violated this code of etiquette. For those who dared to exceed the established limits of interracial contact, the social
ramifications were great. Oftentimes, death by
lynching was the punishment for such unacceptable
behavior.

In Armand's society, association with members
of another race was not merely a <u>faux pas</u>--it was a
flagrant violation of the law. Racism was enforced
by the state of Louisiana to the extent that both
races were forbidden to occupy space in the same
apartment building, even with the existence of
walls separating the races and segregated en-
trances. The only legal exception to this clause
existed where a member of one race was employed as
a servant of the other (Kennedy 74). The legal
system did its best to maintain a stratified class
structure that relegated blacks to the lowest position in society, dehumanizing them in the process.

*Connection
established between
original claims and the
specifics of the story.*

Stanley 5

Since the legal system forbade even such casual
physical contact as handshaking and was known to
punish perpetrators with flogging (Kennedy 212),
interracial sexual relations were clearly taboo.
The language of Louisiana's legislation forbade
"sexual intercourse, cohabitation, concubinage,
and marriage between whites and all 'persons of
color,'" who are "defined by the courts to include
anyone having one-sixteenth or more Negro blood"
(Kennedy 66). However, this racist legislation was
not limited to the state of Louisiana, or even to
the deep South.

Quotation within a quotation: The phrase "persons of color" was in quotation marks in original source, and this is indicated by placing it in single quotation marks within the full quotation.

Legislation that restricted relations between
the races were commonplace in state and federal
laws across the nation. The United States' racial
precedent was set early on when Article I, section
2, of the Constitution specified that each black
was to be counted as three-fifths of a white person
in the determination of the number of each state's
representatives in Congress. However, legalized
racism did not end with the addition of the Fourteenth Amendment to the Constitution, despite its
guarantee of "life, liberty, and property" to every
citizen. Before and after the Fourteenth Amendment
was added, the U.S. Supreme Court repeatedly con-
doned the dehumanization of blacks in its rulings,
as evidenced in such cases as the Dred Scott decision (1857) and Plessy v. Ferguson (1896). The earlier decision was an outright denial of the black
race's humanity, in which the Court sought to bar
the entire race from the benefits of citizenship
and withhold the rights which are guaranteed to all
through the Constitution (Scott v. Sandford). The
subsequent decision sanctioned the forced segre-
gation of the races (Plessy v. Ferguson). As long
as the involved party rendered lip-service to the

Summaries of constitutional articles and court cases.

Stanley 6

Constitution by stipulating that the facilities
provided were "separate but equal," the U.S. government turned a blind eye to blatant racial injus-
tices (Kennedy 167-69) and relegated blacks to
their inferior position in society.

*Brief summary of
multiple pages in
original source.*

Succumbing to pressure from a social structure
and legal system so permeated with racism, Armand
forces his wife and their child to leave. Countless
happy homes, such as that of the Aubigny family,
have been torn apart by this demon of racism
throughout history. Some individuals in today's
society argue that the problem of race relations,
as well as the controversial issue of racial identity, are merely past conflicts that have been
overcome by a more enlightened people. However,
Louisiana--the very state in which the Aubigny family lived--was the location of a recent racial controversy, proving that the issue of race still
divides American society.

In 1983, an individual named Susie Guillory
Phipps requested that the Louisiana Bureau of Vital
Records change her racial classification from black
to white and attempted to sue the bureau after its
refusal to do so. Since Phipps is a descendent of
an eighteenth-century white planter and a black
slave, her birth certificate automatically classi-
fied her as black in accordance with a 1970 state
law that declared anyone with at least one-thirty-
second "Negro" blood to be black (Omi and Winant
13). Although Phipps's attorney argued that most
whites have at least one-twentieth "Negro" ancestry, the Court maintained its support of the
quantification of racial identity, and "in so
doing, affirmed the legality of assigning individuals to specific racial groupings" (13). Even as
late as 1986, Louisiana passed another racially

*Specific evidence
provided to support a
debatable claim.*

Stanley 7

divisive ruling in which a woman with "negligible
African heritage" was legally defined as black
(Cose 78).

These modern court rulings raise the specter of
racism which has haunted the South, and the entire
country to a lesser extent, since the country's
inception. It is the very same system that exists
in Chopin's world, where, according to Michele
Birnbaum:

> The "black," the "mulatto," the "quadroon,"
> and the "Griffe" are subtle indices to social
> status in the white community. Named according
> to the ratio of "Negro blood" in their veins,
> these representative figures function not as
> indictments of an arbitrary colorline, but as
> reminders and reinforcements of cultural tier-
> ing. (308)[1]

The legal system's recent support of classification
based upon percentages of racial heritage only
maintains the rift that has divided the races by
stressing differences and has granted equality a
lesser significance. Countless potential relationships have been thwarted, and even terminated, by
the legal system and the social system's racial
codes. At times, the grounds for interracial
couples' painful separations have been entirely
false.

The agony of rejection undoubtedly breaks
Désirée's heart as she bids farewell to the
husband who has brought her much joy and the happy
home they once shared. The rays from the October
sunset illuminate the golden strands in her tresses
like a halo, and the thin white dress dances in the
breeze like an angel's robe. It is appropriate that
Chopin uses light imagery in her description of
Désirée, for the young woman is truly the only

*Superscript numeral
refers reader to
endnote.*

sunshine that the miserable Armand has ever known.
Like the sun, the beautiful Désirée is as glorious
in her departure as she is in her arrival. However,
unlike the sun, there is no hope for her return
tomorrow.

A few weeks after Désirée's dramatic farewell,
the miserable Armand presides over a great bonfire
in the backyard of L'Abri. This scene conjures up
vivid images of the devil and is consistent with
the dark imagery that Chopin uses throughout
"Désirée's Baby" to describe Armand. As he sits
high above the spectacle, a half dozen blacks feed
the flames with every reminder of his love affair
and previously joyous existence. After the willow
cradle and the baby's <u>layette</u> as well as Désirée's
silk and velvet robes have been devoured by the
blaze, only the couple's love letters from their
days of espousal remain. Among them lingers a
curious scrap of paper scrawled in his own
mother's handwriting. In the note, she thanks God
for blessing her with the love of her husband. In
conclusion, she declares, "But, above all . . .
night and day, I thank the good God for having so
arranged our lives that our dear Armand will
never know that his mother, who adores him, belongs
to the race that is cursed with the brand of slavery" (779).

One may wish that Armand had only known in time
that it was he--not Désirée--who shared a common
heritage with the slaves! Chopin drops hints about
Armand's black ancestry throughout the story, fore-
shadowing the ending with dark and evil imagery
that mirrors common stereotypes of the black race.
However, the awareness of his own heritage eludes
Armand, who makes the mistake of a lifetime based
upon societal prejudices. That knowledge would also

save Désirée, and the blacks of L'Abri, from the
misery that Armand has inflicted upon their lives
by treating them as second-class citizens. Readers
may wish he had only realized the "negro blood"
coursing through his veins is no different than the
"white," because the ending would have turned out
so differently. The regrets will undoubtedly haunt
Armand forever.

It is easy for the reader to judge Armand for
rejecting someone he regards as an inferior, yet
countless American citizens and the legal system
are guilty of committing the same crime. American
society has relegated an entire people to second-
class status, while ignoring the fact that the
only difference between the races is skin color.
Most individuals regret America's dark past, if
only due to the selfish realization that a countless number of Mozarts, Einsteins, and Shakespeares
were branded with a stamp of inferiority and
silenced by the legal and social systems. However,
the daily paper reveals that acts of racism are
still being committed, and the lesson of racial
equality has yet to be learned. American society
has done itself an immense disservice by making an
issue of skin color in the past, and it continues
to do so in the present. Until the world is perceived through color-blind eyes, barriers will
divide the races and peace will remain an unattain-
able goal.

Note

[1]Birnbaum is referring here to racial classifi-
cations in Chopin's novel <u>The Awakening</u>, but
clearly the same system applies in "Désirée's
Baby."

*Endnote provides
information that could
not be easily integrated
into text of paper.*

Works Cited

Birnbaum, Michele A. "'Alien Hands': Kate Chopin
    and the Colonization of Race." <u>American Litera-</u>
    <u>ture</u> 66 (1994): 301-23.

Chopin, Kate. <u>The Awakening</u>. 1899. Ed. Nancy A.
    Walker. Boston: Bedford/St. Martin's, 1993.

- - -. "Désirée's Baby." <u>Making Literature Matter: An</u>
    <u>Anthology for Readers and Writers</u>. Ed. John
    Schilb and John Clifford. Boston: Bedford/St.
    Martin's, 2000. 776-79.

Cose, Ellis. "One Drop of Bloody History." <u>Newsweek</u>
    13 Feb. 1995: 78+.

Evans, Patricia. "Southern Women Writers, An His-
    torical Overview." <u>Literature of the South</u>.
    World Wide Web. <http://falcon.jmu.edu/~ram-
    seyil/southwomen.htm> (8 Mar. 1998).

Kennedy, Stetson. <u>The Jim Crow Guide: The Way It</u>
    <u>Was</u>. N.p.: Lawrence & Wishart, 1959. Boca
    Raton: Florida Atlantic U, 1990.

Omi, Michael, and Harold Winant. "Racial Forma-
    tions." <u>Race, Class, and Gender in the United</u>
    <u>States: An Integrated Study</u>. Ed. Paula Rothen-
    berg. New York: St. Martin's, 1995. 13-22.

Plessy v. Ferguson. 163 US 537. US Supr. Ct. 1896.

Scott v. Sandford. 60 US 393. US Supr. Ct. 1856.

US Const. Amend. XIV, sec. 1.

*Citation for an article
in a scholarly journal.*

*Citation for a work in
an anthology. Note
style for multiple works
by the same author.*

*Citation for an article
in a general-circulation
periodical.
Citation for a World
Wide Web source.*

Citation for a book.

*Citation for a chapter
in a book.*

*Citation for court
cases.*

*Citation for a
government document.*

Index of Authors,
Titles, and Terms

The boldfaced page references indicate where a key term is highlighted in the text.